TRIUMPH
OF THE
BANKERS

Money and Banking in the
Eighteenth and Nineteenth Centuries

WILLIAM F. HIXSON

Westport, Connecticut
London

Library of Congress Cataloging-in-Publication Data

Hixson, William F.
    Triumph of the bankers : money and banking in the eighteenth and
nineteenth centuries / William F. Hixson
        p. cm.
    Includes bibliographical references and index.
    ISBN 0-275-94607-X (alk. paper)
    1. Money supply—United States—History—18th century.   2. Money
supply—Great Britain—History—18th century.   3. Money supply—
United States—History—19th century.   4. Money supply—Great
Britain—History—19th century.   5. Banks and banking—United
States—History—18th century.   6. Banks and banking—Great Britain—
History—18th century.   7. Banks and banking—United States—
History—19th century.   8. Banks and banking—Great Britain—
History—19th century.   I. Title.
HG501.H53 1993
332.1'0973—dc20   93-296

Copyright © 1993 by William F. Hixson

Library of Congress Catalog Card Number: 93-296
ISBN: 0-275-94607-X

First published in 1993

Praeger Publishers, 88 Post Road West, Westport, CT 06881
An imprint of Greenwood Publishing Group, Inc.

Printed in the United States of America

The paper used in this book complies with the
Permanent Paper Standard issued by the National
Information Standards Organization (Z39.48—1984).
10 9 8 7 6 5 4 3 2 1

The author gratefully acknowledges the following permissions:

Extracts from David Hume's *Writings on Economics* edited by Eugene Rotwein
reprinted with permission of Thomas Nelson & Sons Limited.

Extracts from Frank Whitson Fetter's *Development of British Monetary Orthodoxy*
reprinted with permission of Augustus M. Kelley Publishers.

To the memory of my grandfather,
Isaiah (Zare) Hixson,
a Bryan enthusiast in 1896 and the source of my interest
in money and banking

Contents

Tables and Graphs

GRAPHS

Acknowledgments

In the research necessary for this book and in the writing of it, I have benefited greatly from conversations and correspondence with my Canadian economist friends, John H. Hotson and William Henry Pope.

Gratitude of another sort is due to James R. Dunton, Praeger's Editor-in-Chief, and to John Beck, my Production Editor.

For preparation of graphs and tables I owe thanks to my son Clarence Hixson.

The domestic serenity that makes possible the researching and writing of a book I owe to my wife of now very nearly fifty years, Allie Corbin Hixson.

Civil society is little more than
the result of a conspiracy of the rich
to guarantee their plunder.

—Rousseau

Introduction

Analyzing the disaster that befell the U.S. economy between 1928 and 1933, Professor Henry C. Simons at the University of Chicago declared that "the major proximate factor in the present crisis is commercial banking." He went on to write, "Given release from a preposterous financial structure, capitalism might indefinitely endure its other afflictions" (1948, pp. 54 and 80). However this may be, the reforms of the 1930s and since were essentially trivial; and a "preposterous" financial, banking, and monetary structure remains. And because it remains, another major financial crisis, already bad, grows worse.

Between December 1928 and March 1933, 44 percent of the commercial banks in the United States collapsed; 40 percent of all checkable deposits in commercial banks simply vanished. These deposits had arcanely appeared in previous years via the process of deposit-creation on the basis of fractional reserves. By 1933 they had almost as astonishingly and disconcertingly disappeared.

Checkable deposits created by bank loans obviously constitute a means of payment by check—the much-used alternative to payment by cash or legal tender created by government. The sum of checkable bank deposits plus legal tender held by the public constitutes what is called the M-1 money supply. Between December 1928 and March 1933, 23 percent of the M-1 money supply of the United States vanished, the 40 percent fall in checkable deposits being offset by the government increasing the amount of legal tender by 44 percent.

What Simons meant by declaring the financial structure "preposterous" was our having a money supply of such a nature that a large a part of it could disappear in a crisis—the checkable deposit part created by banks. For as money disappeared, aggregate demand shrank, unemployment soared, and deep depression ensued. What we should have, Simons contended, was a money supply consisting entirely of legal tender created by government — money that is replaced as it becomes too worn but does not disappear in a crisis.

He likewise considered it absurd that the government often borrowed, and paid interest to them on, money the banks created. Instead, the government should have created interest-free money for itself.

The essence of Simons's view (also the view of Yale's Irving Fisher, Harvard's Lauchlin Currie, Princeton's Frank D. Graham, Columbia's James W. Angell, Wisconsin's John R. Commons, and numerous other Depression-era economists) was that the government, not private commercial banks, should have the task of creating the nations money supply and that the government, not private commercial banks, should receive the profit resulting from the money-creation process.

In a previous book, *A Matter of Interest: Reexamining Money, Debt, and Real Economic Growth,* I presented and evaluated the views of Simons and his associates in detail and gave consideration to the history of the United States economy from World War I to 1990. In this volume, I describe and discuss a number of the crucial monetary events between 1690 and 1914 — events that culminated in "the present preposterous financial structure."

In a broad, general way this book is also a history of a perennial and unrelenting "class struggle" between creditors and debtors. This makes of it a history of conflict between bankers and entrepreneurs, the former being the principal creditors and the latter being the principal debtors.

The first six chapters deal with several general characteristics of money and its function, with a money supply that consists of gold or silver, and with the way a change in the quantity of money affects the real output of an economy and the level of prices of goods and services. Chapters 9, 10, 14, and 15 concern money-creation and banking in Britain. All other chapters concern money-creation and banking in Colonial America and the United States.

This book and *A Matter of Interest* taken together provide a three-century history of money, banking, and money-creation in the United States. They show in detail why our finanancial system is indeed "preposterous" and suggest a number of things that might be done to improve it.

I have referred so frequently to "Bureau of the Census 1975" that I have chosen to abbreviate it as "BC 1975."

Chapter 1

"Smith's Law" and "Fisher's Equation of Exchange"

As is almost universally acknowledged, one of the truly great books in the history of economics is Adam Smith's *The Wealth of Nations,* published in a year memorable in the United States for quite another reason — 1776. Harvard's Joseph Schumpeter called it, "the most successful not only of all books on economics, but, with the possible exception of Darwin's *Origin of Species,* of all scientific books that have appeared to this day" (1954, p. 181). Schumpeter went on to say that while *The Wealth of Nations* "contained no really novel ideas [it] comprehensibly and forcefully summed up the thinking of the best scholars of the preceding century."

Enriched as we are by more than two centuries of experience not accessible to Smith, it is easy for us to find occasion to differ with a number of his propositions. Many of his other ideas, however, have well withstood the test of time. This chapter and those immediately following are concerned primarily, but not exclusively, with what I regard as some of the more important of Smith's contentions.

A most satisfactory place to begin a study of the history of money is with one of Smith's views — one so important in his estimation that he saw fit to state it repeatedly in various forms.

When . . . the annual produce of [a nation] becomes gradually greater and greater, a greater quantity of coin becomes necessary in order to circulate a greater quantity of commodities. (1937, p. 188)

The quantity of money . . . must in every country . . . increase as the value of the annual produce increases. (1909, p. 280)

Smith's proposition that *the size of a nation's money supply must increase in step with its output of goods and services* is profoundly true and is of fundamental importance. It will be referred to hereafter as "Smith's Law." This arbitrary and presumptuous designation is made for convenience in reference and is chosen despite the fact that it is somewhat unfair to writers who said much the same thing and said it earlier than Smith. I believe, however, the usage is justified by the emphasis Smith gave the matter and its prominence in the inclusive system of thinking about economic matters he developed. Be this as it may, let it be noted that as early as 1705 John Law wrote:

Domestic trade depends on money. A greater quantity employs more people than a lesser quantity. . . . More people cannot be set to work without more money to circulate so as to pay the wages of a greater number. (1966, p. 13)

Benjamin Franklin approached the matter in only a little different way in 1729:

There is a certain proportionate quantity of money required to carry on the trade of a country freely and currently, more than which would be of no advantage to trade, and less, if much less, exceedingly detrimental to it. (1907, 2: 134)

Similar statments embodying the gist of Smith's Law but antedating *The Wealth of Nations* were expressed by John Locke, William Petty, and David Hume among others.

In order quickly and easily to come to an appreciation of Smith's Law, consider the volume of buying and selling that today occurs in Athens or Rome and try to find it credible that the same volume of trade could occur with no more money in circulation than was available in the time of Pericles or Caesar. Think of the enormous volume of goods and services exchanged in Britain in 1990 and imagine the difficulty — the impossibility — of exchange on such a scale occurring if the money supply were no larger than that of 1790 or 1590. Recall that between 1940 and 1990 the real gross domestic product (GDP) of the United States a little more than quadrupled and reflect on what might have happened had "the means of exchange," the money supply, been held fixed at the 1940 level instead of quadrupling (and more), as was the case.

What has happened in actual economies during the past four centuries shows beyond question that a growing economy requires an increasing supply of money — shows the unquestionable applicability and significance of Smith's Law. As we proceed, we will find occasion to look closely at the history of money in Britain and the United States; but, for the moment, suffice it to say that nothing is quite so rare, during any era in the modern history of any economy anywhere in the world, as a case when output of real goods and services in an economy reached a new all-time high while the size of its money supply did not also post a new all-time high.

Although Smith's Law is the beginning of wisdom concerning the relationship between money supply and real growth, it is not beyond controversy. Smith arrived at his law by making certain assumptions that other economists have not always considered warranted to the same extent that Smith appears to have believed.

Why, it may be asked, is it not possible to circulate an increasingly large volume of goods and services, not by increasing the size of the money supply but by increasing the rate of circulation of money? In the course of a month or year, a coin may be involved in several transactions; if the number of transactions per coin per unit of time could be increased, no increase in the number of coins would be required, even though the number of transactions increased because of increases in output. Some economists assert that Smith's Law is oversimplified, to say the least, because it ignores "the velocity of circulation" (V) of the money supply (M). What is important, according to those who dissent, is not M alone but M *and* V or M × V or MV — "the circulating money supply." A million shillings turning over ten times a year and two million shillings turning over five times a year both provide a circulating money supply (MV) or a "purchasing power" or "debt repayment power" of ten million shillings.

Now it is beyond all doubt that the velocity of circulation of money is not perfectly constant, as Smith's Law might be taken to imply. In times of optimism, people quickly spend every coin they earn (and quite often borrow and spend even more); in times of pessimism, they delay every purchase as long as possible and even sometimes hoard money over long intervals of time. "Adam Smith never discusses velocity" (Hegeland 1969, p. 48), but the fact that velocity fluctuates makes it necessary for us to qualify Smith's Law by saying that it is an approximate law quite appropriate for long-run or secular periods but less appropriate for short-run or cyclical periods. Although not a constant for all periods of time, velocity is nevertheless either astonishingly invariant in the long run or changes only with remarkable slowness. Insofar as secular considerations are concerned, Smith's Law, despite its silence with respect to velocity of circulation, gives a very good first approximation to what happens in the real world.

No acceptable statistics with regard to the velocity of circulation of money were kept until long after Smith's era; and thus for evidence supporting the relative constancy of velocity, we must resort to statistics of a more recent period. From 1900 to 1970 in the United States, for example, the M2 money supply increased 6.04 percent per annum whereas the velocity of circulation declined at an annual rate of 0.22 percent. That is to say, in absolute terms the rate of change of M was nearly 27 times as great as the rate of change of V (BC 1975, pp. 224, 992). It follows, therefore, that Smith was largely justified in dealing in terms of M alone, rather than MV, inasmuch as this greatly simplifies matters without introducing unacceptably large errors.

Another objection to Smith's Law is that the amount of money supply required to circulate a given output depends not solely on whether the volume of goods and services increases but on how they are priced. If, for example, the quantity of real goods and services or real gross domestic product (GDP or Q) increased 10 percent but the average price of goods and services (P) decreased 10 percent, then no increase in money supply would be necessary (we continue to assume that velocity remains constant). It is not merely Q that is important in determining the necessary size of the money supply, say a group of dissenters from Smith's Law, but P as well, or Q × P or QP—the nominal GDP, or the purchasing power necessary to clear the market at prevailing prices of what is produced. Obviously, by omitting any mention of prices, by encompassing only Q rather than QP, Smith's Law oversimplifies the matter.

Now it is undoubtedly true that if the price level regularly declined by the same proportion that output increased, no increases in the money supply would be required. Any serious objection to Smith's Law on this account, however, is misconceived. An economy only rarely increases its output when prices are falling. We go into the reasons why this is true in Chapter 4; for the moment, however, the reader who may be in doubt is asked to take this assertion on faith. In the longer term, a growing and thriving economy is characterized either by a steady price level or, perhaps even more often, by a rising price level; it is very rarely indeed characterized by a falling price level. As a secular phenomenon, a growing economy along with a price level that declines in such a way that money supply increases are unnecessary is such a rarity that we may simply disregard it.

In contrast to what he said about velocity, Smith had a great deal to say about prices; and in subsequent chapters what he wrote will be considered at some length. It is evident from all that he said, however, that in enunciating what I have called Smith's Law he was quite explicitly assuming a constant price level as well as implicitly assuming a constant velocity of circulation of money.

Summarizing, after consideration of the two objections to Smith's Law discussed above, we see that "purchasing power needed to clear the market" in an economy is given by QP and "purchasing power available to clear the market" is given by MV. When the two are in balance, then MV = QP. This equation, in the form shown or in some other form amounting to the same thing, is of such fundamental importance to our study as to justify a brief digression.

In most cases, textbooks on economics attribute the equation MV = PQ to fairly recent scholarship. The equation is often identified with Irving Fisher or A. C. Pigou. It is frequently called "Fisher's Equation of Exchange," and I will follow that practice. As we have seen, however, several of the ideas embodied in the equation have a history antedating Adam Smith. It may now be added that a close approximation, M = PQ, can be traced back as far as 1694 and the works of John Briscoe in England. In 1811 a German economist, Joseph Lang, employed different symbols but nevertheless expressed correctly all the relationships embodied in MV = QP, making him apparently the first economist to do so (Humphrey 1984, p. 13).

Other terminology than that used in the paragraphs immediately above is often employed by various authors. For example, I find a book in which it is said that, "the level of nominal income parallels with great fidelity the level of the nominal quantity of money" (Friedman and Schwartz 1982, p. 7). "The level of nominal income" in the sense used in the quotation is given by QP and "the level of the nominal quantity of money" is given by M. Hence the sentence says, in effect, M = QP and V is assumed constant. Many text-book authors define "nominal gross domestic product" by the equation GDP = QP and thus find occasion also to write MV = GDP.

Let us now note that in terms of rates of change (denoted by the subscript r) MV = QP, Fisher's Equation of Exchange, becomes $M_r + V_r \cong Q_r + P_r$. In a case when the velocity of circulation of money is constant ($V_r = 0$) and when the general price level remains unchanged ($P_r = 0$) then we get $M_r \cong Q_r$ — Smith's Law in "shorthand" or in the form of a simple equation. Since $V_r = 0$ is usually true for secular periods and since most economies set $P_r = 0$ as a target for policy, Smith's Law may, in many contexts, be substituted for Fisher's Equation of Exchange and excessive pedantry thereby avoided.

The great importance of what has thus far been said in this chapter — the great importance of Fisher's Equation of Exchange and its simplification, Smith's Law — follows from the fact that for centuries most national economies have stated as their objective an annual growth rate of Q of 3 or 4 percent with prices constant. In the long run, therefore, a money supply that automatically increases, or that somehow can be increased, 3 or 4 percent per annum has been a necessity in such national economies.

The implications of this fact are simply staggering. At a rate of growth of 3.5 percent per annum, Q would double about every 20 years, increase by a factor of about 32 every century, increase by a factor of about 1000 in two centuries, and increase by a factor of about 1,000,000 in four centuries. If we think in terms of the economic objective having been to increase Q by a million-fold over the past 400 years, then it would have been desirable to have domestic money supplies M capable of increasing, or of being increased, a million-fold in the same number of years.

The point of the previous paragraph is that during the past four centuries a fundamental problem in economics has been to discover or devise a domestic monetary system capable of expansion at what appear modest annual rates but at rates that imply absolutely enormous actual amounts of increase in money over long periods of time. The history of money during the past four or so centuries amounts to recounting various efforts to discover or devise a domestic money supply of such a nature that it would satisfactorily meet the requirement stipulated by Smith's Law or Fisher's Equation of Exchange. The requirement is extremely challenging, and there is little to be wondered at that meeting it has not proved to be a simple matter.

Chapter 2

The Impracticality of a Gold or Silver Standard

Early-day economists were aware that from time immemorial the customary form of money had been specie, that is to say, coins of gold or silver. They assumed, without giving any considerable thought to the matter, that the system that prevailed in the past could and would similarly characterize the future. They failed to take into account the difficulty — the impossibility — of increasing the world's supply of money M in the form of specie at the same rate that it proved possible to increase the aggregate output of goods and services Q of progressive domestic economies.

Neither sufficiently aware of nor properly impressed by the difficulty of increasing the world supply of precious metals at suitable rates, Adam Smith wrote:

The currency of a great state, such as France or England, generally consists almost entirely of its own [gold or silver] coin. (1937, p. 446)

A country that has no mines of its own [such as France or England] must undoubtedly draw its gold and silver from foreign countries. [A] country that has the wherewithal to buy gold and silver, will never be in want of those metals. They are to be bought for a certain price like all other commodities, and as they are the price of all other commodities, so all other commodities are the price of these metals. We trust with perfect security that the freedom of trade, without any attention of government . . . will always supply us with all the gold and silver which we can afford to purchase or employ. (1909, p. 333)

The implication seems to be that Smith trusted "with perfect security" that France or England could always enjoy a supply of specie of sufficient or optimum size. He seems to have believed that M would increase in step with Q more or less spontaneously—that Smith's Law, $M_r \cong Q_r$, operated automatically—and that the economy and its money supply would grow steadily and at constant or nearly constant prices and constant velocity of circulation.

The great trouble here is that Smith gave scant attention to the fact that there was little probablity that the world supply of gold or silver could be increased a million-fold every four centuries. Giving little heed to this fact, Smith likewise largely ignored its profound implications.

The overwhelmingly important reason for the eventual discarding of a monetary system based on coins of precious metal was the difficulty—the longer-term impossibility—of making the supply of specie increase by 3 or 4 percent per year or increase a million-fold every four centuries. This impossibility was the result of two matters usually not given the consideration they deserve: (1) the all-important fact that gold and silver occur very rarely in the earth's crust and (2) the fact of lesser importance that whatever the supply of coins at any given time it tends naturally to decrease through loss and wear.

An economy embracing a coins-only system and growing at the rate of 3 or 4 percent per annum requires a net annual increase in precious metals in circulation of 3 or 4 percent. Thus the mines and placers of the world must yield an annual output of new metals of more nearly 5 or 6 percent to offset annual decreases to loss and wear. The choice of a system in which the money supply tended naturally to decrease because of loss and wear can hardly be called a happy one.

Irrecoverable losses of coins made of the precious metals are inevitable— losses from simple carelessness, ship sinkings, burials, hoards cached and never found, and so forth. The decrease in the supply of coinage through such factors was a matter of special interest to C. C. Patterson who studied it intensively. According to an especially interesting example given by Patterson, Alexander the Great plundered 2,200 metric tons of silver and released it into circulation in southwest Asia in 329 B.C. "We can easily show that Alexander's 2,200 tons of silver declined to 90 tons through irrecoverable loss over a period of 160 years," writes Patterson (1972, p. 222). The annual rate of loss, if Patterson's figures are to be credited, was about 2 percent.

Not all scholars would take this as a typical example, and thus it may be worthwhile to note that even if Patterson's estimate is twice as high as other investigations might reveal, a loss of coins at the rate of only 1 percent every year would mean the disappearance of half a given supply of coins in only about 70 years, three-quarters of the supply in about 140 years, seven-eighths in about 210 years, and so on.

Patterson goes on to say:

Classical Greek stocks [of silver] had returned to the earth . . . before the much larger Roman stocks began to accumulate, and these also returned to the earth before the very small medieval stocks of silver accumulated. (p. 208)

Athenian power lasted no longer than the silver. The Roman Empire repeated the process in the west, growing upon silver from Spain and declining when it was exhausted. (p. 225)

The short lives of silver stocks were intimately related to the decline of the Roman Empire and to the economic chaos of the Dark Ages in Europe. (p. 228)

The historical fact that economies regressed (that Q_r turned negative) as their supplies of gold and silver decreased (as M_r turned negative) from the era of the Roman Empire until the influx of gold and silver from the Americas and that the economies therafter grew rapidly lends further credibility to Smith's Law.

Circulating coins of precious metals are subject not only to loss but to wear. This also is a matter of considerably greater importance than is usually appreciated. The loss in weight of silver coins due solely to abrasion has been studied by William Jacob, as well as Patterson and others. Jacob estimated that the British silver coins of the early nineteenth century would lose weight by 1 part in 150 in the course of a year, that is to say, by about 0.67 percent per year (1968, p. 187). At this rate of loss, a given supply would be reduced to half in about 100 years by wear alone. Patterson believed that more recent, better silver-alloyed coins would lose weight by wear at only about half Jacob's estimated rate—by only 0.33 percent per year—or be reduced by half in about 200 years.

Older readers will no doubt remember that some of the silver dimes, quarters, and half-dollars in circulation in the United States became so worn as to render the stampings almost illegible after only 50 years or less. Gold coins, although softer than silver, tended to circulate less rapidly and on that account to lose weight by wear somewhat more slowly.

Coins not only were subject to abrasion but also were often scraped, filed, bored, and otherwise mutilated for bits of metal that could be collected and traded by weight or made into counterfeit coins. Even the most stringent laws against defacing the coinage never succeeded in putting a stop to this practice.

Regarding loss of weight of silver coins in England we find that "During the months of May, June, and July 1695 . . . the officers of the Exchequer . . . weighed £57,000 [face value of coins]. The [legal] weight ought to have exceeded 221,418 ounces [Troy], it was actually 113,771 ounces" (Andreades 1966, p. 93). The loss in weight of the coins thus amounted to about 48.6 percent but we are told neither over what period of time this loss occurred nor what part of the loss was due to wear and what part to defacement.

The usual but not invariable practice of governments was to melt coins down for recoinage before wear or defacement resulted in more than a 20 or 25 percent loss. The process of meltdown and recoinage also involved small but irrecoverable losses.

Decreases in weight due to mutilation plus decreases incidental to meltdown and recoinage almost certainly amounted to 0.17 percent per year at minimum. Adding to this a minimum 0.33 percent decrease in weight due to wear and a minimum 1 percent decrease in aggregate weight due to simple losses suggests a minimum annual decrease in weight of coins of 1.5 percent. That is to say, the disappearance of half the weight of the circulating coinage in somewhat less than 50 years or the disappearance of 90 percent of the weight in about 150 years.

An economy growing at 3.5 percent per year and needing a net increase in gold and silver of 3.5 percent would thus require new acquisition of precious metals amounting to not less than 5 percent, assuming that the money supply consisted solely of silver coins.

To prevent the disappearance of specie owing to the processes discussed above, the coins-only system was sometimes partly abandoned. There emerged instead the practice of locking up the metals in vaults in the form of ingots and issuing and circulating paper money backed by the metals in storage. This practice, however, was not common enough to make a great difference, and it seems certain that 3.5 percent per year real growth would necessitate not less than 4.5 percent growth in the supply of precious metals.

One widely recognized scholar, Frank W. Fetter, observed that the advocates of a monetary system based on precious metals "rarely asked the fundamental question of the world-wide adequacy of the supply of gold or silver to serve as a monetary standard" (1978, p. 3). Another writer observed:

The eighteenth century, which was so deeply concerned with the influence of the [rapid] influx of precious metals on [higher] prices, paid no attention whatever to the inverse problem—an insufficiency of the precious metals [in the long run] for the maintenance of the price level. (Rist 1966, p. 121)

The Swedish economist Gustav Cassel remarked upon "a lag in the increase in gold production" (Palayi 1972, p. 124). Karl Polanyi wrote "that the gold standard . . . meant danger of deadly deflation, and maybe, a fatal monetary stringency in a panic" (1957, p. 138).

Net growth rates of the supply of monetary gold and monetary silver over the past several centuries cannot be calculated very accurately for a number of reasons. (1) Both gold and silver have uses for items other than money, and whether the ratio of monetary to nonmonetary uses is constant or erratic is not very well known. (2) Losses from causes discussed above have probably declined slowly over the past few centuries as the metals have been taken out of circulation and replaced by paper money backed by ingots stored in vaults, as improved alloys have been developed, and perhaps for other reasons; but actual losses are not very well known. (3) Although the amount of world production of gold and silver since 1500 is known with reasonable accuracy, the amount of the metals in Europe at the time of the discovery of the Western Hemisphere is a matter of controversy.

Although, for the reasons just recited, all scholars would not agree on the

Table 2.1
Stocks of Gold and Silver in Metric Tons

Year	Gold	Silver
1500	156	2333
1600	910	25168
1700	1823	62402
1800	3723	119437
1900	15257	277694

Note: Amounts shown for annual production of gold and silver from 1500 to 1900 are taken from the *Encyclopaedia Brittanica,* 11th ed., S.V. "Money." The Bureau of Mines of the United States Department of the Interior, in numerous publications, gives the same figures as the *Brittanica* for 1800 to 1900. The difficult problem is deciding what amounts to show as the stocks existing in 1500. Del Mar (1975, p. 178), gives an estimate by Gregory King in 1696 that "the entire European stock of the precious metals, coin and plate, at the time of the discovery of America" was £45,000,000 ($219,000,000 at the rate prevailing until well into the twentieth century). Jacob (1968, p. 70) estimated only £34,000,000 ($165,000,000). I have arbitrarily assumed $200,000,000 as a proper amount. I have further assumed 5,000,000 troy ounces of gold at $20.67 per ounce, worth $104,000,000. This leaves $96,000,000 in silver which at $1.29 per ounce (also the average legal rate until well into the twentieth century) gives 75,000,000 ounces. Troy ounces are converted to metric tons by dividing by 32,151. Although I have clearly made a number of arbitrary assumptions, I do not believe other reasonable assumptions would yield conclusions significantly different from those I draw.

Table 2.2
Average Annual Growth Rates of Gold and Silver Stocks

Period	Gold	Silver
1500-1600	1.78%	2.41%
1600-1700	0.70	0.91
1700-1800	0.72	0.65
1800-1900	1.42	0.85
1500-1700	1.24	1.66
1500-1800	1.06	1.32
1500-1900	1.15	1.20

Source: Calculated from amounts in Table 2.1

amounts of gold and silver stocks shown in Table 2.1, the amounts are not so grossly innacurate as to invalidate the conclusion I will presently draw from them. How the figures used in the table were determined is discussed in a footnote to the table.

Table 2.2 reveals that whereas a growth rate of not less than 4 or 4.5 percent would seem essential, actual growth rates fell disastrously short of the mark. The 1.15 percent growth rate of gold between 1500 and 1900 was roughly a third of the minimum needed rate, and this might leave the impression that about a third as much gold was produced as was needed. The short-fall, however, was far worse. Just how far short the production of the precious metals fell is perhaps better revealed by observing from Table 2.1 that for these 400 years the growth multiple for gold was 97.8 and the growth multiple for silver was 119.0, whereas a growth multiple of 1,000,000 was more or less optimum if economies were to use only specie for money and nevertheless grow at 3.5 percent per annum in real terms with constant prices and constant velocity of circulation; assuming, additionally, no loss or wear of coins. A proposition of surpassing importance to the history of economic development is thus fully vindicated by the tables above—the proposition that *the supply of gold and silver does not tend to increase nearly fast enough to keep economies growing at their potential or even near their potential.*

The same conclusion may be reached by considering an altogether different data source, Pierre Vilar.

In 1905 the statistician DeFoville was astonished to discover that all the gold in the world taken from the earth by that date could be confined within a 10-metre cube (1000 cubic metres). Yet a similar block made of all gold available in Europe in 1500 would have measured only 2 metres each way (8 cubic metres). (1976, p. 19)

In terms of U.S. measure, the cube of gold of 1500 would have been about 6.5 feet to the side and the cube of 1905 about 32.8 feet. DeFoville's astonishment seems fully warranted.

Vilar, however, did not state the matter quite as accurately as he might. It is probably near to the mark to say that a block made of all gold available in Europe in 1500 would have measured only 2 meters to the side; but the block of 1905 measuring 10 meters to the side appears to have represented not "all the gold in the world taken from the earth by that date" but rather all the gold in the world that remained at that date after the disappearance of gold due to loss, wear, defacing, and remelting.

Be that as it may, according to DeFoville the growth multiple of gold from 1500 to 1905 was 1000/8 or 125 compared to the growth multiple of 97.8 for 1500 to 1900 calculated from Tables 2.1 and 2.2. DeFoville's compound per annum growth rate of gold for 405 years was thus 1.20 percent, compared to the growth rate for 400 years of 1.15 percent given in Table 2.2.

If we define being on a "gold standard" as meaning that there is in place a money supply that cannot increase except at the rate of increase of the monetary gold supply (whether as coins or ingots), then it is certain that all the countries of the world could not have embraced a gold standard and yet grown at anywhere near their potential during the four centuries discussed above. This is essentially why the gold standard has everywhere been discarded and will remain in disuse so long as desired growth rates of real GDP remain far greater than the growth rate of the world's supply of monetary gold. The same remarks apply if silver is chosen for the standard.

There are obvious historical reasons why there emerged the idea of a money supply based at first on gold and silver coins, later on paper money 100 percent backed by a precious metal, and still later on paper money with a fixed "fractional reserve" of specie. Given the facts of the matter, however, and the good historical reasons notwithstanding, there is no *logical* reason for advocacy of a gold or silver standard. There is every reason, on the contrary, to pronounce a precious metals standard "simply impractical."

The idea that a domestic money supply consisting of coins of precious metal is impractical does not exhaust the reasons why a money supply of such a nature should be discarded. It should be discarded not only because of its impracticality but also because of its undesirability, even had it proved practical. So let us now turn to a consideration of the reasons why a gold standard or silver standard is undesirable.

Chapter 3

The Undesirability of a Gold or Silver Standard

As an economic system grows and monetary transactions become not only more numerous but ever larger in size, a "coins only" system may be faulted on account of sheer cumbersomeness. A transaction in the early nineteenth-century United States involving only $10,000,000 would require the loading, hauling, unloading, and storage of nearly 16 metric tons of gold or over 240 metric tons of silver. Thus David Hume observed, "Many people . . . having large sums of money, would prefer paper with good security; as being of more easy transport and more safe custody" (Hume 1970, p. 35).

If "easy to transport paper money" is wanted, and at the same time a gold or silver standard, then the amount of paper money in circulation must be constrained to increase at an annual rate no greater than the rate of net increase in the quantity of specie serving as reserves. But as has been pointed out, a system wherein the quantity of money is constrained to grow no faster than the gold or silver supply must be considered an impractical system owing to the low growth rate of the world supply of these precious metals. It is also an undesirable system from other points of view.

Recall now Adam Smith's observation cited at the beginning of the preceding chapter that "a country that has no mines of its own must draw its gold and silver from foreign countries." This surely is as obvious as anything can be; but some of its implications, despite their far-reaching nature, are considerably less obvious. Furthermore, some of the more important of these implications were largely ignored by Smith and likewise only infrequently commented upon by subsequent economists.

If a would-be prosperous nation adopts a gold standard, it must of necessity increase its gold supply by upwards of 4 percent per year. Yet if the world supply of gold increases by only about 1.2 percent per year, no nation can increase its supply by 4 percent without requiring other nations to make do with even less than 1.2 percent. Thus in the 1930s John Maynard Keynes was prompted to comment:

Never in history was there a method devised of such efficacy for setting each country's advantage at variance with its neighbours' as the international gold (or, formerly, silver) standard. For it made domestic prosperity directly dependent on a competitive pursuit of markets and a competitive appetite for the precious metals. (Keynes 1964, p. 349)

Or as Scotsman John Law lamented in 1705, the world's supply of money, of specie, "is not in our power, but in the power of our enemies" (Law 1966, p. 118).

Thus, it is often insufficiently appreciated that an important cause of countries becoming enemies was that they adopted a gold standard for their domestic money supplies. In other words, they became enemies because each could increase its money supply optimally only by making certain that other countries increased theirs far less than optimally. This is not to say, of course, that the adoption of a gold standard for domestic money supplies was the only cause of conflict between nations; merely that it was one important cause and that there was no necessity for it.

So long as they insisted on a money supply consisting of specie or of paper money backed or offset by some fixed percentage of gold or silver, and in view of the fact that they had no precious metal mines, the British had only two choices if they were to bring into their island the increase in its money supply without which industry could neither grow nor prosper to the limit of its potential to obtain the precious metals: (1) by piracy on the high seas or the plunder of weaker countries or (2) by selling a part of their production of goods and services to foreigners in order to obtain (by purchase, as it were) the foreigners' silver or gold.

For centuries the preferred method of countries for the obtaining of more gold or silver was forcible seizure rather than purchase. From time immemorial, looting has been the preferred method of all powerful countries. This fact was not, however, a matter upon which Adam Smith chose to dwell. His lack of frankness in dealing with a preeminently important way of increasing a nation's money supply must count as a mark against both the frankness and the comprehensiveness of his exposition.

Thus it came about that Britain became the bane of Spanish galleons en route to Europe from Mexico and Peru. "The channel of circulation necessarily draws to itself a sum sufficient to fill it," opined Smith (1909, p. 338). "The quantity of coin will increase from necessity," he declared (1937, p. 188). But, complained the Spanish pamphleteer Quevedo, "[They] go for gold and silver to our fleets the way our fleets go to the Indies for it" (Vilar 1976, p. 196).

In due time, Britain went on to conquer most of the world worth looting of gold and silver (or of anything else of value). And in due time, Britain went on to become (for a time, at least) the world's foremost producing and exporting nation. The early primacy in predation was a necessary, although not sufficient, condition, for the early primacy in industrial development — a proposition that will be more fully considered in due course.

Smith's *Wealth of Nations* is not just an exposition of his ideas on how an economic system could and should be structured but also a polemic against a school of economists called mercantilists. The much written-about distinction between Adam Smith and the mercantilists was, however, less about ends than about means. Mercantilists are ordinarily thought of as wanting their nation's supply of gold and silver to increase as an end in itself. The view usually attributed to them, not without reason but neither with total justification, is that the importance of gold and silver resided in the fact that these metals constituted genuine wealth per se. On the other hand, Smith is thought of as wanting the increase not as an increase in wealth but because it would make possible the circulation of a larger annual output of goods and services — the proper measure of the wealth of a nation in his view.

Motivations aside, both the mercantilists and Adam Smith agreed in wanting the supply of gold and silver to increase. The really significant difference between them was that the mercantilists advocated "restraints upon importation [of goods and services] and encouragements to exportation [of goods and services]" (Smith 1909, p. 346). That is to say, mercantilists advocated restraints upon the exportation of gold and silver and encouragements for their importation. Adam Smith, on the contrary, opposed "encouragements and restraints" of all kinds (subsidies or tariffs, for example) and advocated "free trade."

We trust with perfect security that the freedom of trade, without any attention of government . . . will always supply us with all the gold and silver which we can afford to purchase or employ. (1909, p. 333)

The sovereign is completely discharged from a duty, in the attempting to perform which he must always be exposed to innumerable delusions, and for the proper performance of which no human knowledge or wisdom could ever be sufficient; the duty of superintending [encouraging or restraining] the industry of private people, and directing it towards the employments most suitable in the interest of the society. (1909, p. 456)

Every individual is continually exerting himself to find out the most advantageous employment for whatever capital he can command. It is his own advantage, indeed, and not that of the society, which he has in view. But the study of his own advantage naturally, or rather necessarily, leads him to prefer that employment which is most advantageous to the society. (1909, p. 349)

But the entirely self-regulating economy imagined by Adam Smith is not only far less automatic than might at first appear and is too frequently assumed, it is also considerably less beneficient to all concerned. This is true from many points of view, but only one is pertinent in the present context. When Smith says that "the study of his own advantage . . . leads the individual to prefer that employment which is most advantageous to the society," he means by the word *society* what might better be called "domestic society" or "the national economy." Obviously, even assuming that the pursuit of the individual's self-interest invariably promotes the interest of his nation (a completely gratuitous assumption), if the nation's interest requires a net inflow of scarce gold and is thus opposed to the interest of other nations (since they are thereby deprived of the inflow of gold they need), then an individual's self-interest does not "naturally, or rather necessarily" promote the interests of people of other nations; and therefore it does not promote the interests of "society" in its broadest connotation. Hence Smith's book is more nearly about the wealth of *a nation* (viz., Britain) considered apart or individually than about the wealth of *all nations* considered collectively, as the title he used seems meant to imply. The idea that what is good for one nation is necessarily good for all nations is equal in absurdity to the idea that what is good for one individual is necessarily good for all individuals.

Smith's belief that the economy of every separate nation would be optimally self-regulating if only individualism were given free rein was misconceived from many points of view, one of which is particularly pertinent here. It is misconceived in that it imagined that the money supply of every separate nation could be optimally self-regulating. But given the growth potential of all individual nations, given the dependence of the aggregate of nations wishing to achieve that growth potential on impossible increases in the world's supply of gold and silver, "Smith's idea of a self-regulating system is a utopian vision . . . an aberration in the history of mankind" (Wilbur and Jameson 1983, p. 165).

In the world as it actually exists rather than as we might wish it to be, Smith's ideas about "free trade" constitute an ideology appropriate only to the world's lowest-cost producer. It is an ideology by which the lowest-cost producer attempts to persuade other nations to sacrifice their home industries and domestic money supplies to the advantage of the lowest-cost producer. As Friedrich List was to write:

A country like England, which is far in advance of all its competitors, cannot better maintain and extend its manufacturing and commercial industry than by a trade as free as possible from all restraints. . . . This explains the favor with which the most enlightened economists of England regard free trade. [It likewise explains] the reluctance of the wise and prudent economists of other countries to adopt this principle. (Cited in Lekachman 1977, p. 163)

"Free trade" was thus the ideology (and to a remarkable extent the policy) of Britain during the era when it was the world's lowest-cost producer. It was not, during that era, an ideology that greatly or effectively discouraged protectionist policies in the United States, for example. Subsequently, with its emergence as the world's lowest-cost producer, the United States unfurled the banner of free trade. If, as appears likely at the time of this writing, Japan soon becomes the world's lowest-cost producer, then it is not altogether unlikely that Japan may find occasion to praise the free trade ideology it so wisely disdained so long as it was not.

The doctrine of free trade envisages a fictitious world in which each nation is perfectly contented to rely on whatever advantages nature and history have accorded it and to allow all other nations freely to do the same. It over-looks the inveterate tendency of all nations to seek as much self-sufficiency as is attainable. In practice, it has come to amount to a doctrine to the effect that countries of the tropical zones should be world suppliers of bananas and coconuts and leave to countries of the temperate zones the task of being world suppliers of manufactured items.

How different might have been the history of the last several centuries had the British realized at an early date that an adequate and satisfactory domestic money supply in no way need be dependent on an ever increasing stock of gold or silver — dependent on plunder (so long as that passed a mini-mal cost-benefit test) or, subsequently, dependent on selling goods and services abroad that could have been more equitably and happily consumed at home. Acceptance of a specie standard gave the emerging private enterprise system of Britain (and countries that followed the British example) a baleful twist — one from which it has not yet recovered — by turning it outward instead of inward.

The bizarre idea that came to prevail was the belief that the people of Britain should be constrained to consume less than they produced, that is to say, they should be constrained to produce more than they were permitted to consume. "Consumption is the sole end and purpose of production" could be heard recited ad nauseam by English economists, but the policies that were implemented in practice necessitated that domestic consumption be curtailed and firmly held below the level of domestic production. Only thus could an economy on a specie standard achieve a "favorable balance of trade" and thereby acquire an adequate quantity of specie for an optimally sized money supply.

No matter what level of deprivation and misery might prevail among the common people of Britain, whatever they produced but had not the money to buy was proclaimed "overproduction" or "surplus." It was then shipped abroad to be consumed by others than those who produced it — shipped in exchange for gold or silver (preferably produced cheaply by slave labor). Gold and silver were commodities unfit for consumption but foolishly believed to be necessary in order to provide an adequate medium of exchange and medium for the payment of debts.

All this occurred despite the fact that specie or paper money backed by specie was in no way a necessity for a domestic economy. At as early a date as the writing of Plato's *Laws* it was understood that "for domestic trade a token-money established by law should be used, gold and silver being restricted to transactions with foreigners" (Monroe 1965, p. 7).

The point of the preceding chapter was that a domestic money supply based on the precious metals is unachievable for all nations or for very many, if any, of them. The point of this chapter has been that even the attempt of several economies to operate on a gold and silver standard became a cause of wars abroad and cruel deprivation at home. The attempt at institutionalization of the specie standard (1) virtually guaranteed conflicts between nations for a larger share of the inadequate world production of the precious metals (or, as is sometimes said, for markets for their "overproduction") and (2) virtually guaranteed that the people of a nation would never be permitted to raise the level of their consumption to their level of production. And this, of course, virtually guaranteed class conflicts on the domestic front.

We will begin a discussion of alternate and far better ways of providing a medium of exchange than the way dictated by a specie standard with Chapter 7. Before undertaking that task, however, several misconceptions regarding the relationships between money supply, production, and prices remain to be cleared away.

Chapter 4

Low Growth Rates of Money Supply

Let us imagine a period during which, for some combination of circumstances, the real output of an economy Q increases 4 percent per annum and the economy's money supply M increases only 2 percent per annum. What is the result? Obviously, if there is increasingly less money per unit of output, each unit of money must perform a larger task. The purchasing power of money must increase; in other words, the prices of goods and services P must decrease.

Perhaps this may be seen more clearly if we recall a form of Fisher's Equation of Exchange under the assumption of constant velocity of turnover of money: $M_r \cong Q_r + P_r$. Using the values assumed above, the equation becomes $2 = 4 + P_r$ or $P_r = 2 - 4$ whence $P_r = -2$. That is to say, the growth rate of P must be negative and this means that prices on average will decline in the event that the money supply growth rate is less than that of real output.

What is the effect on an economy of the falling general level of prices that results from a too slowly increasing money supply? A principal purpose of this chapter is to answer and discuss this question. First, however, some references to Adam Smith bearing on the topic.

Smith reports, for example, that over the two centuries between roughly 1325 and 1525 the price of silver in England doubled. We may assume that this occurred either because output Q remained about the same and the amount of silver M became scarcer due to loss, wear, and defacement or because it so happened that Q increased faster than M. In any event, Smith says that the price P of "a quarter of corn" was 4 ounces of silver in 1325 and only 2 ounces of silver in 1525 (1937, p. 176). What Smith says on the matter fully accords with our conclusion above that the result of a too slow increase in money supply is an increase in the price of money and, inversely, a decrease in the average price of everything else.

Elsewhere Smith writes:

So far as their quantity [i.e., the quantity of gold/silver] in any particular country depends upon . . . the fertility or barrenness of the mines which happen to supply the commercial world, their . . . price . . . will, no doubt, sink more or less in proportion to the fertility, and rise in proportion to the barrenness, of those mines. (1937, p. 236)

In other words, if the barrenness of mines is such that the money supply of the commercial world does not increase as rapidly as output, then the price of gold and silver will rise and other commodity prices will fall.

A different terminology is often employed to say much the same thing as has just been said. An increasing scarcity of money is often called "deflation of the money supply" and is said to cause "deflation of the prices of goods and services" or simply "price deflation." Note, however, that with deflation of the money supply it is prices of goods and services that decrease, or are said to be deflated, not the price of money; it increases.

The above citations of Smith show his appreciation of the phenomenon that early-day economist William Petty had in mind when he wrote that "the value of silver rises and falls of itself" (1963, p. 183). His remark is, of course, equally applicable to gold, and it is clear that Smith fully agreed with Petty.

Smith, no doubt, would also have agreed when Petty went on to say that "the fact the value of silver [or gold] rises and falls of itself consequently takes from it the perfect aptitude for being an uniform and steady measure of all other things" (1963, p. 183). This calls for another slight digression.

It is worthwhile to dwell briefly on the fact that neither gold nor silver is, in fact, a uniform and steady measure of all other things since their value may rise or fall "of itself," as Petty says, or because of changes in the "fertility or barrenness" of mines, as Smith says. There is a widespread belief that the adoption of a gold (or silver) standard provides a guarantee against widely fluctuating prices of goods and services. History provides ample evidence to dispel such a belief. Smith has been cited above to show a case when the purchasing power of silver doubled, but other and more recent examples abound.

From 1814 to 1849 the wholesale price index in the United States fell 55 percent. Following the discovery of gold in California and Australia the index rose—by 66 percent between 1849 and 1872. From 1872 to 1896 the index fell 50 percent. Following the discovery of gold in Alaska, the Yukon, and South Africa and the perfection of improved methods of extracting gold from ores the index again rose—by 49 percent between 1896 to 1913. (Council of Economic Advisors 1982, Table 3-1, p. 71)

Although the adoption of a gold or silver standard is no guarantee against price deflation (or inflation), neither is there a guarantee against price fluctuations if the size of the money supply is left to the discretion of private banks or the printing presses of government; but discussion of any type of money supply other than one pegged to specie has been postponed until later chapters. The sole point of this discussion is that the adoption of a gold or silver standard in no way provides a guarantee against a widely fluctuating price level.

Let us now return to the original question: What is the effect on an economy of a falling price level due to slow growth of the money supply? And let us begin by considering the answer given by Adam Smith. Should there occur an increasing scarcity of specie, with the result of a fall in the prices of goods and services, Smith writes that this would be

of very little importance to the real wealth and prosperity of the world, the real value of the annual produce of the land and labour of mankind. . . . The quantity of gold or silver by which this annual produce could be expressed or represented, would, no doubt, be very different; but its real value . . . would be precisely the same. (Smith 1937, p. 237)

Here Smith is gravely mistaken, and his mistake became one of enormous importance in the history of economics because so many subsequent economists accepted his altogether incorrect proposition as truth.

The inescapable and most obvious consequence of falling prices of goods and services is a failure of entrepreneurs to make acceptably large profits, but Smith appears not to have appreciated this fact or its great importance. The consequence of smaller entrepreneurial profits is the closing of factories, unemployment, bankruptcies, and decreased output Q. Thus when prices fall, "the real value of the land and labour of mankind" will *not* in the aggregate "be precisely the same" but will be less. For Smith to assert that a falling price level "is of . . . little importance to the real wealth and prosperity of the world" is grievously to misconceive the way the world works.

Because the distinction Smith makes in the quotation given above between nominal value (price P) and real value (however difficult to measure it may be) is one frequently made by economists, it deserves a few further remarks. A loaf of bread has what we may call real value in that it requires real labor and real materials to produce. Likewise, an hour's work certainly has real value to a worker. Whatever the scarcity or abundance of the precious metals, the real value of bread or work may be assumed to remain essentially unaffected. At any particular time, however, the bread will have a nominal value or price (say, an ounce of silver) for which a person must work one hour. At another time (owing, for example, to an increased scarcity of silver, a rise in its price, and a fall in all other prices) the nominal value of the loaf of bread might be one half ounce of silver, for which a person must work one hour. The fact that the nominal values of bread and work have fluctuated may appear to make little real difference since one hour's work still equals one loaf of bread. From such a consideration (among others) emerges the notion that nominal values are of little real significance.

One way in which nominal values are significant, however, is that the process of going from the first equilibrium (loaf of bread = one ounce of silver = one hour work) to the second equilibrium (loaf of bread = half-ounce of silver = one hour of work) requires the passage of time. What happens during the transition from one equilibrium to the other may be, and usually is, of great importance. If wages should fall faster than the price of bread, for example, it is absurd to say that nominal values have little real significance to the wage earner needing to buy bread.

Let us imagine a case in which an entrepreneur borrows 100 ounces of silver at a time when he would have to sell 100 pairs of shoes to repay it. Let us imagine further that by the time repayment comes due the entrepreneur would have to sell 200 pairs of shoes in order to repay (owing to a scarcity of silver, a rise in its price, and a fall in the price of shoes and wages) and, worse still, that the wages of the buyers of shoes have fallen. It cannot be said that nominal values would be of little real significance to the entrepreneur. It is not impossible that the increased burdensomeness of his debt would bankrupt him.

Falling prices of goods and services (including wages) tend to affect entrepreneurs and other borrowers of money adversely. On the other hand, falling prices tend to affect bankers and other lenders of money favorably. Entrepreneurs and debtors generally tend to be devastated by falling prices (deflation). Bankers and creditors generally prefer falling prices since the money with which they are repaid will buy more than the money they lent.

Smith's assertion that nominal values at this or that time have little significance diverts attention from the fact that changes in nominal values from one time to another can have great real significance. Both Smith and many economists after him exhibited the tendency to place undue emphasis on "equilibrium conditions" and to give far too little consideration to what happens during the transition from one equilibrium state to another. Equilibrium states are usually rare and of short duration; most of "economic time" is a time of transition. It is a time of dynamic movement, not of static equilibrium.

The tendency of Smith and other economists was also, on one hand, to think of changes in the output of goods and services in the economy as being determined by "real factors" (e.g., availability of raw materials and labor), but, on the other hand, to think of changes in prices as being determined not by real factors (e.g., cost of production) but solely by "monetary factors." The tendency is to be deplored. The fact is that both nominal and real factors affect both the quantity of output and the price level. Too slow a growth of money supply means falling prices; falling prices mean lower profits, more bankruptcies, more unemployment, less production, and hence a decrease in Q_r. Slow growth of M affects not only P but Q as well.

We must also note that Smith deals most frequently with situations in which he assumes P is constant and that he assumes causation to run from Q to M: "the quantity of money must increase as the value of the annual produce increases." But it is also possible for causation to run from M to Q (and/or P). In particular, it is possible for M_r, when it is small, to result in Q_r being small as a result of insufficient profits.

The impossibility of increasing M, when it consisted of specie, at rates corresponding to the rates at which Q could more or less easily grow, was shown in Chapter 2. This means that the normal expectation under a rigid gold or silver standard is slow real growth—a principal thesis of this chapter.

A closely related point, as we have seen, is that the normal expectation under a rigid gold or silver standard is a falling price level or price deflation. The entire period from the depletion of the mines that supplied the Roman Empire to the discovery of the Western Hemisphere was a period of deflation. That is also partly the cause of it being a period of extremely slow Q growth. Growth, however, is a many-faceted matter, and the extent to which the slow Q growth of the period was due to deflation rather than to other factors will long remain a subject of controversy.

A silver (rather than gold) standard prevailed in most of the world until early in the nineteenth century. Gold was used as well as silver, but its price was quoted in terms of silver or in terms of national monetary units (shillings, franks, marks) that were defined in terms of silver. The change from a silver standard to a gold standard did not alter matters decisively inasmuch as both are commodities with a cost of production that "rises and falls of itself." Thus it should occasion no surprise to read: "The gold-standard period was very deflationary on the whole. For the period 1814 to 1913 the fall in the wholesale price index in the United States was 44 per cent" (Council of Economic Advisors 1982, p. 71).

Two factors of importance other than the existence of the gold standard, however, affected the performance of the price index between 1814 and 1913. One of these factors, as we shall see later, was that the gold standard was not rigidly adhered to; and the effective money supply in Britain, the United States, and most other countries, was made to increase far faster than the gold supply. Had this not been the case, the wholesale price index would have fallen much more than 44 percent.

The other factor of importance is that between 1814 and 1913 prices declined, in part at least, not on account of any monetary factor at all but because the Industrial Revolution brought about enormous reductions in the cost of production of goods and services and made possible lower prices without reduced overall profitability.

This introduces a new aspect of the matter of prices. It is certainly true that, other things being equal, a decrease in the supply of money necessarily raises the price of money and pushes down prices of goods and services. But the converse is not necessarily true: a decline in the prices of goods and services does not necessarily mean that deflation of the money supply is occurring or has occurred. Falling prices may be the result of falling costs of production (due to the introduction of new materials or processes, lower taxes, or lower interest rates on borrowed money, and so on). When prices fall because of falling costs of production, saying that the prices are being "deflated" involves a word of misleading, or at least questionable, connotations. "Deflation" implies, or is usually taken to imply, that prices earlier were inflated and that the excess of "hot air" they contained is being let out. It is also questionable in that it implies, or is usually taken to imply, that monetary deflation is the cause of falling commodity prices, although the cause is altogether different. Fluctuating prices may under certain circumstances be "purely a monetary phenomenon," but under other circumstances they might not in any sense be a monetary matter.

In brief summary, it may be repeated that in order to prosper a private enterprise economy needs a money supply that increases or may be increased at least as rapidly as the production of goods and services. A too slow growth of the money supply means falling commodity prices; and a falling price level, in turn, means falling profits, layoffs, factory closings, and suboptimum economic performance.

Chapter 5

More Rapid Growth Rates of Money Supply

Now let us imagine a period during which, owing to some combination of circumstances, the real output Q of an economy increases at 4 percent per annum and the economy's money supply M increases 6 percent per annum. What is the result? Obviously, if there is increasingly more money per unit of output, the purchasing power of money must decrease. In other words, the prices of goods and services P must increase.

Recall again the form of Fisher's Equation of Exchange under the assumption of constant velocity of turnover of money: $M_r \cong Q_r + P_r$. Using the values assumed above, the equation becomes $6 = 4 + P_r$, or $P_r = 6 - 4$ whence $P_r = +2$. That is to say, the growth rate of P is positive; and this means that prices on average will increase in the event that money supply increases faster than real output.

What is the effect on an economy of a rapidly increasing money supply and, in consequence, an increasing price level? The answer is discussed at some length later on; first, however, some references to Adam Smith bearing on the topic need to be examined.

Smith reports, for example, that during the century between roughly 1525 and 1625 the price of silver in England fell by 75 percent. We may assume that this occurred either because output Q remained about the same and the amount of silver M became more plentiful (because of large importations from the Americas) or because it so happened that Q increased but M increased faster. In any event, Smith says that the price P of "a quarter of corn" was 2 ounces of silver in 1525 and 8 ounces of silver in 1625 (1937, p. 176). What Smith says on the matter fully accords with our conclusion that the result of a too rapid increase in money supply is a decrease in the price of money and, inversely, an increase in the average price of everything else.

The fourfold rise in the price of corn is an outstanding example of "price inflation" of goods and services, owing principally to a fall in the price of silver, owing, to "inflation of the supply of silver," owing, in turn, to the conquest of the Aztecs by Cortez and of the Incas by Pizarro.

The effect of the influx of coin was not solely that prices increased, however. The all-important additional effect was that it stimulated entrepreneurs to produce more goods and services now that the money supply was increasingly abundant. That increasing abundance of money made it possible for more products to be sold profitably; and this in turn encouraged the hiring of more workers and the building of more or larger factories.

When the amount of money in the hands of potential consumers increases, when, as economists nowadays commonly say, aggregate demand increases, then entrepreneurs either raise the prices of their products or increase output of their products or both. The increase in M may be said sometimes to cause an increase in P or sometimes to cause an increase in Q (or both).

The writings of David Hume, Smith's friend and fellow Scotsman, describe the dynamics of the situation more fully and more satisfactorily than Smith's.

Prices of all things [wrote Hume in 1752] have only risen three, or at most, four times, since the discovery of the West Indies. But will anyone assert that there is not much more than four times the coin in Europe, than was in the fifteenth century, and the centuries preceding it? . . . No other satisfactory reason can be given, why all prices have not risen to a much more exorbitant height, except that . . . more commodities are produced by additional industry. (1970, p. 44)

In order to impart a more full appreciation of the differences between Smith and Hume, another citation from the former may be helpful.

As the value of the annual produce increases . . . a part of the increased produce . . . will be employed in purchasing, wherever it is to be had, [i.e., from some foreign country] the additional quantity of gold and silver necessary for circulating [the increased produce]. The increase in those metals will . . . be the effect, not the cause, of public prosperity. (1909, p. 280)

As previously discussed, selling abroad the goods and services that could not be sold domestically because of a scarcity of specie was virtually the only method of acquiring coin that Smith thought worth giving attention. This led him to believe that an increase in the supply of gold or silver M was invariably an effect rather than a cause of prosperity. In other words, Smith thought of Q as the independent variable and M as the dependent variable. That M might under certain circumstance be the independent variable and Q the dependent variable he regarded as too exceptional a circumstance to warrant discussion.

In order to deal with the matter more thoroughly, although he found no time or place to do so, Smith should also somewhere have written something like the following:

As our fleets or the vessels of our privateers captured Spanish ships returning from the Indies laden with gold or silver, or as the result of our raids on Spanish ports in the New World, or our plundering other countries anywhere in the world, there ensued an inflow of huge amounts of coin. The result was more spending of money, more demand for goods and services, and more production of them. The increase in the supply of precious metals was then the cause, not the effect, of public prosperity.

Or Smith might have engaged in a little wishful thinking and ventured to say:

If within the shores of our island there should be discovered an unsuspected silver mine of large proportions, the result would be a greater abundance of coin, more spending, more demand for goods and services, and more production of them. The increase in the supply of silver would then be the cause, not the effect, of public prosperity.

Smith saw fit to deal almost exclusively with the case when increased product output occurs first, followed by foreign sales, and then by the inflow of precious metals. Any other process by which a greater abundance of precious metals in England might be brought about did not fit well into his overall conception of a self-regulating money supply and therefore an economy that as a whole was self-regulating.

Hume, on the other hand, gave full recognition to the fact that an inflow of precious metals could occur from a cause or causes other than the foreign sale of increased output and could itself be a cause of increased output (as well as sometimes a cause of higher prices, depending on circumstances).

Since the discovery of the mines in America, industry has encreased in all the nations of Europe . . . and this may justly be ascribed, amongst other reasons, to the encrease of gold and silver. Accordingly we find, that, in every kingdom into which money begins to flow in greater abundance than formerly, everything takes a new face: labour and industry gain life; the merchant becomes more enterprising, the manufacturer more diligent and skillful, and even the farmer follows his plow with greater alacrity and attention. (Hume 1970, p. 37)

[It] is as pernicious to industry when the quantity of money diminishes as it is advantageous when it encreases. (p. 40)

[Good] reasons . . . can be given for a gradual and universal encrease . . . of money. (p. 39)

More than a hundred years after Hume, Alexander Del Mar viewed the matter similarly.

The spoil [gold and silver] was first obtained by the Spaniards and the Portuguese. The earliest rise in prices [P] and the earliest social progress [rise in Q] which followed it occurred in Spain and Portugal. No rise in prices [P] and no signs of a renaissance [rise in Q] are to be observed in France, Holland, or England, until after these phenomena had appeared in the Iberian peninsula. But no sooner did the northern nations—no matter by what means—manage to secure a share of the American spoil, and turn it into money, than there at once followed a similar rise in prices [P] and a similar renaissance [rise in Q]. (1975, p. 179)

Another facet of the difference between the viewpoints of Hume and Smith becomes evident when we consider the following passage from Hume:

The good policy of the magistrate [or sovereign] consists . . . in keeping [the nation's money supply] encreasing; because by that means, he keeps alive the spirit of industry in the nation. (1970, p. 39)

This is a statement Smith could never endorse since it is so completely out of keeping with his conviction that "the sovereign is completely discharged from any duty" of trying to influence the size of the money supply (1909, p. 456). Hume did not find convincing the Smithian ideology that insisted that the money supply and the economy are optimally self-regulating and that there is no fitting, proper, or significant role for government to play.

Let us now consider in somewhat greater detail the case of an increasing abundance of gold and silver, M, resulting in a decrease in their prices and a rise in the prices of goods and services, P. The most obvious consequence of rising prices is that entrepreneurs' profits tend to rise. Smith appears not to have appreciated fully the importance of this fact, the consequence of which is increased production by existing factories and the opening of new factories, a decline in unemployment, and increased output Q. Thus "the real value of the land and labour of mankind" will *not* "be precisely the same" as before the increasing abundance of specie, as Smith believed. It will be greater. For Smith to assert that a rising price level, P, "is of little importance to the real wealth and prosperity of the world" is to misconceive greatly the way the world works.

Let us imagine a case in which an entrepreneur borrows 100 ounces of silver at a time when he would need to sell 200 pairs of shoes to repay it. And imagine that by the time repayment came due (owing to an increased abundance of silver, a fall in its price, and a rise in the price of shoes and wages) the entrepreneur would need to sell only 100 pairs of shoes to repay and, better still, that buyers of shoes have higher wages with which to buy them. It can hardly be said that nominal values would be of little real significance to the entrepreneur.

As observed in only slightly different words in the previous chapter, price inflation tends favorably to affect entrepreneurs and other borrowers of money. On the other hand, it tends adversely to affect bankers and other lenders of money. Entrepreneurs find to their advantage a period when prices are rising—a period of inflation. Bankers and other creditors find to their advantage a period when prices are falling—a period of deflation. Thus, because he quite properly preferred the welfare and prosperity of entrepreneurs over that of money lenders, "Hume preferred slowly rising to steady prices" (Schumpeter 1954, p. 713). Money lenders, in Hume's view, constituted a class of people "prone to sink into the lethargy of a stupid and pampered luxury, without spirit [or] ambition" (Hume 1970, p. 98).

Smith's erroneous belief that changes in the quantity of M result only in changes in P and do not result in changes in Q even appealed to Karl Marx at times. In *Capital* he writes, "It is a popular delusion to ascribe stagnation in the production and circulation [of commodities] to an insufficiency in the circulating medium" (1977, p. 218). On another occasion, however, Marx expressed a quite contrary view:

The most common observation shows that an increased demand [increased money supply] will, in some instances, leave the market prices of commodities altogether unchanged, and will, in other instances, cause a temporary rise of market prices followed by an increased supply, followed by a reduction of the prices to their original level, and in many cases below their original level. [In some instances] an increase of demand produces an increase of supply instead of an ultimate rise of market prices. (Marx and Engels 1955, p. 408)

This example of Marx being of two minds about the matter reminds me that on one occasion, and I believe on only one occasion, Smith conceded (with obvious reluctance) that owing to an increase in the size of the money supply, "the commerce and industry of the country . . . may be somewhat augmented" (Smith 1909, p. 259).

Smith's more frequently expressed view that changes in M result only in changes in P, not in Q, retained its popularity into the twentieth century. Astonishingly and quite unfortunately, it remains a widely held view. Milton Friedman and Anna Schwartz, for example, begin an impressive and in many ways valuable book by saying much the same thing as did Smith: "The dominant influence and ultimately the whole influence of monetary change is on price rather than output." More than 600 pages later their view is reiterated: "[Our] theory supposes output to be determined by predominantly nonmonetary forces and supposes . . . changes in money to be reflected ultimately entirely in prices" (1982, pp. 8 and 623).

Hume's alas, has exerted less enduring influence than Smith, despite his deeper insight. It is nevertheless true, as Hume believed, that increases in the money supply, or increases in aggregate demand, not only tend to raise prices but also act as an incentive, an inducement, a spur to greater output; act as a generator, precipitator, promoter, or nourisher of increased production.

Perhaps an analogy from the natural sciences will be useful in showing the perverse onesidedness of the view that changes in M result solely in changes in P rather than in changes in P and/or Q. If one begins with any fixed number of molecules of a gas (oxygen, neon, or whatever) placed within a sealed container of some sort, and then one increases the temperature of the gas, the result will be either an increase in the pressure exerted on the walls of the container or an increase in the volume occupied by the gas provided the container is flexible, or possibly a change in both pressure and volume. If the pressure is held constant, the change in volume will be closely proportional to the change in the absolute temperature. If the volume is held constant, the change in pressure will be closely proportional to the change in the absolute temperature. Or the constraints on the system might be such that the effect of the increased temperature will be some change in both pressure and volume. There is no way to know whether an increase in temperature will affect pressure or volume or both except by knowing what constraints are put on the system. Likewise, there is no way to know whether an increase in money supply will affect output or prices or both except by knowing a long list of initial conditions. To expect that no matter what the initial conditions an increase in money would affect only prices is as absurd as to expect that no matter what the initial conditions an increase in temperature would affect only pressure or only volume in the case of a confined sample of some gas.

Another matter of importance must be noted. It is certainly true that increases in the size of the money supply often produce decreases in the price of money and hence increases in the prices of goods and services. This cannot, however, be taken to mean that increases in the prices of goods and services are always to be attributed, or only to be attributed, to increases in the size of the money supply. Rising prices, for example, may be the result of rising costs of production (due to the depletion of sources of cheap raw materials, due to higher taxes, due to higher interest rates on borrowed money, due to cartel profits, and so on). When prices rise because of rising costs of production, saying that the prices are being "inflated" is a highly questionable procedure. Fluctuating prices may under certain circumstances be "purely a monetary phenomenon," but under other circumstances they may not in any sense be a monetary matter.

Recall now Smith's Law of Chapter 1: "The quantity of money . . . must in every country . . . increase as the value of the annual produce increases." When the rate of increase of the money supply M_r equals the rate of increase of real output Q_r the price level P tends to remain constant. An increase in M does not necessarily or always cause an increase in P. An increase in M is thus not necessarily a cause of "price inflation" in any proper sense of the words. Likewise, the fact that M for some reason increases is not a sufficient reason to warrant the assertion that the money supply is being "inflated." An increase in the money supply that does not result in higher prices of goods and services is entirely possible, sometimes does occur, and must occur if Q is regularly to increase at constant prices. And from this it follows that the practice, so often encountered, of characterizing as "inflationary" any and all cases of increases in the money supply deserves the strongest disapproval. It is only when M_r exceeds Q_r that there is the slightest excuse for calling the money supply increases "inflationary"; but even when M_r exceeds Q_r, there is no way of knowing from this fact alone whether it is the size of M_r that causes prices to rise or the prices are rising due to other causes, so that the size of M_r is merely an accommodating factor rather than a causal one.

Chapter 6 _____

Money as a Legal and Psychological Matter

Any economic system deserving of the term, even one of minimal sophistication, involves a division of labor — between town and country, woodsmen and carpenters, miners and manufacturers, producers and distributors, and so on. Likewise, it involves trade or exchange between the participants in the division of labor.

Trade may be conducted by direct barter — a farmer's corn for a cobbler's shoes, for example. But if the farmer does not want shoes or the cobbler does not want corn, barter must involve third parties and becomes very complex and time consuming. Thus early on there developed the practice of the farmer and cobbler first bartering their produce for silver coins and then using the coins to barter for the produce of others.

A basic principle of trade has always been that items are exchanged only for other items of equal value; and this principle led to the belief that when shoes or corn are bartered for silver coins the amount of silver in the coins should be of equal value to the shoes or corn. In other words, it was presumed that silver money should have an intrinsic value equal to that of the product for which it is exchanged. When a commodity such as silver is used as money and when it is exchanged on the basis of its intrinsic value, what we have is still a system of barter, albeit a more sophisticated and handier one.

Over a period of many centuries, the concept of money having an intrinsic value has been gradually phased out and replaced by a concept of money having no intrinsic value. People today accept paper money that is valueless in itself for their goods and services simply because they are satisfied that the money will, in turn, be accepted in payment for the goods and services of others or accepted in payment of their debts. The paper money of the

United States, for example, bears the words, "This note is legal tender for all debts, public and private." It is accepted in payment of wages, for example, because workers know that it must, as an enforceable legal matter, be accepted by their creditors or by the vendors of the goods and services they may be induced to buy.

We know from Chapter 2 that money of intrinsic value (gold or silver) necessarily had eventually to be phased out because of the impossibility of increasing the quantity of the precious metals in step with increases in output of goods and services and thus in step with the need for an ever larger "medium of exchange" or "medium of repayment of debts." The evolution of the monetary system from one based on a commodity of intrinsic value to one based on "legal tender" without intrinsic value is what much of this book is about, and some of the earlier phases of this evolution is the subject of this chapter.

The earliest silver or gold coins were introduced as a method of providing traders with a known and uniform quantity and quality of precious metal — as a method of rendering it unnecessary to assay and weigh every piece of metal. Early coins usually bore the seal or the likeness of the sovereign of the issuing country as a guarantee of weight and fineness. The English shilling of year 1300 or thereabouts contained one-twentieth of a pound weight (troy) of silver (roughly 18.7 grams of silver in today's terms).

In England the practice quickly developed of quoting prices in terms of shillings and of making contracts and loans in terms of shillings rather than ounces of silver or other units of weight. Thus even at an early date in the evolution of an economic system, we find not only a role for the individuals who buy and sell, enter into contracts, lend and borrow, and so on, but also a role for "the sovereign," for government, not merely as a recorder of deeds to property or as an arbitor of disputes over property ownership but also as an enforcer of contracts, a collector of debts, a superintendent of debtor's prisons, and so on.

"Commerce and manufactures," wrote Adam Smith, "can seldom flourish long in any state . . . in which the faith of contracts is not supported by law, and in which the authority of the state is not supposed to be regularly employed in enforcing the payment of debts" (1909, p. 578). Nothing, in fact, figures more prominently in the history of money than the problem of paying debts. Debtors' prisons characterized all population centers for centuries and endured in western economies until late in the 1800s.

Debts, as a matter of custom or common practice, came to be denominated in terms of "coin of the realm" or "legal tender money" and repayable in the same. As Adam Smith remarked, "In England . . . all accounts are kept, and the value of all goods and of all estates is generally computed in silver" (1937, p. 39).

In order to gain a better appreciation of the significance of the emergence of legal tender money or coin of the realm, let us now imagine a sovereign who becomes indebted to the amount of, say, 100,000 shillings. In other words, imagine that he has borrowed what amounts in modern units to about 1,800,000 grams of silver. He then begins a process of withdrawing from circulation all existing shillings and replacing them by a new "coin of the realm" essentially identical in appearance, and still called a shilling, but, let us imagine, containing only 9 grams of silver and a greater amount of cheap alloy. Eventually twice the original number of shillings may be issued. He then repays his debt with 100,000 of the new shillings. That is to say, he repays his creditors not with 1,800,000 grams of silver but with 900,000 grams. From one point of view, this is an obvious case of defrauding creditors. Looked at the other way, however, the sovereign borrowed 100,000 in coin of the realm and repaid with 100,000 in coin of the realm.

Such a procedure came to be called "debasing the coinage"—a literally accurate yet somewhat pejorative way of expressing the matter—and occurred again and again in virtually all countries. By 1600 the silver content of the English shilling had been reduced to only about a third its earlier value (Petty 1963, p. 51), but in a legal sense the shilling all the while remained a shilling and a basic coin of the realm. What we see here is that what counts as money, as "legal tender for the payment of all debts" is very much a matter of sovereignty. Money, in significant respects, is what the government, as enforcer of contracts, says is money.

Thus, about 1600, when a creditor tried to refuse payment in shillings because their silver content had been reduced since the contracting of the debt, an English court ruled as follows:

As the King by his prerogative may make money of what matter and form he pleases and establish the standard for it, so he may change his money in substance and impression and enhance or debase the value of it or entirely decry and annul it. Although at the time this contract was signed pure unalloyed silver was current in this kingdom, since alloyed money was introduced before the day payment came due, the creditor is required to accept it. (Dunn 1960, p. 4)

With the passage of time, the prerogatives of kings were subject to ever larger limitations, and eventually in England "sovereignty" came to reside in Parliament rather than in the person of the king. But the principle that "money is what the sovereign authorities say it is" remains essentially unchanged to this day.

As recently as the 1930s, the U.S. government revalued ("debased") the dollar from 1.672 grams of gold to 0.987 grams. People holding so-called "gold bonds" bought by legal tender dollars with which 1.672 grams of gold could be purchased were required to accept in repayment legal tender dollars with which only 0.987 grams of gold could be purchased. This all came about as a result of legislative enactments, executive policies, and a series of decisions by the United States Supreme Court. According to the court, clauses requiring payment of 1.672 grams of gold per dollar "interfere with the exertion of the power granted to the Congress to choose a uniform money system" wherein the dollar is valued at 0.987 grams of gold. "The frustration of contracts" such as those requiring repayment of 1.672 grams of gold per dollar, "may be a lawful exercise of power when such contracts are in conflict with public welfare" (Dunn 1960, pp. 91–94).

Although the sovereign may by decree determine that a shilling of 9 grams of silver is legal tender for the payment of debts incurred when the shilling contained 18 grams (or determine that a dollar of 0.987 grams of gold is legal tender for payment of debts incurred when the dollar contained 1.672 grams), it cannot, however, determine the purchasing power of the new shilling (or dollar) with respect to goods and services. The purchasing power of money is determined by bid and asked prices in the marketplace.

"The value of money" thus has two aspects. On the one hand, the value of money as "legal tender in payment of debts" may be decreed by the governing authorities. On the other hand, the value of money as "purchasing power for goods and services" cannot be determined by decree but can only be settled by what private people are willing to give or take for it. It is crucial constantly to bear in mind both the legal and the psychological aspects of money. In part it is a legal matter subject solely to decisions by government and in part it is a psychological matter involving decisions by interacting individuals.

Our shillings and sixpences, which are almost our only coin [in England in 1769] are so much worn by use that they are twenty, thirty, or forty per cent below their original value; yet they pass currency which can arise only from a tacit convention. Our colonies in America . . . used a paper currency [which] passed in all payments by convention. (Hume 1970, p. 214)

In a certain sense, it may be said that money can be anything that people generally will accept as money. And it will have whatever purchasing power people generally are willing to attribute to it. It will be hoarded when there is an expectation that it will rise in purchasing power (whether or not the expectation is rational) and spent as promptly as possible when there is an expectation (rational or irrational) that it will fall in purchasing power. In an altogether different sense, however, it may be said that money is whatever the government says is money. And it will have that power to pay debts that the government says it has.

The area over which a government has jurisdiction is obviously limited. The instantaneous effect of reducing the silver content of the shilling from 18 to 9 grams of silver was to reduce its purchasing power and its debt-liquidating power by half in all foreign countries. That is to say, the shilling was revalued immediately and solely on the basis of the weight and fineness of its silver content in all areas controlled by foreign governments, by all parties not bound by the national conventions or habits or laws of the country reducing the silver content of its coinage. Its legal tender value or purchasing power in the issuing country was a matter of no interest or concern to traders or lenders or money market experts in other countries.

English merchants, having now to pay two shillings for foreign goods where they previously paid only one, were therefore constrained to raise their selling price on the home market more or less accordingly. Hence, with indeterminate rapidity depending on widely differing circumstances, all prices of goods and services tended to rise in terms of the new shillings to one degree or another.

It would be an altogether unwarranted oversimplification, however, to say that the only effect (or the immediate effect) of halving the silver content of the shilling, hence doubling the number of shillings in circulation, was the doubling of all commodity prices. The passage of time was required before everyone accustomed to dealing in "old" shillings became accustomed to "new" shillings. The common or popular view that "a shilling is a shilling is a shilling" could be dispelled only slowly.

Rising prices made it easier for entrepreneurs to realize profits, reduced the burdensomeness of their debts, encouraged them to borrow and invest more, enabled them to hire more employes and thus produce more. The increase in M was reflected not solely in an increase in P but also in an increase in Q. "Debasement of the coinage," on account of the concomitant increase in the quantity of shillings (M) in circulation, benefited entrepreneurs and their newly hired employees. In general, it stimulated the economy and resulted in faster real growth. On the other hand, "debasement of the coinage" was a disaster from the point of view of creditors, who could buy less with the shillings with which they were repaid than with the shillings they originally loaned.

"Debasement of the coinage," since it stimulated the economy to higher employment and increased production, might be regarded as "one of the prices of progress." It is not customary to so regard it, perhaps because of the influence of creditors on the thinking of economists, lawyers, and historians. Many of "the prices of progress"—child labor, death or incapacitating injury in industrial accidents, lockouts to drive down wages, and so on—have been regarded as perhaps deplorable but nevertheless entirely tolerable, but not "debasement of the coinage." It seems probable that this attitude came about because the thinking of commentators has been less influenced by children, victims of industrial accidents, and the unemployed than by the creditor class. A century or so ago, it was not considered immoral to enslave children in mines and mills as a price of progress. Why at the same time should it have been considered immoral to reduce the precious metal content of the coinage, since this amounted in practice to little more than a special tax on creditors?

"Debasement of the coinage" originally appeared odious because it was frequently associated with the conniving of overindebted kings. It would be a mistake, however, to think of all reductions of the gold or silver content of coins as due entirely to the venality of monarchs or the desire of governments to reduce the burdensomeness of their debts. We must also remember the ongoing loss and wear of coins that tended inexorably to reduce the quantity of silver available for coinage.

Imagine a case in which the silver content of the total coinage of a country was reduced by, say, 20 percent, through loss and wear over a period of several decades. A recoinage that brought the shilling back to its original silver content would decrease the number of shillings in circulation by 20 percent. The reduction of the size of M would result partly in changing prices, P, but also partly in a declining output, Q — the decline in Q resulting from the greater difficulty entrepreneurs encountered in realizing profits, the greater burdensomeness of their debts, and so on. On the other hand, a recoinage that reduced the silver content of the shilling by 20 percent but brought the number of shillings in circulation back to the original amount punished money lenders rather than entrepreneurs, creditors rather than debtors. If a recoinage there must be, is not a recoinage favorable to entrepreneurs preferable to one favorable to money lenders?

David Hume, for one, saw some merit in "debasement" when the periodically necessary recoinages due to loss and wear occurred.

Were all our money, for instance, recoined, and a penny's worth of silver taken from every shilling, the new shilling would probably purchase everything that could have been bought by the old . . . and domestic industry, by the circulation of a greater number of pounds and shillings, would receive some increase and encouragement. . . . As a recoinage of our silver begins to be requisite, by the continual wearing of our shillings and sixpences, it may be doubtful whether we ought to imitate the example of King William's reign [1689–1702] when the money was raised to the old standard. (1970, p. 39)

The ever-present problem in an economy wherein money consists of coins of the precious metals is how to achieve fulfillment of Smith's Law and keep M increasing in step with Q. Leaving out of account matters of motivation, devaluation of the coinage may be regarded as simply a procedure that resulted in increases in M and that in turn stimulated increases in Q.

The whole of the history of money over the past few centuries is little more than the history of "debasing money" (reducing its precious metal content by legal enactments). The final result has been that money today may be said to be totally debased (since it now bears no legal relationship whatever to the precious metals). This is intended as a simple statement of fact; it should not be taken as a derogatory remark about today's money.

The crude but simple method of debasement employed by bankrupt kings has been replaced by refined and complex methods engineered by parliaments and congresses. Chapter 7 will begin a study of what appear to be the good and the bad of these methods. Before proceeding, however, two points made earlier in this chapter bear repeating with emphasis. The first is that the private sector must rely on a government sector for the enforcement of contracts, and the second that government must stipulate what shall constitute the money in terms of which it will enforce contracts. Thus money must be regarded as a legal as well as an economic matter, a government sector matter as well as a private sector matter. From this follows the fundamentally important conclusion that the private sector cannot be independent of government and cannot be self-regulating or controlled solely by the principle of laissez faire. At the same time, psychological evaluations of money in the marketplace are enormously important. They determine what value will be assigned to monetary units in the exchange of goods and services as contrasted to the value that the government may assign to them when the payment of debts is concerned.

Chapter 7

Paper Money Created by Colonial Governments: Background and the Pennsylvania Experience

The conclusions in the preceding chapters, of the greatest importance as background for the material of this chapter, may be listed as follows. (1) If an economy is to experience sustained and relatively uniform growth at the rate of, say, 3.5 percent per year, as is easily possible, then a relatively uniform net money supply growth rate of approximately 3.5 percent must be sustained. (2) There is no way even one economy, much less all economies of the world, can increase the supply of gold or silver anywhere near 3.5 percent per year in a sustained and uniform manner and therefore no way any economy can adopt a rigid gold or silver standard and maintain its real growth potential. (3) Historically, all economies nominally on a gold or silver standard, in order to make it possible more nearly to achieve and to maintain their real growth potential, have supplemented their specie supply by recourse to issues of paper money, large parts of which were, despite all claims to the contrary, neither 100 percent backed by stocks of precious metal nor 100 percent redeemable in gold or silver coin.

The possible issuers of paper money fall into two, and only two, categories: (1) government agency or (2) private agency. The primary purpose of this chapter and the one following is to consider selected examples of the methods and results of the issuing of paper money by the governments of British colonies in North America in the period preceeding the War for Independence. The following chapters will then deal with the paper money issued by private agencies in Britain during essentially the same era. But first a few other general remarks about paper money.

In 1690 the Massachusetts Bay Colony made its first issue of "colonial notes." This was, if not the very first, one of the first cases of government-issued paper money of the modern age. As one historian remarked, "Paper currency issued under government auspices originated in the thirteen colonies; and during the eighteenth century there were laboratories in which many currency experiments were performed" (Nettles 1934, p. 265). Paper money, however, is known to have been used in China long before the colonial experiments (Perkins 1980, p. 106; Ferguson 1961, p. 1).

The Bank of England was chartered as a private corporation or private agency in 1694 and in that year brought forth its first issue of paper "banknotes." This was not the first case of paper money issued by private banks in the modern era, but it was the first of great and lasting significance in the English-speaking world. Thus government-issued and privately-issued paper money appeared in the British Colonies and in Britain respectively at very nearly the same time.

Both types of issue are usually attributed to the same proximate cause: military adventures brought about an urgent need for money, but the government thought it either impossible or unwise to try to raise money by taxation or borrowing. The underlying cause in both cases, of course, was the slow growth of both the world and the domestic supplies of gold and silver.

In both cases the pieces of paper money that were issued were called *notes* — that is, promises to pay. The Massachusetts notes were declared to be redeemable in specie if and when sufficient coin could be raised by taxation; and the banknotes of the Bank of England were declared to be redeemable on demand in specie, a promise not always kept. The issue of the notes in both cases tended to stimulate real production in the private sector, although in different ways; and at one time or place or another, both types sank in value with respect to gold and silver — that is, resulted to one degree or another in higher prices of goods and services. It may also be noted that up to the 1780s there were no private banks of any significance, if any at all worthy of the designation, in the colonies of North America. Thus banknotes issued by private banks played no significant role in the money supply of any colony during the colonial period. Similarly, notes issued by government played no significant role during the same years in England. In terms of their incipient monetary policies, the motherland and the colonies were clearly headed in quite different directions.

The single most important fact of colonial economic experience was an acute and chronic shortage of gold and silver coins. British settlers in the New World were, on the whole, a far from wealthy lot who could bring with them only very modest amounts of specie. Furthermore, because of the need to keep the money supply of Britain growing at an optimum rate and because of the difficulty of doing so, one ministry after another banned the export of silver or gold to the colonies (Lester 1938, p. 326).

Benjamin Franklin was perhaps the most remarkable and original economic thinker of the New World until at least the middle of the nineteenth century, and several of his remarks regarding the plight in which the colonies found themselves are pertinent here.

Gold and silver are not the produce of North America which has no mines; and that which is brought in cannot be kept in sufficient quantity for a [domestic] currency.

The balance of [the colonies'] trade with Britain being generally against them, the gold and silver is drawn out to pay that balance. . . .

Britain, an independent great state . . . can, and frequently does, make laws to discourage . . . importations [which draw away its specie], and by that means can retain its cash. The colonies are dependent governments and their people . . . cannot be restrained [from making importations] by any province law; because such a law, if made there, would immediately be repealed [by Britain] as prejudicial to [its] trade and interest. . . .

Every colony was ruined [by its specie being drawn away by the purchase of imports from Britain] before it made paper money. (1907, 5: 2–7)

As was the case with Britain, the colonists, in order to try to amass an adequate supply of gold and silver, were constrained to rely on either (1) plunder or (2) international trade. We may now consider in the stated order these two ways by which settlers acquired specie coins.

The fact that the colonists could not import gold and silver from England

led to the quest for Spanish . . . coin. The colonies during this search dealt gently with pirates who came ashore with their stolen treasure. Nearly all of the colonies raised the value of foreign coin in the hope of attracting as much of it as possible: doubtless the acts for this purpose were passed in part to encourage pirates to bring their money to ports where it had the highest value. . . . The colonies that saw the most of the pirates—South Carolina, New York, Pennsylvania, and Massachusetts—placed the highest value on the money the pirates brought. (Nettles 1964, p. 280)

Not content with merely maintaining friendly dealing with freebooters, encouraging their depredations, and paying them a premium for their loot, some colonies considered the ships of Spain fair game for vessels sailing under a colonial banner rather than the jolly roger. In 1740, for example, Governor Ward of Rhode Island boasted that his colony had "equipped and manned five privateers now cruising against the Spaniards" (Hammond 1957, p. 19).

The rather bizarre result of these activities was that although the colonists normally kept accounts in terms of shillings (or pounds sterling) the greater part of the coinage was not of English origin or denomination.

By 1690 every colony had created a special currency of its own, called "current money of the province." This currency consisted of foreign coins (principally Spanish "pieces of eight" or "dollars") which were valued by provincial law in terms of shillings.

Thus a Massachusetts act of 1692 defined pieces of eight . . . of seventeen penny-weight as worth 6 shillings each in the colony [although] a piece of eight [was] worth less than 4s. 6d. [4.5 shillings] in English coin. (Nettles 1964, p. 256)

Although the colonies were constrained by law to import virtually all manufactured goods solely from England and pay for them in specie, they were permitted to export commodities not only to England but to other countries and thus acquired not only Spanish but French and Portuguese coins and even, it is said, coins of "Arabian gold." Quite often, however, "trade" consisted of pure barter (say of hardwoods for sugar in the West Indies) that yielded no coins.

Throughout the entire colonial period, a shortage of specie tormented the colonies. Hence, in addition to resort to other expedients, there occurred various experiments with seashells, beaver pelts, tobacco, and other commodities as a domestic medium of exchange. More important, there occurred numerous experiments with paper money.

Here is the basic attitude of Benjamin Franklin, and of numerous other colonials, in regard to paper money:

However fit a particular thing [such as gold or silver] may be for a particular purpose, wherever that thing is not to be had, or not to be had in sufficient plenty, it becomes necessary to use something else, the fittest that can be got in lieu of it. (1907, 5: 6)

The fittest thing that could be obtained in lieu of gold or silver, was, in Franklin's view, "a paper currency" issued by a colonial government. We will consider the paper money issued in 1690 by Massachusetts and that issued subsequently by other colonies in the next chapter. Let us first, however, consider the paper money issued by Pennsylvania beginning in 1723. There are several reasons for dealing first with the various issues of Pennsylvania — reasons not equally applicable in the cases of the issues of other colonies: (1) the Pennsylvania issues were subject to cogent comment by Franklin; (2) they were also commented upon by Adam Smith; and (3) they were exceptionally successful.

In 1721 Francis Rawle published in Philadelphia a pamphlet entitled *Some Remedies Proposed for Restoring the Sunk Credit of the Province of Pennsylvania*.

He advocated the issue of "stamped paper" whose value would be "secured" by "some visible fund" of loans "on real security," the loans of paper money to be made "at an office appointed by public authority for that purpose," and the interest on the loans becoming "the public's advantage." (Lester 1938, p. 333)

Rawle's prescription was fairly closely followed, as may be seen from comments by Adam Smith:

The government of Pennsylvania without amassing any treasure [i.e., any stock of gold or silver], invented a method of lending, not money indeed, but what is equivalent to money, to its subjects. [It advanced] to private people at interest, upon security on land to double the value, paper bills of credit . . . made transferable from hand to hand like bank-notes, and declared by act of assembly to be legal tender in all payments from one inhabitant of the province to another. (1937, p. 772)

Smith goes on to say that the interest Pennsylvania received on account of the loans of the paper money it created defrayed much of the cost of the government and made taxes largely unnecessary.

In May 1723 Pennsylvania loaned into circulation, with mortgaged real estate as security, notes to the amount of £15,000; and another £30,000 was issued in December. It was enacted that, "counterfeiters were to be punished by having both their 'ears cut off,' being whipped on the 'bare back with thirty lashes well laid on,' and fined or sold into servitude" (Lester 1938, p. 338). All colonies experienced serious problems as a result of counterfeiting; and the Pennsylvania law, harsh though it may seem, was mild compared to the death penalty provided for counterfeiting by Massachusetts in 1714 (Nettles 1964, p. 269).

Within a few years from 1723, a remarkable revival of the economy of Pennsylvania had taken place. It was reported, for example, that in 1726 in Philadelphia twice the number of ships were built as in any year previous to the introduction of paper money. For the quadrennium 1725–1728, compared to 1720–1723, Pennsylvania's imports soared 91 percent and exports 47 percent (Lester 1938, p. 341). So successful was the issue of notes considered that additional issues were made from time to time. From £15,000 early in 1723 the value of notes in circulation increased to £81,500 in 1754—the eve of the French and Indian War. The annual growth rate of the note circulation over thirty-one years was moderate, 5.6 percent. In 1755 the British forces were defeated at Fort Duquesne (now Pittsburgh); and in order to contribute to the war effort, the Pennsylvania authorities increased the value of the colony's notes from £81,500 in 1754 to £456,000 by 1764—an annual rate of 18.8 percent. With the war ending in 1764, notes were burned as loans were paid off; and the amount in circulation was reduced to £421,700 by 1774. Thus from 1723 to 1774 the average per-annum growth rate in the note supply over fifty-one years was 6.8 percent (Lester 1938, p. 353).

The purchasing power of the Pennsylvania notes remained remarkably constant. According to Adam Smith, Pennsylvania's "paper currency . . . is said never to have sunk below the value of the gold and silver which was current in the colony before the first issue of paper money" (1909, p. 266). Smith here acknowledges (rather surprisingly in view of less favorable comments by him cited later) that successive issues of paper money over a period of nearly half a century need not result in higher prices.

Smith's remark was not without foundation. From other sources it appears that in 1723 it took 1.33 Pennsylvania £ notes to equal an English £ note in London and in 1775 it took 1.66 Pennsylvania notes. The Pennsylvania notes thus depreciated in terms of British paper money only about 0.4 percent per year (BC 1975, p. 1198). Thus Franklin was prompted to remark that "paper money does not have the ruinous nature ascribed to it [by critics in Britain]. Far from being ruined by it, the colonies that have made use of paper money have been and are all in a thriving condition" (1907, 5: 2–3).

Since the rate of growth of the supply of paper money was 6.8 percent and the rate of depreciation of the Pennsylvania notes was 0.4 percent, the annual growth rate of the Pennsylvania economy from 1723 to 1775 may have been something on the order of 6.4 percent if we follow the equation $M_r \cong P_r + Q_r$. No very accurate calculation can be made, however, owing to the absence of reliable statistics on the change in the amount of specie during the period. It is said that in Pennsylvania around 1750 "paper money comprised from one-third to one-half of the money stock" but there are no adequate data on the rate of change of the total supply of money (specie plus paper) (Perkins 1980, p. 114).

A number of matters mentioned above more or less in passing now perhaps deserve further comment. First, Rawle and others were seemingly following ideas advanced by John Law in 1705 in *Money and Trade Considered*. Law proposed "coining land instead of coining metals" in order to bring about increases in the money supply. He was later to become infamous for carrying his idea to an absurd extreme in France, but colonists in Pennsylvania showed greater discretion.

Second, it is perfectly clear from all that they wrote that Rawle, Franklin, and their compatriots, although they believed in a system of private enterprise, at the same time did not believe private enterprise could thrive if the money supply were left to control itself or to pirates, to "the money market," "the precious metals market," or any other market mechanism. They believed that Q growth necessitated M growth and that M growth would stimulate Q growth. They believed the government had an obligaton to provide the "plentiful supply of money" that the markets failed to supply. They believed that in so doing the government simultaneously served the interest of private enterprise, workers, consumers, and the government itself. The insight they showed deserves applause.

Third, they recognized that, if error there must be, it is better to err on the side of too much than of too little money. If a country should have too little domestic money, this would be "exceedingly detrimental to trade" whereas too much money would merely be "no advantage in trade" (Franklin 1907, 5: 134). In other words, they seem to have felt, as did David Hume, that it is better to risk or tolerate a little price inflation than to take a chance on any price deflation, which is always crippling, although it is better, insofar as it is possible, to increase the money supply in proportion to real growth and maintain a steady price level. In the case of Pennsylvania, the decision makers seem to have been rather amazingly adept in maintaining steady prices in the absence of reliable statistics.

Fourth, the Pennsylvanians recognized, far more clearly than their English counterparts, a clear distinction between a domestic money supply and a money supply for international trade. The first should be "a paper money that could not (or would not) be carried away" to become a part of the money supply of some other country (as happens with gold/silver) and thereby be lost to the country of origin (Franklin 1907, 5: 7). Only international dealings required specie for settling imbalances in trade.

The significance of certain technical aspects of the Pennsylvania note issue deserves elaboration. First, the notes were declared by the issuing government to be legal tender for all transactions, including the payment of taxes. Making the bills acceptable in the payment of taxes was an important inducement to their general and widespread acceptance. The proclamation that the bills should be legal tender also assured their acceptance in domestic trade and in the settlement of private debts. Second, as Franklin wrote:

> He that trades with money he hath borrowed at eight or ten per cent cannot hold market with him that borrows his money at six or four. . . .
> A plentiful currency [of colonial bills loaned at moderate rates] will occasion interest to be low; and this . . . will tend to enliven trade exceedingly, because people will find more profit in employing their money that way than in usury, and many that understand business very well but have not a stock sufficient of their own will be encouraged to borrow money to trade with when they can have it at a moderate interest. (1907, 2: 135)

By the issue of notes at 5 percent interest, the government tended to set an effective upper limit on the rate of interest in the colony. At the time of the first issue, the highest legal rate was 8 percent; but by various ruses what amounted to even higher rates were common.

All things considered, the Pennsylvania experiment with paper money proved a great success. The colony's money supply was increased without dependence on an increase in the amount of specie; the economy was stimulated to fairly steady real growth; and "the price level during the 52 years prior to the American Revolution and while Pennsylvania was on a paper standard was more stable than the American price level has been during any succeeding fifty-year period" (Lester 1938, p. 325).

As observed earlier, Pennsylvania was not the first of the colonies to issue paper money, nor was it the last. It is to the experiments of other colonies that we now turn.

_____

Chapter 8

Paper Money Created by Colonial Governments: Other Examples and Summation

The experiences with paper money in the English colonies of North America other than Pennsylvania varied from being only a little less successful to being very much less successful. All told there were about 250 separate issues of colonial notes by the various colonies between 1690 and 1775, and each issue varied from all others either in minor detail or in some significant way (BC 1975, p. 1200). It would be both tedious and unproductive to discuss in detail all the different monetary measures enacted and the results, but there is something to be gained by a look at a few of them.

The notes of Massachusetts Bay Colony of 1690, the first note issues of any colony, were not secured by mortgages on land as in the case of Pennsylvania but by being declared redeemable by the colonial government in specie, not on demand and at any time, but only as soon as sufficient coin to redeem them could be raised by taxation. So inadequate was the supply of specie in Massachusetts, however, that despite only this vague promise of eventual redemption the notes were readily accepted and "for twenty years the notes circulated side by side with gold and silver of equivalent denomination" (Galbraith 1976, pp. 61–62).

It was the apparent success of the Massachusetts issue over a period of two decades that encouraged other colonies to follow a more or less similar procedure. South Carolina brought forth its first issue in 1703. By 1709 New Jersey, New York, New Hampshire, and Connecticut had their separate issues of paper money in circulation. Rhode Island followed in 1710, North Carolina in 1712, and other colonies still later.

By 1712, however, Massachusetts had added several additional issues to that of 1690; and its paper money was beginning to slip in purchasing power. In 1690 the price of an ounce of silver in terms of the Massachusetts paper shilling was 7.0; by 1712 the price had risen to 8.5; and worse was to come. Massachusetts continued to issue notes in varied amounts and at irregular intervals and to postpone the promised date of redemption in specie. An increasing loss of confidence in the Massachusetts notes was a result. The price of silver rose to 17.5 paper shillings by 1735 and to 57.5 by 1748 (BC 1975, p. 1199). The Massachusetts experiment is accordingly often cited as a horrible example of overissue of "the printing press money of government" with the result of "runaway inflation" in commodity prices.

By and large, a harsh judgment against Massachusetts is probably warranted; but a closer look at some of the statistics is revealing. According to the source just cited, the amount of notes outstanding in 1704 was £32,000 and in 1748 (a peak year), £2,135,000. This would mean a compound annual growth rate of 10 percent in the supply of notes over the period of forty-four years, that is, an average rate of "monetary inflation" of 10 percent. Since, as noted above, in 1704 it took 7 colonial notes to purchase an ounce of silver and in 1748 it took 57.5, this increase in the price of silver indicates an average annual rate of "price inflation" of about 4.9 percent — considerably less than the rate in the United States from 1978 to 1988 when the issue of "bank credit" rather than the issue of government printing press money was culpable. In any case, it seems certain that the rate of "price inflation" was only about half the rate of "monetary inflation."

Using Fisher's Equation of Exchange and assuming constant velocity of circulation of money and that the Massachusetts colonial notes were the sole form of money in circulation in both 1704 and 1748 (that is, using $Q_r = M_r - P_r$) the average real growth rate of the Massachusetts economy must have been on the order of 10.0 minus 4.9 or 5.1 percent per annum. Since these assumptions greatly oversimplify the matter and cannot be verified, neither can it be verified that the real economy grew at 5.1 percent although this is by no means an unbelievable rate. Even if we discount this figure considerably, it must be said that a monetary policy that results in even 3 or 4 percent annual real growth can hardly be considered totally bad (real growth was only 2.6 percent per annum in the United States from 1978 to 1988).

The experience of New York was more satisfactory than that of Massachusetts. Issues outstanding in 1711 totaled £23,000. According to Franklin, by 1767 the issues outstanding of that colony totaled "£600,000 or near it" (1907, 5: 11). The annual growth rate of the money supply over a period of fifty-six years was thus 6 percent — a much more moderate rate than the one prevailing in Massachusetts and slighly more moderate than that in Pennsylvania.

All the available evidence indicates that New York did not suffer from the severe depression during the period from 1720 to 1723 as did the mother country and the other colonies like Pennsylvania, Delaware, and Maryland, that had as yet issued no paper money, or New Jersey where all previous currency issues had been retired.

In October 1720 the new governor of New York spoke of the "flourishing state" of the province and added: "We live in the happiest of times. . . ." Later he spoke of "the success of [New York's] currency," which he thought was "much surer than Bankers Bills in London." (Lester 1939, p. 202)

Reviewing the New York experience for the entire 1711–1767 period, Franklin wrote:

Nor has any alteration been occasioned by the paper money in the prices of the necessaries of life. When compared with silver, prices have been for the greatest part of the time no higher than before paper money was emitted, varying only by plenty and scarcity according to the seasons or by a greater or less foreign demand. (1907, 5: 11)

If New York experienced money supply growth of 6 percent per annum and concurrently experienced no price inflation, it is possible that real growth was 6 percent or nearly that amount, although the absence of knowledge of fluctuations in the supply of specie make impossible any accurate calculation. From 1711 to 1767, the population growth rate of New York was about 3.4 percent. We may guess then that the per-capita rate of growth of the economy was perhaps 2.6 percent per annum—a figure it is not unreasonable to believe although impossible to verify from other data.

In regard to the issue of paper money, Rhode Island was widely regarded as the most profligate of all the colonies (Hammond 1957, p. 17). The available evidence, however, does not reveal that Rhode Island behaved very badly in the years before the War for Independence—certainly not as badly as Massachusetts. According to what should be a reliable source, there were outstanding £51,000 in Rhode Island notes by 1715 and £550,000 in 1748; the growth rate thus being 7.5 percent per year—a higher rate than that in New York or Pennsylvania but less than that in Massachusetts (BC 1975, p. 1200).

In 1738 the Rhode Island legislature gave stimulating trade and construction as its reason for another emission of paper money. And in 1740 Governor Ward of the colony wrote:

If this colony be in any respect happy and flourishing, it is paper money and a right application of it that has rendered us so. And that we are in a flourishing condition is evident from our trade, which is greater in proportion to [our size] than that of any [other] colony. (Hammond 1957, p. 20)

Ward added that Rhode Island headquartered more than 120 sailing ships trading with Europe, Africa, the Caribbean, and neighboring colonies.

In Rhode Island, as in most colonies, when notes were issued except for direct payment of expenses incurred by military expeditions against "the French and the Indians," the notes resulted from loans on land and brought in annual interest. The interest received on loans made it possible to keep taxes lower than otherwise would have been the case. Roads, harbor facilities, lighthouses, a building for the seat of government, and other additions to the infrastructure were constructed without any necessity for taxation; and the entire community profited from the colony's act of creating and lending money.

A third way in which colonial bills were put into circulation was practiced on one occasion by Maryland. In 1733, £48,000 "was given away — a certain sum to each inhabitant over fifteen years of age. This was done in order that the paper money might be 'the more useful to the inhabitants' and its circulation might be as speedy and diffusive as possible" (Lester 1939, p. 208).

"The Maryland currency was distributed throughout the colony on a per capita basis to all persons subject to taxation. Every taxable individual was given 30 shillings" (Perkins 1980, p. 109). Maryland seems to have anticipated by nearly two hundred years something closely resembling the "Social Credit" proposals of Major C. H. Douglas in Britain in the 1920s.

"In the year 1751 Parliament passed an act forbidding any more legal-tender paper issues" in Massachusetts and "in 1763 Parliament declared any colonial acts for issuing [legal-tender] paper money void" (Sumner 1968, pp. 38 and 42). That these acts of Parliament were clearly at the behest of the lenders of money, not of the entrepreneurs, is evidenced by the reason given for them: that by the use of the paper money "debts have been discharged with a much less value than was contracted for" (Krooss 1983, 1: 2).

The laws placing limitations on the issue by the colonies of legal tender paper money figured prominently in the growing list of grievances of the colonists against the mother country. As Franklin wrote: "It seems hard [to the colonists for the British] to draw all their [gold and silver] money from them [by the balance of trade being against the colonies], and then refuse them the poor privilege of using paper instead of it" (1907, 5: 7). Diplomat that he was, Franklin did not mention that perhaps one of the greatest reasons for British opposition to colonial money was that British bankers wanted the colonies, rather than creating their own notes, to acquire a colonial money supply by borrowing banknotes in Britain (at interest payable in specie).

Franklin's defense of colonial paper money went unheeded by Parliament and did not result in a repeal of the laws enacted in Britain prohibiting paper money as legal tender for all transactions. It was, however, noted by Adam Smith, who wrote, "No law . . . could be more equitable than the Act of Parliament, so unjustly complained of in the colonies, which declared that no paper currency to be emitted there in time coming, should be a legal tender of payments" (1909, p. 256). It seems strange that on the one hand Smith, as earlier cited, should concede that the system of legal tender paper money of Pennsylvania worked well (1909, p. 311), yet on the other hand declare it should be outlawed.

In the nine years following 1764, compared to the nine years before, the number of new issues of colonial notes by all colonies combined dropped almost by half. Whether any of the new issues were declared legal tender in defiance of Parliament and the Board of Trade, I have been unable to determine. What is certain, however, is that not all outstanding notes declared legal tender were taken out of circulation. And many colonists continued to treat as legal tender even notes not thus labeled. This provides further evidence that money is, in part at least, whatever is accepted as money: intrinsic value and legal edicts are important but are not always the ultimately deciding factors.

Finally, in 1773, Parliament revised the law and permitted colonies to declare their currency issues legal tender in all public payments [colonial taxes, fines, and so on]. The ban on paper-money settlements of private debts remained in force. There the matter rested until the outbreak of the war. (Perkins 1980, p. 115)

On the other hand, obligations payable in the mother country remained payable in specie, not paper. "Taxation without representation" as a principal cause of the troubles between England and the colonies inadequately expresses the matter. "Taxation that draws away gold and silver and diminishes our money supply" is a phrase that more satisfactorily brings into the picture the fact that money, or what was to be treated as money, also figured prominently among the objections of the colonists to British rule.

Because of the large number of issues of colonial notes, and the very different character of many of them, no fully satisfactory summary of the colonial experience with paper money is possible in a few words. Some attempt at doing just this, nevertheless, seems desirable at this point.

The most important single feature of all colonial notes was that they demonstrated that an economy could grow and prosper without a domestic money supply consisting either of gold or silver coin or of paper money exchangeable for coin "on demand" at any time. The belief that money necessarily had to be gold or silver or immediately exchangeable for gold or silver was (or should have been) completely dispelled by the colonial experiments. The lesson was not lost on Karl Marx who cited with approval Bishop Berkeley's observation that "the development of the North American colonies makes it as plain as daylight that gold and silver are not so necessary for the wealth of nations as the vulgar of all ranks imagine" (Marx, 1970, p. 79).

Put another way, the issues of colonial notes were of great historical significance since here for the first time in modern history we find units of government relying on a money that they created out of paper and ink rather than a money that had to be, if and when possible, dug out of the ground. That is to say, governments turned to a money supply the size of which it was within their power easily to control and away from a supply the size of which was almost entirely beyond their control.

A common feature of all colonial notes, it must be emphasized, was that they were "promises to pay" or IOUs of one sort or another. The notes issued

to pay for military expeditions (by Massachusetts, for example) were promises by the issuing government to pay the holder of the notes in coin at some
future date upon receipt of future taxes. The notes unconnected with military
adventures and issued purely to provide a substitute for coin (by Pennsylvania, for example) were promises by the holder of the notes to pay the issuing government and bore the stamp of the issuing government to certify that
the party to whom the note had been issued had mortgaged property of
greater value than the face value of the note.

The colonial "promises to pay" of both sorts, being IOUs, may be looked
upon as an intermediate form of money between the earlier system based
solely on coins of the precious metals (coins, take note, are not IOUs) and
the system later to be embraced (today in the United States, for example,
but almost everywhere else as well) of paper money issued by government
that is not imprinted with any promise to pay or promise to redeem in specie
and thus is not an IOU. The progression in history has thus been from one
type of "no-debt money" to "debt money" of various types and then to a type
of "no-debt money" altogether different from the first.

Obviously, my effort in this chapter and the preceding one has not been
to suggest that the various colonial moneys were ideal forms of money.
Whatever may be said in disparagement of the colonial moneys, however,
they represented a giant forward stride in the understanding of the role of
money in an economy and in the varieties of possible money. At one and the
same time they were a great improvement over the system that preceded them
and over the quite different system that developed concurrently in England
which is considered in the next two chapters.

Finally, from the point of view developed in chapters to follow, perhaps
the single most important lesson of the colonial experience is that it showed
how a private enterprise economy can grow and prosper not only without a
specie standard but without "private banks of issue," that is, without banks
that create banknotes or otherwise increase the effective money supply by
the creation of bank credit as money or a money substitute. What few reliable statistics are available suggest that growth in the British Colonies from
1607 to 1780 almost undoubtedly exceeded 3 percent per annum. It should
never be forgotten that this rate of growth took place in the total absence of
private banks.

It is an article of faith among bankers and among the economists who
have come under the influence of bankers' propaganda that a private enterprise system cannot prosper without private banks. The colonial experience
shows that this is nothing other than an assiduously cultivated but ground-
less myth.

Chapter 9 _____

Paper Money Created by Private Banks in Eighteenth-Century Britain

How to make the economy's money supply grow at the rate of 3, 4, or 5 percent per annum, as the real economy was easily capable of growing but the supply of specie could not easily or generally be made to grow, was only a moderately less urgent problem for the mother country than for the colonies. With well over ten times the population of its provinces in North America in 1700, England faced the need of increasing its money supply annually by roughly ten times the amount needed by the colonies. How to keep the money supply increasing by optimum amounts perplexed Parliament as well as the colonial assemblies.

The method of solving the problem was, in one sense, essentially the same on both sides of the Atlantic, namely, the use of the printing press to create a supply of paper money to supplement the supply of gold or silver coin. In another sense, two essentially opposite methods were used in the two areas. In Pennsylvania and the other colonies, the government issued and loaned money into circulation; and the government, and therefore the general public, benefited from the interest on the newly created money. In England privately owned banks issued and loaned money into circulation, and the owners of these banks benefited from the interest on newly created money. Having examined in the previous chapter some details of colonial methods, we must now do the same with regard to English methods.

Although earlier and on a small scale some goldsmiths performed lending and money-creating functions not altogether different from the functions of banks, the history of banking in England may be said to have begun in earnest with the chartering of the Bank of England in 1694 as a corporation with private individuals as stockholders. King William's War (1688–1697) necessitated the spending of large sums of England's gold and silver on the Continent, plunged the government deeply into debt, and simultaneously greatly diminished the country's specie supply. It was in the midst of such conditions that the Bank of England was conceived.

In the plan for founding the Bank of England, £1,200,000 in gold and silver was to be subscribed as initial capital by the stockholders and loaned to the government. In return the government agreed to pay the Bank £96,000 annual interest (at 8 percent) plus £4,000 in management fees each year. That is to say, the government contracted to double the money lenders initial capital every 9 years.

The really interesting part of the story, however, is that the government also granted to the bank the authority to issue "banknotes" to the amount of its capital and lend that printing-press money into circulation. The principle upon which the bank was founded appeared to be, as the English economist Macleod was later to say, "that every loan made to the government was to be attended by an equivalent increase in the paper currency" (Andreades 1966, p. 124).

On the assumption that £1,200,000 in banknotes could be loaned to private borrowers at the same rate as to the government, the stockholders of the bank would receive £96,000 from private borrowers (in addition to £100,000 from the government) for a total return of 16.33 percent on their capital. In other words, Parliament gave money lenders a deal whereby they could double their money about every 4.5 years. Money lenders had learned early in the game that it pays to have friends in Parliament. Members of Parliament simultaneously perceived the wisdom of becoming stockholders in the bank. "The precise purpose which the Government had in view in permitting their circulation [i.e., the circulation of banknotes, was] that of subsidizing the banker in return for the facilities he provided" (Powell 1966, p. 126). That the size of the subsidy was of usurious proportions was deemed a matter best quietly swept under the carpet.

The plan was not truthfully described as a scheme for enriching the stockholders of the bank, of course, but (1) as a patriotic means of assisting in the finance of the war and (2) as a method of helping to mitigate the shortage of a circulating medium in the realm. As to the second reason, William Paterson, one of the founders of the bank, declared:

If the proprietors of the Bank can circulate . . . twelve hundred thousand pounds [in banknotes] without having more than two or three hundred thousand pounds [of specie with which to redeem banknotes on demand] lying dead at one time with another, this Bank will be in effect as nine hundred thousand pounds or a million of fresh money brought into the nation. (Andreades 1966, p. 66)

What we see from the quotation are two important things. The first is that Paterson believed that the banknotes would circulate as money only if the promise were made that they could be redeemed at the bank in coin at any and all times and that for this purpose "two or three hundred thousand pounds of coin" would have to be held as "reserves" at the bank. Clearly, Paterson believed that the bank would need to raise as capital not only £1,200,000 to lend the government but an additional £200,000 or £300,000 as reserves for redeeming on demand some part of the £1,200,000 in banknotes it would lend to private borrowers. Thus the bank was to be a "fractional reserve bank," and the reserve fraction was to be between 1:6 and 1:4. All private commercial banks ever since and everywhere have been fractional reserve banks.

The second thing of importance in Paterson's statement, a matter of greatest significance, was that here was a way of side-stepping or overcoming the dearth of specie in England and providing the nation with a larger, more adequate money supply. Here, in effect, was a way of creating new money and putting it into circulation. In both the mother country and the colonies there was a strong desire to see "the value of the annual produce of the country increase"; and on both sides of the ocean it was realized, in accordance with Smith's Law, that "the quantity of money must increase as the annual produce increases."

The differences between the inducements to the public to accept the notes of the Bank of England and the colonial notes as a medium of exchange are significant. Colonial notes were made legal tender, and redemption in coin was promised only at some future date if at all. Notes of the Bank of England were not made legal tender on the assumption that since redemption in coin was promised "on demand" they would pass as an acceptable tender for all transactions.

On the face of it, the claim that "banknotes are as good as gold" seemed to make the ready acceptance of them by the public more reasonable than the ready acceptance of colonial notes. What seemed to go unnoticed was that if the reserve ratio of the bank was, say, 1:5, then only one fifth of the banknotes issued could in fact be redeemed in coin. The bank's promise to redeem in coin all banknotes offered for redemption was predicated on the assumption that not more than one fifth would be so offered at any one time. The claim that *all* banknotes were as good as gold was clearly fraudulent, designed as a cover-up for the fact that unredeemable paper money was being created to supplement the supply of coin.

In practice, the idea that banknotes could be redeemed in gold also broke down time and again. Virtually all the original capital raised by the Bank of England was loaned to the government, and precious little of it was actually retained as a reserve for redeeming banknotes. "It seems incredible that the bank took no [sufficient] precaution to ensure the convertibility of its notes," remarked one historian (Andreades 1966, p. 85). "Two years after the opening of the Bank, it was forced to suspend payments [in coin for its banknotes]," remarked a second chronicler of the era (Nettles 1964, p. 169). A third reported that "the paper of the Bank . . . was often at a discount of 20 per cent" in the early years of the Bank (Powell 1966, p. 213). Over the course of the next two centuries, the word "suspension" (that is, the suspension of the practice of redeeming banknotes in specie) became so characteristic of every "crisis" that the words could be used almost interchangeably.

"By the year 1725 all the basic essentials of the modern financial mechanism were in being" in England (Powell 1966, p. 197). By 1725 the bank had increased its capital, its loans to the government, its issue of banknotes, and its "fractional reserves" for redeeming banknotes on demand. By 1725 most of the start-up problems of the bank had been disposed of and its status as a going concern firmly established.

On account of the Bank of England's unique charter, it long maintained a virtual monopoly on banking in London. By 1750, nevertheless, there were 12 banks outside London. This number increased to 150 by 1776, 350 by 1790, and 721 by 1810 (Powell 1966, pp. 117–118). The banks outside London, called "country banks," often kept their reserves in banknotes of the Bank of England, not in gold or silver coins or ingots. "As late as 1826 it was possible for Lord Liverpool to say that the law permitted any shopkeeper, however limited his means, to start a bank . . . and issue banknotes purporting to be payable on demand" in Bank of England notes that were, in turn, payable by the bank in specie on demand (Powell 1966, 127–129).

Note that if on the basis of £20,000 in gold and silver reserves the Bank of England could print and lend £100,000 in its banknotes into circulation; and if, say, £20,000 in these notes were withdrawn from circulation and used by country banks as reserves for the creation of £100,000 in their banknotes, then there could result a circulation consisting of £180,000 in the two kinds of banknotes combined on the basis of only £20,000 in specie.

In view of such explosive possibilities, the rate of banknote expansion in eighteenth-century England seems to have been moderate. On the basis of not wholly satisfactory data it appears that from 1694 to 1751 the number of outstanding banknotes of the Bank of England increased from about £1 million to about £5.2 million or by about 2.9 percent per annum. The population growth rate for the same period may be estimated at 1.4 percent (Mitchell 1978, pp. 8, 354). The yearly increase in banknotes per capita in England thus appears to have been about 1.5 percent. For comparison, from 1725 to 1765 the growth rate of the colonial note issues outstanding in Pennsylvania was 6.8 percent, the population growth rate, 4.6 percent (1720 to 1760), and thus the per capita growth rate of notes was about 2.2 percent (BC 1975, pp. 1168, 1200).

From 1755 to 1795, the notes of the bank increased at an average annual rate of 2.8 percent. There are no satisfactory statistics for the comparable increase in the note issues of the country banks or for the increase in specie. In any event, according to one historian, "by the end of the eighteenth century practically the whole employing class [in England] had come to depend on borrowed capital," most of which was borrowed from banks and consisted of banknotes. In other words, most of the employing class had come to depend not on coin but on paper money created by banks (Powell 1966, p. 123).

In eighteenth-century England, therefore, it became possible, owing to the nature of the private banking system, to increase the nation's money supply more or less fivefold even if there was no increase in the supply of gold or silver. In its initial stages, the introduction of fractional reserve banking permitted the total money supply (specie plus banknotes) to increase very much faster than the specie supply. Once all banks had issued banknotes to the limit permitted by the self-imposed reserve requirement, however, the growth rate of the total money supply could again be no greater than the growth rate of the specie supply.

The amount of reserves that a bank should maintain was left to the discretion of each individual bank until well into the nineteenth century, when governments began to legislate minimum reserve requirements. Meanwhile, the reserve requirement of very conservatively managed banks was sometimes as high as 1:3; less conservative managements required perhaps as little as 1:10. All managements, nevertheless, promised the impossible — redemption on demand in specie of all their banknotes.

The most widespread idea of how banks operate seems to be that they are simply intermediaries between depositors and borrowers. Banks, it is said, receive deposits and therefrom make loans, and that is the end of the matter. It seems poorly understood that the essential function of banks is not to receive and disburse parts of a money supply that remains at a constant size but to preside over the expansion of the money supply — to create money.

The key to understanding the money-creation process is to perceive that only fractional reserves are required for issues of banknotes. It has been shown in this chapter how the original capital of a bank (e.g., in gold) can be used as reserves. When the reserve requirement is one to five, then five times as much money in banknotes can be created as existed in the form of original capital.

If we now think in terms of a bank still having a requirement of "reserve money" amounting to one fifth of the notes it issues, then a customer's deposit of £100 in reserve money permits the issue of £500 in notes. The deposit of new reserve money gives the same result as an increase in bank capital.

In more recent and sophisticated banking systems with many banks, the system as a whole functions much as a single bank. The introduction into the system of £100 in new "reserve money," or "high-powered money," as it is sometimes called, may result in £500 in newly created money when the reserve ratio is one to five or generate £1000 in newly created money when the reserve ratio is one to ten, and so on.

In these same more recent and sophisticated banking systems, instead of creating money by printing banknotes to lend to borrowers, creditors create money by issuing a deposit in the name of the borrower. A century or so ago, a borrower received the loan in banknotes. Today, the borrower gets a slip of paper showing that amount has been deposited in his or her checking account. The change, however, is in form rather than content. "A banknote and a deposit in a checking account are fundamentally the same thing" (Schumpeter 1954, p. 319).

It is important never to forget that, whatever other function banks may serve, so long as they issue banknotes or create checking account deposits they are also factories creating new money. Assuming a balance in international payments and no domestic mines, only to the extent that they create money does the nation's money supply increase and only to the extent that the nation's money supply increases is the demand for new products increased, and only as demand increases will new production be stimulated or sold at a profit — regardless of why produced.

In modern banks, virtually all deposits consist of money originally created somewhere in the banking system in the process of making loans on the basis of fractional reserves. In an important sense, it is loans that give rise to deposits, not deposits that give rise to loans as most people seem to believe.

The widespread misunderstanding that sees banks only as intermediaries between savers (depositors) and investors (borrowers) is closely related to the widespread misunderstanding that it is saving and investing that make the economy grow. But by Smith's Law, the economy grows only as its money supply grows; and no amount of saving and lending of the same money will increase the money supply by a farthing. The investment of money that people have saved can build new factories or increase the output of the factory system; but this increased output cannot be sold, the market cannot be cleared, and demand for commodities cannot equal the supply of commodities — unless the money supply increases in proportion to the increased output of the factory system. Increasing the money supply involves a process of money creation, a process entirely different from the process of money saving.

It remains to be made as explicit as possible that the notes of private banks, like the notes issued by the various colonies, were issued with the understanding that they would not be accepted by the public unless something of value "backed them up" or "stood behind" them. Specie, it was accepted, stood behind the notes of private banks, mortgages on land stood behind the issues of some colonies, and the taxing power of government behind others. Custom or convention or habit had so far evolved that paper money was acceptable in place of specie, but only so long as it was paper with "solid backing" redeemable in some specific amount of some specific commodity. Custom or convention or habit had not yet so far evolved that each individual accepted paper money simply because it would in turn be acceptable for payment of taxes or debts or because everyone else accepted it, and accepted it despite the absence on the paper money of any promise that it could be redeemed by any given amount of specie. Whatever else one may think of the notes of both private banks and colonial governments, they must be thought of as a stage in the evolution of money from coins of precious metal to "unredeemable" paper money.

Likewise, the notes (or deposits) of private banks, like the notes of colonial governments, appeared with the creation of loans and disappeared with the repayment of loans. Both, then, were forms of impermanent money and therefore transitional forms between earlier money of gold or silver and forms of permanent paper money that were to appear later.

_____

Chapter 10

Adam Smith on the Bank of England and Banking in General

Before the founding of the Bank of England in 1694, banknotes played no role of any significance in the daily buying and selling that took place in Britain. During the period embraced by the next several decades, however, the nature of the medium of exchange was dramatically transformed; and by 1767 Benjamin Franklin could say, "Bank Bills and Banker's Notes are daily used as a medium of trade [in England], and in large dealings perhaps the greater part is transacted by their means" (1907, 5: 7).

Adam Smith seems to have been less aware than Franklin of the drastically altered character of the circulating money supply, for in 1776 he still believed that "the currency of a great state, such as France or England, generally consists almost entirely in its own [gold or silver] coin" (1937, p. 446). Such a statement, undoubtedly true in 1694, was woefully out of date by the time it was written.

Whether or not the "greater part" of transactions of the time involved paper money, as Franklin thought, Smith undoubtedly exaggerated when he said the currency consisted "almost entirely" in coin. What percentage of all transactions in England in 1767 or 1776 was made in paper and what percentage in coin is not easily determined. We do know, however, that even as early as 1767 there were in circulation banknotes of the Bank of England to the amount of over £5,500,000 (Mitchell 1978, p. 354). The "currency" also included the notes of 150 country banks of a total value I have been unable to determine. Thus we know enough to say that Smith in 1776 failed to attribute to the role of paper money anywhere near its proper significance.

Harvard's Joseph Schumpeter believed he found sufficient cause to speak of "Marx's distinctly weak performance in the field of money" (1950, p. 22).

As far as I know, he made no similar remark about Adam Smith although Smith's "performance in the field of money" must be regarded as even weaker than Marx's. Smith seems to have understood not at all the magnitude of the role paper money was coming to play in the operation of the English economy. It was obvious to Franklin, although apparently not to Smith, that paper was rapidly replacing specie as the principal medium of English trade. Smith's treatment of the subject of paper money and banking, therefore, leaves much to be desired.

It is noted in Chapter 7 that Smith was aware of the way the government of Pennsylvania created and loaned into circulation paper money and that the interest thereon "went a considerable way toward defraying the annual expense . . . of that . . . government" (1937, p. 772). He was accordingly aware that there was a great difference between the paper money issued in England and that issued in the colonies. Likewise he knew that the significant difference between the two types of paper money resided in the fact that in England the money was issued by private banks to the profit of stockholding private individuals and in the colonies it was issued by governments to the profit of all their citizens. Yet he did not hesitate to say that "there are several different sorts of paper money; but the circulating notes of banks and bankers are the species . . . which seems best adapted to this purpose" (1909, p. 241).

It is almost incredible that Smith should conclude that paper money created so as to enrich private individuals was superior to paper money created so as to provide a substitute for financing the government via taxation. His perverse conclusion may be attributed in part to his perverse ideological conviction that an "invisible hand" somehow guarantees that the behavior of private individuals will always be such as to serve desirable social ends. In part, however, his conclusion was based on a belief that paper money should be redeemable "on demand" in gold or silver and that banknotes appeared to meet this requirement more satisfactorily than did colonial notes.

Smith's conception of the nature and operation of private banks was essentially the same as Paterson's (cited in the previous chapter) when he proposed the organization of the Bank of England. Here is Smith:

> Though the banker has generally in circulation . . . notes to the extent of a hundred thousand pounds, twenty thousand pounds in gold and silver may, frequently, be a sufficient provision for answering occasional demands.
>
> [Bank] notes come to have the same currency as gold and silver money, from the confidence that such money can at any time be had for them. (1909, p. 241)

Smith appears altogether too ready to ignore the fact that if a bank has put into circulation £100,000 in banknotes it has printed while it has only £20,000 in gold or silver with which to redeem them (that is, if "bank reserves" amount to only a fifth of the note issue), then obviously the bank has created £80,000 in banknotes that it cannot possibly redeem. Smith's "confidence that gold or silver money can at any time be had for the banknotes" can be based solely on the probability that holders of more than £20,000 in banknotes will not try to redeem them at the same time. Sometimes this "confidence game" works well from the point of view of both the bank and the public, and sometimes it does not.

When the holders of banknotes of greater total value than the reserves in specie request redemption of their notes, a bank must "suspend payment" and may, on that account, be forced to close its doors. But whether sufficient confidence prevails for the bank's doors to remain open or not is beside the point. The inescapable fact is that in the case of the Bank of England and the country banks a private company was granted government permission to create large sums of money in the form of banknotes it could not redeem, lend them into circulation, and collect interest on them for private gain. Why should the government of England or any other country charter a private group to create money when it could create the paper money itself? The government could create money, lend it into circulation, collect interest on it, and use the interest in lieu of taxes. The government could also create money and spend it into circulation in lieu of taxes. Why should Adam Smith neglect even to mention such alternatives?

Leaving aside for a time further discussion of the relative merits of paper money issued by governments vis-à-vis money issued by private banks, let us look further into Smith's ideas concerning banking in England.

If bankers are restrained from issuing any circulating bank notes . . . of less than a certain sum [Smith believed it important that minor transactions should be made exclusively with coins]; and if they are subjected to the obligation of an immediate and unconditonal payment of [gold or silver coin for] bank notes [presented for payment], their trade may, with safety to the public, be rendered in all other respects perfectly free. (1909, p. 268)

The matter of government restraining the issue of banknotes of small denomination aside, the only really substantive regulation Smith favored was the requirement that banks must be able to redeem their notes in coin on demand. But this merely begs the question of what the minimum reserve requirement of banks should be. The only way a bank can always be positive that it can redeem its notes is to have reserves to the amount of 100 percent. Since Smith is already on record that 20 percent reserves "may, frequently, be a sufficient provision for answering occasional demands," we are left to wonder just where between 20 percent (which Smith does not dare to say will *always* be sufficient) and 100 percent the reserve requirement should fall.

However all this may be, Smith clearly recognizes that "the banking trade" cannot in *all* respects be left perfectly free. He does not really believe any "invisible hand" will satisfactorily regulate banking. "Every particular banking company has not always attended to its own particular interest" and has issued excessive amounts of banknotes, he writes (1909, p. 251). He goes on to say that "those exertions of the natural liberty of a few individuals, which might endanger the security of the whole society, are, and ought to be, restrained by the laws of all governments," and he specifically includes "regulation of the banking trade" as a proper activity of government (1909, p. 263). It is not difficult to believe that he would have raised no great objection had he lived to see the day when minimum reserve requirements were imposed on banks by government.

But this whole area of discussion is one that makes Smith uncomfortable. For if banking is not self-regulating, then the nation's money supply is not self-regulating; and if the money supply is not self-regulating, then the economy as a whole cannot be self-regulating. In view of Smith's ideological commitment to the proposition that the economy is self-regulating, his discomfort over the necessity for bank regulation is understandable.

Another quotation from Smith is of both interest and importance: "It is not by augmenting the capital [money supply] of a country, but by rendering a greater part of that capital [money supply] active and productive than would otherwise be so, that the most judicious operation of banking can increase the industry of a country" (1909, p. 258).

This sentence, completely false in its essence, contains elements of truth in that it mentions the two functions performed by private banks: (1) "augmenting the capital of a country," which translated means creating money in the form of banknotes out of paper and ink and lending the money at interest to borrowers who will put it into circulation, and (2) "rendering a greater part of the capital of a country active and productive than would otherwise be so," which translated means paying interest (say, 3 percent) in order to attract deposits of money that might otherwise lie idle in private hoards and lending at interest (say, 5 percent) the money thus attracted to borrowers who will spend it into circulation. These two functions may be described more tersely as: (1) putting newly created money into circulation, and (2) putting erstwhile hoardings (savings) into circulation.

Smith's statement is essentially false inasmuch as it asserts that the most important way banking serves to increase the industry of the country is by lending savings rather than by lending newly created money. Exactly the opposite is the case. The way to increase the production of the industry of a country to a new high is to increase aggregate demand for the products of industry to a new high, and the way to do this is to increase the amount of money in circulation to a new high. Increasing the amount of money in circulation to a new high means "augmenting" the money supply. Putting savings or erstwhile hoardings into circulation will keep the circulating money supply from decreasing, but it can never raise it to a new high. The only way to make industrial activity reach and sustain a new high is to make the size of the country's money supply reach and sustain a new high. Thus Smith's statement about the matter contains not merely an assertion of what is untrue but an explicit denial of what is true. A greater disservice to economic theory is hardly imaginable.

In his proposal for the founding of the Bank of England, Paterson displayed a far better understanding of the matter in 1694 than did Smith eight decades later. Whatever ideas Paterson may have entertained about the role the bank might play in "rendering a greater part of that money supply active and productive than would otherwise be so," he had no doubt that the all-important role of the bank was augmenting the money supply. "This bank will be in effect as nine hundred thousand pounds or a million of fresh money brought into the nation" (Andreades 1966, p. 66).

Different from but closely related to the last quotation from Smith is his observation that "The . . . money which can be lent at interest in any country is . . . regulated . . . by the value of that part of the annual produce which . . . is destined for replacing a capital, but such a capital as the owner does not care to be at the trouble of employing himself" (1909, p. 292).

The distinction Smith makes here between money that is saved and invested directly by the person saving it and money that is saved, then loaned, then invested by a borrower, is a useful distinction and one employed by many economists including, for example, Keynes when he says, "It is open to the individual to employ his wealth by [1] hoarding money or [2] lending money [or 3] purchasing actual capital assets" (1964, p. 160). Taken as a whole, however, the quotation from Smith is profoundly false. It completely misses a point of utmost significance—that a large part of "the money which can be lent at interest in any country" is money newly created by banks on the basis of fractional reserves.

It is a common belief, one shared by Smith apparently, that before money can be loaned it must first be earned and then be saved. This common belief is utterly and completely false. Banks create and lend money that was never previously earned or saved by anyone. Thus Smith again misinforms his readers and misses an opportunity to stress the importance of banknote creation by banks.

A word must also be said about Smith's remarks concerning the early years of the Bank of England. Only about 3 of the 900 pages of *Wealth of Nations* are devoted to the history of the bank, and only about 10 pages contain even the slightest mention of it (1909, pp. 256–258). Much of what he has to say about the bank consists of a mere recitation of the amounts of its loans to the government and its capitalization in various years. Along with the bland selection of statistics, however, a very distinctive point of view is repeatedly expressed. The Bank of England, we are informed, is "the greatest in Europe," it is an astute "manager of other people's money," it is a "great company," it "advances money to the public," it is "a great engine of the state," and so on. The all-important fact that the bank was a private corporation authorized to print paper money to the amount of its loans to the government and thus was a creator of paper money is nowhere simply and unambiguously stated, nor is its significance adequately discussed. Indeed, one could read every word of Smith and never gain a clear idea about the true nature and significant role of the Bank of England.

Smith notes that by 1746 the government had borrowed from the bank, and still owed, a total of £11,690,000. He finds no occasion, however, to mention that between 1694 and 1746 the government handed over to the bank more than £23,000,000 in interest — twice the amount it had borrowed but nevertheless still owed. The idea that a government that can charter a private corporation to create money can also create money itself apparently seemed to Smith a subject unworthy of discussion. Why a government that can create money should borrow from and pay interest to a private corporation that creates money is a question he apparently considered unworthy of discussion.

In fairness to Smith it may be contended that 1776 was too early a date in the history of money and banking to expect from him a really cogent treatment of the relative merits of government-created and private-created paper money. If the contention is warranted, then it must also be said that 1776 was too early a date for Smith to conclude in favor of private-created money — too early for him to write that "there are several different sorts of paper money; but the circulating notes of banks and bankers are the species . . . which seems best adapted to this purpose" (1909, p. 241).

_____

Chapter 11

Financing the War
for Independence of
the United States

Paul Revere's famous ride the night of April 18, 1775 followed by the the battles of Lexington and Concord, small as they were, marked the beginning of the War for Independence. In a practical sense, the surrender of Cornwallis at Yorktown on October 19, 1781, signaled the end of the war although no peace treaty was signed until September 1783, and General Washington did not totally disband the remnants of his army until November 1783.

As is shown in Chapters 7 and 8, in the period up to 1775 the British colonies in North America never succeeded in making their supply of gold and silver grow in proportion to their increasing output of goods and services — grow according to "the needs of trade" as it was customarily phrased. They therefore found it expedient to print and put into circulation paper money; and when the issues of paper money were made with due circumspection, the overall money supply (specie plus paper) was made to increase in proportion to output with the result that the paper was exchanged at par with specie. That is to say, the issue of paper money did not result in price inflation.

In the period of the War for Independence, 1775–1783, the United Colonies — the United States as they came to be called — found it more difficult than ever before to increase their supply of specie, especially because of the blockade of international trade imposed by the British Navy. Simultaneously, the need for money to pay for the war skyrocketed. The separate states and the United States acting through the Continental Congress did what they had always done when specie proved to be in short supply; they issued paper money. But now they issued it not in proportion to the relatively slow-growing needs of trade but in response to the fast-growing needs of war. There were two results: (1) the war was paid for to a remarkable extent by the issue of paper money, and victory over the British was achieved despite the acute shortage of specie; and (2) the issue of paper money in quantities out of all proportion to the increase in output of goods and services caused the paper money to lose value in terms of specie — caused runaway price inflation.

It is the second of these two results that historians ideologically opposed to the issue of paper money by governments have chosen to emphasize and to implant indelibly in the minds of their readers; it is the first of the two results, however, that deserves the emphasis. The war of national liberation waged by the United States against Britain could not have been won without the issue of paper money. We owe our independence to government-issued paper money.

This is not to say that we do not owe our independence to other factors as well. The war could not have been won (1) without the purchase of goods and services with the government-issued paper money, (2) without the gifts, loans, and military assistance on land and sea provided by France, and (3) without Washington's army and the militias of the several states seizing goods and commandeering services from the citizens of the country when necessary and "paying" with IOUs called "loan certificates" — in effect another form of paper money.

In 1786 Thomas Jefferson estimated that for the period 1775–1783 paper money issued by the Continental Congress had permitted purchases equivalent to $36 million in specie, that paper money issued by the states had also permitted purchases amounting to $36 million, and that the debt resulting from the issue of IOUs was $43 million for the Congress and $25 million for the states. The total cost of the war according to Jefferson's estimate was thus $140 million (Bullock 1979, p. 174). At about the same time, "Samuel Osgood, who was well informed, estimated expenditures through 1783 at $150,000,000 in specie" (Ferguson 1961, p. 28).

Historians have since estimated that the cost of the war in terms of specie was as low as $100 million or as high as $168 million (BC 1975, p. 1140 and Ferguson 1961, p. 334). The lower estimate, made by the Department of Commerce's Bureau of the Census, which shows no breakdown into components, is almost certainly too low. The higher estimate, made by Ferguson (slightly rounded), may be detailed as follows:

Specie value of paper money issued by the Continental Congress	$ 46,000,000
Foreign debts ($8,000,000 to France, $2,000,000 to Holland and $500,000 to Spain)	10,500,000
Federal debts resulting from issue of IOUs domestically	28,000,000
State debts resulting from issue of IOUs domestically	18,200,000
Additional direct expenditures in support of the war by the states	65,300,000
Total	168,000,000

Ferguson's estimate is about 12 percent greater than Osgood's and 20 percent greater than Jefferson's. But Ferguson is doubtful about the validity of the figure of $65.3 million for allowances to the states and thinks it might have been as little as $55 million so that the total cost of the war would thus have been only $158 million. His estimate in this case would be only about 5 percent greater than Osgood's and 13 percent greater than Jefferson's.

If we assume that expenditures by the states in behalf of the war effort was $55 million and that half was paid for by the issue of paper money by the states, then the total specie value of paper money issued by the Congress and the states amounted to $73.5 million ($46 million plus $27.5 million)—only about 2 percent more than Jefferson's estimate of $72 million. The very significant conclusion is that considerably more than four-tenths, but perhaps a little less than half, of the cost attributed to the war was paid for by the direct and overt issue of paper money.

If we add together Ferguson's estimate of the debts to foreigners and the federal and state debts for domestically issued IOUs, we get a total of $56.7 million for the war debt as of 1783. The state debts were assumed by the federal government in the negotiations leading up to the adoption of the Constitution in 1787, and the debt of the United States as of 1791 totaled $75.5 million (BC 1975, p. 1117). This amounts to $56.7 million in 1783 plus accrued interest at an average rate of 3.64 percent, which suggests that the figure of $56.7 million is probably fairly accurate.

It is important to understand that the domestic debt in 1783 of $56.7 million in terms of specie was for the most part not due to the borrowing of specie—could not possibly have been due to actual borrowing of specie. "Hamilton estimated that before the Revolution [the amount of specie in the 13 colonies] was eight millions [dollars. Pelatiah] Webster's estimate of the coin was ten millions" (Del Mar 1979, p. 110). Perhaps as much as a third of this was spent abroad purchasing materials of war. With no more specie than existed in the country, it is not credible that borrowing of $56.7 million in specie could have occurred; and no historian believes that it did occur.

Most of the domestic debt resulted from issuing IOUs for goods and services and not from borrowing gold or silver coin. "On December 27, 1776, Washington was empowered to seize whatever supplies should be required for his army; to compel the owners to sell them at a reasonable price" (Bullock 1979, p. 128).

An act of February 1780 directed state assessors to inquire how much wheat, above the amount necessary for subsistence, was held by individual citizens. The surplus was to be confiscated and paid for by loan certificates.

The great number of [IOUs or loan] certificates issued . . . did not represent bona fide loans. [They were issued to citizens who] could not collect money immediately from the government officials who bought their goods. . . . Payment in loan certificates [was accepted] rather than wait for money. (Ferguson 1961, pp. 57–61)

Much of the pay of soldiers and officers after 1780 was also in the form of loan certificates.

Not only did the $56.7 million in domestic debt not result from actual borrowing of specie, it was not intended when most of the loan certificates were issued that they would eventually come to represent a debt payable in specie. The loan certificates were made acceptable in payment of taxes, and it was originally expected that in due time they would pay themselves off or be taken out of circulation in that way. As it actually happened, however, great numbers of the holders of certificates were induced to sell them to speculators, often at heavy discounts. Thereafter the speculators, to their great profit, induced the government to turn the certificates into an interest-bearing debt denominated in specie.

So much, for the moment, as to how the war was financed by debt. It is also especially noteworthy that the war was financed by taxation only to a small extent. Heavy taxes were impossible because one of the reasons the colonies rebelled was their opposition to taxes imposed by Britain. They were likewise opposed to taxes imposed by their own assemblies. Most colonial governments had in the past financed themselves not by taxation but either by spending into circulation their issues of paper money or by lending paper money into circulation and depending on the income from interest on the loans to take the place of taxes. Colonists unused to paying domestic taxes and in rebellion against taxes imposed by Britain were very little inclined to impose taxes on themselves in order to finance the war.

Taxation great enough to figure importantly in financing a war is unpopular even in the case of a long-established and fully sovereign government with a time-honored system of taxation already in place and enforced by accepted judicial and police forces. In the War for Independence, however, each of the colonies was jealous of its sovereignty and reluctant to grant full sovereignty to the Continental Congress. Although meetings of representatives of the several colonies for the purpose of taking concerted action against Britain began much earlier, the Articles of Confederation were not even provisionally adopted until November 1777 and not ratified by the colonies until July 1781. During the entire period of its existence (1775–1787), the Continental Congress was not legally authorized to impose taxes for war finance, nor had it any apparatus of courts and constables to guarantee the collection of taxes; it never collected a dollar of taxes in its own right. To the extent that taxation figured in financing the war, the taxes were imposed and collected by the various states and then spent by them or handed over to the Continental Congress for spending. "There is nothing available to show that the returns from taxation [for war financing] were appreciable anywhere before 1781" (Harlow 1929, p. 67).

Since it was impractical to try to pay for the war by taxation or by borrowing specie and since the colonists were habituated to dealing in terms of government-issued paper money, it is scarcely surprising that an attempt was made to pay for the war by government-issued paper money. Because of the size of the issues, however, the purchasing power of paper money declined, gradually at first, then rapidly. Thereafter the costs of war were paid mainly by various units of government issuing IOUs (more paper) for goods and services purchased or "arbitrarily sequestered."

The explanation given above on how the war came to be financed in so large a measure by paper money is fully in accord with the comments of Benjamin Franklin in 1784:

When Great Britain commenced the present war upon the Colonies, they had neither arms nor ammunition, nor money to purchase them or to pay soldiers. The new government had not immediately the consistence necessary for levying heavy taxes; nor would taxes that could be raised within the year during peace have been sufficient for a year's expense in time of war; they therefore printed a quantity of paper bills, each expressing to be of the value of a certain number of Spanish [silver] Dollars, from one to thirty. With these they paid, clothed and fed their troops, fitted out ships, and conducted the war. (1907, 9: 231)

Franklin then discusses the fact that paper money, although essential to the conduct of the war, experienced over the years a drop in purchasing power.

The paper money thus issued, passed current in all the internal commerce of the United States at par with silver during the first year; supplying the place of the gold and silver . . . which was sent out of the country to purchase arms, etc. . . . But the great number of troops necessary . . . to defend a coast of near 500 leagues in length against an enemy, who, being master of the sea, could land troops where they pleased, occasioned such a demand for money, and such frequent emissions of new bills, that the quantity became greater than was wanted for the purpose of commerce. . . .

It has been long and often observed, that when the current money of a country is augmented beyond the occasions for money as a medium of commerce, its value as money diminishes. . . .

Thus the excessive quantities which necessity obliged the Americans to issue for continuing the war, occasioned a depreciation in value, which, commencing towards the end of 1776 has gone on augmenting, till at the beginning of the present year, 50, 60, and as far as 70 dollars in paper were reckoned not more than equal to one dollar in silver.

Before the depreciation commenced, the Congress, fearing it, stopt for a time the emission of new bills and resolved to supply their occasions by borrowing. . . .

Those loans not being sufficient, the Congress were forced to print more bills and the depreciation proceeded. (1907, 9: 231-233)

The depreciation to the point of worthlessness of the paper money issued by the states and by Congress is accounted for in part by the huge quantity they issued. Another cause of the eventual rapid depreciation, however, was the enormous amount of counterfeiting that occurred. In the days before the extensive use of watermarked or carefully restricted types of paper, exotic inks, or elaborate engravings, counterfeiting flourished both in the colonies and in England.

Counterfeiting of American money, in fact, was perhaps the most important and successful of the British counterinsurgency efforts, and little secret was made of it. The following quotations are only a few of the many that may be found on this subject.

In the same newspaper in New York in which the official British documents were printed [during the British occupation under the command of General Howe] there were also printed advertisements proposing to supply counterfeit money to persons going to other Colonies — [countefeit bills] "so nearly and exactly executed that no risk attended their circulation. . . ."

On July 3, 1777 it was recorded in the Secret Journal of Congress that a large amount of counterfeit Continental bills had been fabricated in England and brought to America in British men-of-war operating on the Delaware; and that the bills had been put into circulation. (Del Mar 1979, pp. 102–103)

How much the American money supply was increased by counterfeit issues is, of course, unknown and unknowable. Del Mar describes the amount of counterfeit as "immense" and "prodigious." In 1779 John Jay issued "An Address to the People on the Currency" in which he defended the issues of paper money and blamed depreciation on widespread counterfeiting operations by the enemy (Morris 1987, p. 105). Much of the adverse effect of counterfeit paper came about simply because everyone soon became aware of its existence. Thus even the genuine issues of money were accepted warily or at a discount out of fear that they might be counterfeit. The recognized presence of counterfeit was probably as much an important factor undermining the confidence in American paper money as the actual amount of counterfeit or the actual amount of money, counterfeit and genuine added together.

In retrospect, and taking account of all the factors militating against the success of the issues of paper money, it is astonishing how successful they proved and surprising that one of the more respected historians of the period could write:

Paper money provided the sinews of war in the first five years of the Revolution and other incomes were secondary to it. . . . Indeed currency finance sustained the war and survived in an attenuated form until the moment of victory. (Ferguson 1961, p. 44)

Other historians have been less approving. Colonists have been reproached for resorting to "the worst of financial expedients, the emission of paper money" (Harlow 1929, p. 46). "Ruinous issues of paper money" is another phrase often encountered in histories of the period (see Ferguson 1961, p. 36).

Paper money, critics have railed, "polluted the equity of laws," "corrupted the justice of public administration," "destroyed the fortunes of those who had the most confidence in it," and "went far to destroy the morality of the people" (Mitchell 1974, p. 88).

Franklin, however, argued not only that there was no practical alternative to paper money issues but also that price inflation (the decline in the purchasing power of the paper money) was far less evil than is usually claimed by economists and historians.

> The general effect of the depreciation [of Continental and state bills] among the inhabitants of the states has been this, that it has operated as a gradual tax upon them. Their business has been done and paid for by the paper money, and every man has paid his share of the tax according to the time he retained any of the money in his hands and to the depreciation within that time. Thus it has proved a tax on money, a kind of property very difficult to be taxed by any other mode: and it has fallen more equally than many other taxes, as those people paid most, who, being richest, had most money passing through their hands. (1907, 9: 134–135)

This appraisal of the effect of the necessary "overissue" of continental currency was not a hurried one. Earlier (April 22, 1779) Franklin had written from France to Samuel Cooper:

> The effect of paper currency is not understood on this side of the water. And indeed the whole is a mystery even to the politicians, how we have been able to continue a war four years without money [specie], and how we could pay with paper, that had no previously fixed fund appropriated specifically to redeem it. The currency as we manage it is a wonderful machine. It performs its office when we issue it; it pays and clothes troops, and provides victuals and ammunition: and when we are obliged to issue a quantity excessive, it pays itself off by depreciation. (1907, 7: 294)

Franklin's analysis suggests that the horror of inflation, so often expressed by bankers and by moneyed people in general, stems precisely from the fact that it is in a sense a tax on money — "a kind of property very difficult to be taxed by any other mode." Inflation is opposed by moneyed people, who always portray it as a calamity, and by economists and journalists subservient to them, for precisely the reason that the people who hold the most money in their hands the longest time are the "people who pay most" of the cost of inflation. Thus inflation has been called "a tax of the most unjust and objectionable sort" by one historian (Bullock 1979, p. 138).

It is as absurd to contend that a war could always be conducted in such a way that no one suffers financial loss as to argue that it should be conducted in such a way that no one suffers physical injury or death. War is a matter in which injuries, financial and otherwise, are inevitable and inevitably inequitable. It is astonishing, however, that so many historians have shed more tears over the financial losses of moneyed people from a depreciating currency than over the soldiers who gave life or limb to the cause of the War for Independence.

So much for the indispensable role played by paper money in the War for Independence and how that paper money eventually became worthless. It remains to be observed that, whether the cost of the war from 1775 to 1783 was $140 or $158 or $168 million, a war debt of $56.7 million or thereabouts existed in 1783 and because of accrued interest amounted to $75.5 million by 1791. It may be estimated that before the $56.7 million debt of 1783 was finally liquidated early in the 1830s about $70 million interest had been paid on it — about 1.25 times the original debt. By another estimate, $90 million in interest on the debt and veterans' pensions must be added to the original war debt to obtain the ultimate cost of the war (BC 1975, p. 1140). The ultimate cost to the United States, then, would have amounted to roughly $250 million.

It is interesting to try to make some comparison between the cost of the war to Britain and the cost to the United States. The highest estimate of the cost to Britain that I have found is $532 million for 1775–1783 (Mitchell 1962, p. 390). The lowest estimate I have encountered is $475 million for 1776–1785 (Andreades 1966, p. 119). Let us take as the cost of the war to Britain as $500 million through 1783, or between three and four times the cost to the United States for the same period.

The much greater cost to Britain may be attributed in part to the much longer lines of communication and the attendant higher costs of transport. It may be attributed in part to the British use of mercenary troops. It may also to some extent be attributed to corruption and war profiteering that were more widespread among the British than among the Americans, although these factors were far from absent in the United States.

If the original war cost Britain more than three times what it cost the United States, what about its ultimate cost? No two historians or econonists are likely to agree on an answer to this question. My answer begins with the fact that instead of financing its war in such a way as to minimize the amount of debt at the end of the war, Britain relied almost entirely on borrowed money. By 1783, the British national debt was roughly $500 million greater than in 1774. But here is the really interesting fact: Britain's national debt has never since 1783 been less than it was at the end of that year (Mitchell 1962, pp. 401–403). The conclusion I draw from this is that Britain has not even yet finished paying for the war it lost attempting to suppress the emerging United States.

British taxpayers have now been paying annual interest on the $500 million cost of the war for more than two hundred years. How much interest has been paid by the British to their moneylending class of 1783 and its heirs? It would be tedious to attempt an exact calculation. Instead let us estimate the average rate of interest over the past two centuries at the low figure of 4 percent. Even at this moderate rate, the interest on the debt for twenty-five years would equal 100 percent of the debt. This means that by 1983 the war debt of 1783 had required payment of over $4 billion in interest although the original debt was still owed in full. Put another way, the British have now paid for the war more than eight times over, and yet today they owe every penny of the expenditures the war occasioned.

The ultimate cost of the war to U.S. taxpayers was estimated earlier at $250 million. By 1983, British taxpayers had paid sixteen times the U.S. amount, and the ultimate cost of the war was increasing by interest on the unpaid debt every year. The average rate of interest on British public debt is now far above 4 percent. The probability seems to be that in the next hundred years the British will have to pay for the 1775–1783 war not merely four times but more nearly eight times. What the ultimate cost of the war may turn out to be no one knows.

This effort to compare the ultimate war costs to the United States and Britain is advanced to challenge the many scholars who assert that Britain followed "sound fiscal policy" during the war (Ferguson 1961, p. 121). On the other hand, the same scholars insist that the United States resorted to "the worst of financial expedients, the emission of paper money" (Harlow 1929, p. 46). But to the extent that the United States financed the war by paper money, it was left with no debt; whereas Britain was left with an enormous debt on which interest has had to be paid ever since. The definition of sound financing procedures according to these scholars seems to be those financing procedures that assure moneylenders or bondholders the greatest long-run return and prove in the long-run the most burdensome on taxpayers. This seems a rather bizarre way of viewing the matter.

There remains to be reemphasized here the importance of money as a causal factor in bringing about the War for Independence. For reasons about which it would be easy to speculate but difficult to prove anything, historians have usually played down the central importance as a cause of the war the dispute about who should create money for the Colonies. On the other hand, "Franklin cited restrictions upon paper money as one of the main reasons for the alienation of the American provinces from the mother country" (Ferguson 1961, p.16).

To a significant extent, the war was fought over the right of the Colonists to create their own money supply. When the Continental Congress and the states brought forth large issues of their own legal-tender money in 1775, they committed acts so contrary to British laws governing the colonies and so contemptuous and insulting to British sovereignty as to make war inevitable.

The right of a people to create their own paper money through their government was an issue that played a principal role in the real growth of the Colonial economies before 1775. It was, among other things, to secure the right of the people to create their own paper money that the revolt against England occurred. The decision of the people, through Congress and state assemblies, to create their own paper money made possible the winning of the War for Independence.

_____

Chapter 12

The 1780s in the United States

The years immediately following upon the War for Independence were not happy ones for the people of the United States. In the decade of the 1780s, the country experienced its first great depression. "Indebtedness and unemployment [occurred] to a degree of severity Americans had never previously experienced . . . Workmen walked the streets seeking jobs, . . . fishermen by the thousands were idle, and foreclosures and bankruptcies occurred on a scale unparalleled in the [previous] history of the country" (Morris 1987, pp. 131, 134).

With wartime paper money losing its purchasing power and disappearing from circulation, the money supply of the country in the early 1780s was reduced almost solely to specie. Loan certificates at widely fluctuating discounts provided an addition to the means of exchange, although a far from satisfactory or sufficient addition. For the most part, the country was forced into a reliance on gold and silver coins.

As is nearly always the case, the supply of specie was inadequate to meet the needs of trade at prevailing prices, or even at prewar prices, and the great inflation of war time was followed by a great postwar deflation. Debtors who had been able to pay their creditors with cheap money during the inflationary period now had to pay with money that was dear. Thus, "each one of the thirteen states found creditors arrayed against debtors" (Morris 1987, p. 155).

The supply of specie, entirely too small at the beginning of the decade, tended to grow steadily smaller as the balance of international trade remained persistently unfavorable to the United States. Because of the British blackade during the war, some of America's best customers turned elsewhere for their imports, and trade with them recovered slowly if at all. After 1783 ships of the United States were banned from calling on ports in the British West Indies where before the war they had carried on a profitable trade. The extent of the loss of customers at home and abroad is indicated by the fact that "between 1772 and 1775 some 150 vessels were engaged in whaling, largely out of Nantucket. [By 1787] that number had shrunk to a mere 36" (Morris 1987, p. 141).

Some branches of trade, however, recovered quickly. For example, "Between 1783 and 1785 seven thousand blacks were reputed to have been imported into South Carolina. The *Maryland Journal* reported in June 1785 that American vessels, 'mostly from Boston,' abounded on the Guinea coast, carrying New England rum to be exchanged for slave cargoes." But such prosperous branches of trade were rare. "Altogether the per capita value of U.S. exports was less in 1790 than in 1774" (Morris 1987, pp. 161, 135).

The enmities of war time seem to have been quickly forgotten, and the extent to which the new nation almost immediately reestablished Britain as its principal trading partner is astonishing. This is particularly true inasmuch as the trade balance with Britain was unfavorable to the United States in every year of the 1780s. For years 1783 to 1789 inclusive, for example, imports from Britain amounted to $69.3 million and exports to only $24.5 million. With imports 2.8 times as great as exports "gold stocks were quickly depleted (one estimate puts exports of specie for the three years 1784-5-6 at $6,130,000) . . . and a credit [money] crisis proved inevitable" (Morris 1987, p. 132).

What occurred in the 1780s was not a quick deflation in the early part of the decade followed by a stabilization of the price level and then a moderate degree of prosperity but a relentless persistence of deflation. "Urban wage rates dropped from an index figure of 23 in 1785 to 17 in 1789," for example. This 26 percent fall was paralleled by an even greater decline in the prices of commodities produced by farmers (Morris 1987, p. 131).

Given the breadth and depth of the depression, it is not surprising that debtors found themselves in deep trouble. Nor is it surprising that resistance to paying with dear money debts that had been contracted in cheap money became widespread or that resistance turned violent on numerous occasions.

At York, Pennsylvania, debtors forcefully prevented the sale of cattle . . . in November of '86. The previous summer Maryland's Charles County Courthouse was closed down by a "tumultuous assemblage of the people." In South Carolina, farmers attacked the Camden Courthouse. . . . In April 1787 the people of Virginia's Caroline County entered into an association to purchase no property sold at auction, and . . . a mob burned down Virginia's King William County Courthouse, destroying all the records [among others, records of debts and taxes due]. (Morris 1987, p. 265)

In 1785 and 1786 an insurrectionary movement, known as Shay's Rebellion, broke out in New England. It was an insurrection of debtors who were suffering from the collapse of the currency and return to specie values. . . . This insurrection was put down by force, but Massachusetts passed a law delaying the collection of debts. (Sumner 1968, p. 50)

"Debtors in the year 1786 made up 80 per cent of the occupants of Worcester's jail" (Morris 1987, p. 260). Obviously, therefore, penalties imposed upon debtors and creditors were unbalanced to an extreme degree. The most a creditor ever lost was some percentage of his money (most likely obtained by exploitation or chicanery in the first place); a debtor often lost what was infinitely more valuable—his freedom. He was subject not "merely" to jailing but to being "sold into servitude" for whatever period of time might be decided by a judge usually more in sympathy with creditors than debtors. Even "at the time of the adoption of the federal Constitution the elimination of servitude for white debtors was still several decades away, as was the abolition of imprisonment for debt" (Morris 1987, p. 175).

Creditors wanted deflation; they wanted a specie money that could not be expected to increase as the needs of trade increased and therefore guaranteed persistent deflation. Debtors wanted inflation; they wanted a paper money that could be made to increase faster than the needs of trade increased and therefore guaranteed persistent inflation. To believe that either creditors or debtors were dedicated to fairness or justice, however such words might be defined, is to misjudge entirely the character of the type of class warfare that emerged.

Nor must we overlook the fact that the arguments on the side of the debtor class were superior to those of the creditor class, even from the point of view of the creditor class, if a long-term rather than a short-term point of view is taken. The creditor class is usually more prosperous when the members hold claims against a smaller percentage of a large and rapidly growing economy than when they hold claims against a larger percentage of a stagnant or contracting economy. And an economy can be a rapidly growing one or become a large one only if farmers and urban businessmen are willing and able to borrow and expand production, only if interest rates are low and there exists a reasonable probability that debts can be repaid with money no more dear than the money that was borrowed.

In Rhode Island in 1786, the debtors-inflationists carried the election and issued paper money at rates designed and guaranteed to enable the payment of debts and taxes with cheap money. By the end of 1786, seven states had new issues of paper money in circulation—the size and legal-tender status of the various issues reflecting the balance of power between creditors and debtors of the particular states.

New Jersey's legal tender bills were fairly steady, although they passed outside the state at a slowly increasing discount. . . . In New York, Pennsylvania, and South Carolina [paper] currency was not legal tender, and it was being successfully managed despite a slight discount in exchange for specie. (Ferguson 1961, p. 244)

It is significant that after seeing the wartime issues of paper money depreciate to zero, a large constituency still favored government-issued paper money. One might have surmised that the depreciation of the wartime issues would have turned the populace against new issues for all time to come. But it was creditors, not debtors, that came to hate the paper money of units of government. And it was creditors who usually enjoyed the backing of men of influence and position.

Thus, in the first of the Federalist Papers that he wrote, the eminent Virginian James Madison was surprisingly forthright in expressing his pro-creditor bias. "Among the numerous advantages promised by a well constructed Union," he wrote, is that a national government can, far better than separate state governments "break and control the violence of faction." A "most common and durable source of faction," he continued, is the division of society into "those who are creditors and those who are debtors." But since debtors greatly outnumber creditors, one object of the union must be the protection of creditors from "the superior force of an interested and over-bearing majority." Should debtors, for example, develop "a rage for paper money, for an abolition of debts, . . . or for any other improper or wicked project [then] the whole body of the Union [rather] than a particular member [state] of it" could better protect the creditor minority from the debtor majority. A union with an elaborate system of checks and balances was imperative, as Madison saw it, to tip the balance in favor of creditors and to check the "improper or wicked" aspirations of the debtor majority (Beloff 1987, pp. 41–47). One is reminded of Rousseau's contention that civil society is little more than the result of a conspiracy by the rich to guarantee their plunder.

Sentiments similar to those of Madison were expressed in New England as well as Virginia. Elbridge Gerry of Massachusetts, with such "violence of faction" as Shay's Rebellion very much on his mind, declared: "The evils we experience flow from an excess of democracy" (Morris 1987, p. 279).

Overall, however, during the 1780s, the momentum remained with the creditors-deflationists not the debtors-inflationists. Crafty and voluble exponents of a specie standard gained in prominence—Robert Morris and Alexander Hamilton most notably. Morris, who was born in England, refused to vote for the Declaration of Independence although became a signer after its approval by the Congress. Born in the British West Indies, Hamilton displayed uncritical admiration of British laws and institutions to the end of his days.

The plan of Morris and Hamilton for putting an end to government issues of currency was to begin by establishing the "Bank of North America" using the Bank of England as its model. A charter for the new bank was obtained from Congress in May 1781. Morris hoped to increase his bank's capital to the extent that much private wealth in the country would be invested in its stock; and the loans of its capital to the government, as in the case of the Bank of England, could then be matched in size by the issue of banknotes. The banknotes of the Bank of North America were supposedly redeemable in specie, but the bank's charter placed no limit on its issue of banknotes and ignored the ratio of reserves in specie to banknotes. "Notes [of the bank] were made receivable for all taxes and debts to the United States, as Hamilton had proposed" (Morris 1987, pp. 153–154).

It was the hope and plan of Morris and Hamilton that the banknotes of the Bank of North America, together with whatever specie was in circulation, would provide a medium of exchange and debt repayment for the entire nation. Morris hoped to engineer an early retirement of all federal and state currencies, replacing them with the notes of his bank (Ferguson 1961, pp. 123–124).

The vagueness of the charter of the Bank of North America notwithstanding, if the example of the Bank of England were followed, then the size of the banknote issue would depend on the size of the debt of the government to the bank. A banknote issue of adequate size to retire all currencies outstanding would require a large government debt to the bank denominated in specie. If all the loan certificates outstanding could be declared payable in specie, if large numbers of holders of the certificates could be persuaded to buy stock in the bank therewith, then the bank, as holder of a large government debt, could come forth with an adequately sized issue of banknotes.

With notes of the Bank of North America replacing all paper money issued by various units of government, the beneficiaries of the interest on the nation's money supply would become the stockholders of the bank rather than the general public, the ultimate issuer of the paper money that the banknotes would supersede. "A certain amount of funded debt is a national blessing," creditors proclaimed, meaning, of course, a blessing to them. "The creation of a new species of money by this means," since they would profit from the interest on it, they likewise believed would be a national blessing (Ferguson 1961, pp. 289–290). "A domestic debt [of the federal government] would greatly contribute to the Union," Morris told Congress and went on to say such a debt would serve the function of "combining together the interests of moneyed men" in support of the federal government. "Morris's plan of action anticipated the major features of the later Federalist program" and the major features of the "Bank of the United States" that Hamilton was to champion when he became secretary of the treasury in Washington's cabinet (Ferguson 1961, p. 124).

It is unnecessary here to go into the detailed history of Morris's bank except to say that it never lived up to his expectations. What Morris's proposals did succeed in doing, however, was to give encouragement to a coterie of firm and influential believers in the redemption in specie of all debt certificates and loan certificates outstanding and in a federal debt repayable in specie. The ownership of loan certificates and other forms of state and federal debt had become concentrated in the hands of a new and small class that exerted an influence out of all proportion to its size. No complete statistics are available on ownership of the $75.5 million that became the federal debt of 1791; but the evidence that does exist points to a concentration of wealth well beyond what one might guess.

In Massachusetts 61.8 percent of the debt was held by only 7 percent of all holders, 73.7 percent by only 12 percent. Only 21 percent of all debt was in the hands of those to whom it had been originally issued, and 79 percent had been acquired by speculators at some fraction of what turned out to be its ultimate worth. The statistics from Maryland indicate much the same concentration; 71.3 percent of the debt was held by only 14 percent of all holders, and 81 percent of the debt had been acquired by speculators from the original holders. In Pennsylvania 9 percent of all holders of debt held 61 percent of the total, and 59 percent of the debt was held by speculators who had acquired it from original holders. A review of another compilation of statistics reveals that a mere 3 percent of holders held over 40 percent of all debt, while at the bottom of the scale 40 percent of all holders of debt held less than 3 percent of it (Ferguson 1961, pp. 273–284).

The few, but increasingly influential, holders of large blocks of debt naturally favored the redemption of all debts in specie at face value. This prompted the prominent Philadelphia physician and signer of the Declaration of Independence, Benjamin Rush, to remark that a man who expected to get 100 cents on the dollar for securities bought sometimes for a tenth of that amount "had a mind like a highway robber" (Ferguson 1961, p. 301). A very large majority of citizens would no doubt have agreed with Rush, but the matter was never the subject of a plebiscite; and "representative democracy" was then, as forever after, remarkably sensitive to moneyed interests.

The debts for the war assumed by the United States government, although seemingly large, were in fact small compared to the government's assets. One of the great accomplishments of the Continental Congress in the 1780s was the formation of the Northwest Territory and the passage of the Northwest Ordinance. Seaboard states were persuaded to relinquish their claims to parts of the territory now comprising the states of Ohio, Indiana, Illinois, Michigan, Wisconsin, and a small part of Minnesota. The federal government thus came into posession of somewhat more than 160 million acres, the sale of which at only 50 cents per acre would more than liquidate the federal debt.

The Northwest Ordinance contemplated the survey of the territory into "townships" consisting of thirty-six "sections" of one square mile (640 acres) and the sale of land at not less than 1 dollar an acre in specie. Four sections per township were to be retained by the federal government, and one section per township dedicated to the support of public schools. The government also claimed a right to one third of any gold, silver, or copper discovered on land it sold. The ascendancy of a wealthy and greedy class of land speculators was signaled by the failure of the government to retain a right to 100 percent of all minerals and by the decision to sell land in lots of not less than 640 acres—a decision that made it impossible for the poor to purchase land.

In such turbulent times of depression, money stringency, debtor-creditor conflict, and speculation in loan certificates and government land, the Constitution was written. The document that was drafted would necessarily have to address matters of money and debt.

Chapter 13

The Constitution and Paper Money in the Early Decades of the United States

Whatever high degree of wisdom the founding fathers may properly be said to have shown in writing other parts of the Constitution, the sections dealing with a money supply for the new nation reflect no great foresight on their part. It is possible to imagine a more botched job, but not easy to do so. Pure ignorance combined with misconceived ideologies and conflict of interest to produce a mish-mash of compromised monetary provisions that was to plague the country far into the future.

There are only two sections in the Constitution relating to money, both occurring in Article I. Section 8 authorizes Congress "to coin money, [and] regulate the value thereof." Section 10 forbids to the states certain monetary or money related actions: "No State shall . . . coin money; emit bills of credit [paper money]; make anything but gold and silver coin a [legal] tender in payment of debts; . . . or pass any law impairing the obligations of contracts [debt contracts, for example]."

By granting total control of the coinage to the federal government and denying to the states any role in the matter, the framers of the Constitution obviously intended a single nationwide system of coins. So far, so good. By denying the states any right to emit "bills of credit" (paper money) the framers obviously intended that if there were any paper money issues, such issues would be made by the federal government and be uniform nationwide. So far, so good. But when the delegates to the convention that wrote the Constitution were asked to vote on a clause that would give the federal government specific authority to issue paper money, they voted against it. And when the delegates were asked to vote on a clause that would specifically deny the federal government such authority, they again voted against it (Hammond 1961, p. 92).

Thus the Constitution does not authorize the federal government to issue paper money; and the *intent* of the Constitutional Convention seems clearly and beyond question to have been that since the federal government was not granted the specific power to issue paper money it could not do so even though the power was not specifically denied. In the words of the Tenth Amendment: "The powers not delegated to the United States [the federal government] by the Constitution, nor prohibited by it to the states, are reserved to the states respectively, or to the people." As is discussed later, the Supreme Court was eventually to rule that the federal government did have the power to issue paper money, and that ruling stands unchanged.

Taken altogether, the provisions of the Constitution, as originally interpreted, imply that neither the federal government nor the states could issue paper money. We will return to the far reaching consequences of such limitations on the issue of paper money a little later, but first some remarks pertaining to coinage are in order.

The effect of the Constitution, together with the laws enacted by Congress in 1791 to establish the United States Mint, was to put the new nation on a bimetallic gold-silver standard. By embracing bimetalism, Congress displayed an almost incredible lack of understanding or foresight. There was already ample historical evidence to show that the ratio of the value of gold to that of silver may change for any number of reasons and, in fact, always does change in the course of time.

Even more reprehensible, the mint ratio of gold to silver selected in 1791 was not in accord with current market prices. The dollar was defined simultaneously as 371.25 grains of silver and 24.75 grains of gold. Any given weight of gold was thus assigned a value fifteen times that of the same weight of silver. In value terms, the gold-silver ratio was thus 15:1. But the prevailing ratio on the world market was not 15:1 but more nearly 15.5:1. Thus with 371.25 grains of silver one could purchase 24.75 grains of gold in the United States and then sell the gold abroad for 383.63 grains of silver for a profit of 3.33 percent less transaction costs. Although the differential was not great, the effect was the gradual export of gold in exchange for silver and for the country to drift toward a time when the only specie in circulation would be silver. "In fact, until 1834 legal tender currency was composed almost entirely of silver coins" (Harris 1961, p. 108). Compared to other monetary mistakes of the new government, however, embracing bimetalism and choosing a foolish gold-silver ratio were minor matters, as is shown presently.

It should be mentioned in passing, however, that the decision to relate the principal coins of the United States by the number 10 or a multiple thereof represented a great improvement over the cumbersome system involving pounds, shillings (1/20th pound), and pence (1/12th shilling or 1/240th pound) inherited from England. Thus the principal small coins of the United

States were made to equal 5/10ths, 1/10th and 1/100th of a dollar, and the principal large coin equal to ten dollars.

The fact of transcendent monetary importance, however, was that in the period subsequent to the formation of the new government, just as in the colonial period, there was insufficient gold and silver in the country to transact the business of the private and public sectors satisfactorily. Nor was there any practical likelihood that the supply of specie would or could be increased in such a way as to permit the economy to grow as it was capable of growing. The need for some form of paper money as a supplement to specie was as pressing as, or more so than, it had been in the colonial period or in the 1780s. Yet the Constitution forbade the states to issue paper money; and since it delegated to the federal government no specific power to issue paper money, the government was unauthorized to issue any either.

Under the Articles of Confederation, the federal government had authority to issue paper money. An early draft of the new Constitution would have granted the same authority, but this provision was deleted by a vote of nine to two.

The only delegate who avowed himself "a friend of paper money" was John Mercer, a Maryland lawyer. . . . His associate from Maryland, Luther Martin, later said that they both had argued against the deletion, taking the ground that it it would be "a novelty unprecedented" to establish a government without a power that might be "absolutely necessary" in time of war. (Hammond 1957, p. 93)

It seems obvious that if the Constitution in effect forbade both the federal government and the states to issue paper money then it was no part of the intention of the framers of that document that either the federal government or the states could charter private corporations, private banks, to do what they themselves were not permitted to do — issue paper money in the form of banknotes. But charter private banks is what some states had already begun to do and what other states proceeded to do. Meanwhile, the federal government got into the act and issued a twenty-year charter for a largely privately owned "Bank of the United States" together with a promise that a federal charter would be issued to no other bank.

The almost incredible fuzziness of the Constitution with regard to money matters thus permitted the issue of banknotes by private companies on the basis of only fractional reserves in specie. Although neither the federal government nor state governments could print or circulate paper money, private companies proceeded to do so without government interference and with tacit government blessing.

It has previously been noted that all the prodigious economic growth from 1607 to the successful War for Independence had been accomplished without the existence of private banks. Thus, if anything in the field of economics has ever been proved conclusively, it was proved by the experience of the colonies that private banks as creators of banknotes or bank credit are totally unnecessary for economic growth and prosperity. Nevertheless, an unbridled proliferation of private banking began in the decade of the 1790s. The short-comings of the Constitution concerning the way in which the nation's money supply should be structured permitted the emergence and development of a money supply of almost the worst conceivable sort.

The aim of private bankers was not to provide the economy with a money supply that grew in step with the output of goods and services but to create a money supply they could increase or decrease in whatever way promised to optimize profits. The interest on their loans was to be not a fund for public improvements in lieu of taxes, as was the interest on the loans of Pennsyl-vania during the colonial period, for example, but a source of private profit to do with as they pleased. And the rate of interest was not to be kept low in order to encourage investment and growth but to be raised as high as the traffic would bear.

By the end of 1791, state-chartered banks were doing business in Philadel-phia, New York, Boston, Baltimore, and Providence; and the Bank of the United States had opened in Philadelphia. By the end of Washington's eight-year administration, there were twenty-four banks in business in the United States (Hammond 1957, pp. 144–145). There is perhaps nothing surprising that this happened during Washington's administration since he seldom ex-pressed any opinion regarding either the structure of the nation's money supply or private banks. He seemed always ready to do whatever was sug-gested by his secretary of the treasury, Alexander Hamilton. And Hamilton seemed bent on ignoring all colonial history and modeling the United States monetary and banking system on that of England and being in all ways sub-servient to the creditor class.

What should occasion surprise, however, is that during the four years of the administration of John Adams and the eight years of the Jefferson ad-ministration the number of state banks more than tripled. This astonishing twelve-year proliferation occurred despite the fact that neither Adams nor Jefferson had any great admiration for private banks.

Consider first these remarks of Adams:

Our medium [of exchange] is depreciated by the multitude of swindling banks, which have emitted bank bills to an immense amount beyond the deposits of gold and silver in their vaults. . . . Every dollar of a bank bill that is issued beyond the quantity of gold and silver in its vaults represents nothing, and is therefore a cheat upon somebody. (Letter to Vanderkem, 16 February 1809, see Adams 1856, 9: 432)

Our whole banking system I have ever abhorred, I continue to abhor, and I shall die abhoring. (Letter to Rush, 28 August 1811, see Adams 1856, 9: 635)

I have never had but one opinion of banking . . . and that opinion has uniformly been that the banks have done more injury to the religion, morality, tranquility, prop-erty, and even the wealth of the nation, than they have done or ever will do good. They are a delusion of the many for the interest of the few. (Letter to Taylor, 12 March 1819, see Adams 1856, 10: 376)

It is the habit of most historians to deal with the period here under consideration by contrasting Hamiltonian Federalism to Jeffersonian Democracy and to put Adams within the Federalist camp. A case may be made for such a procedure, no doubt, but these quotations show a great gulf came eventually to separate the monetary ideas of Adams and Hamilton.

Thomas Jefferson wrote in much greater detail about monetary and banking matters than Adams, and thus his views may be explored at greater length. At least one historian has declared that Jefferson "thoroughly mastered" the subject of money (Hirst 1926, p. 471). I would hesitate to guess the large number of historians who have proclaimed Hamilton's "mastery" of the same subject. The truth, however, is that although Jefferson almost undoubtedly had a wider acquaintance with the monetary literature available at the time than did Hamilton and although his opposition to private banking was more soundly based than Hamilton's promotion of it, Jefferson, as well as Hamilton, entertained highly questionable ideas about money.

Although taking exception to some of Smith's views after reading *Wealth of Nations,* Jefferson called it a "rational and systematic work" and thought Smith's presentation "able and of the first degree of merit" although "prolix and tedious" (Padover 1943, p. 369). Jefferson grasped the importance of what I have earlier called Smith's Law and understood that "our medium of exchange" must increase in proportion to "the whole value of the annual produce of the United States." Elsewhere he repeats "our medium should be proportioned to our produce" (Padover 1943, pp. 360, 368).

But Jefferson seems not to have appreciated the impossibility of increasing the nation's supply of specie at the rate at which the economy was capable of growing. Thus he repeatedly praised a precious metals standard. In one place he advocated that "the medium of gold and silver be universally restored" (Padover 1943, p. 367). In a second he spoke of "the great advantage of specie as a medium" (Padover 1943, p. 359). In a third he declared that "specie is the most perfect medium, because . . . having intrinsic and universal value, it can never die in our hands." And he thought that "the trifling economy of paper . . . weighs nothing in opposition to the precious metals" (Padover 1943, p. 368).

No one was more aware than Jefferson that in the states then in existence there were no gold or silver mines of significance and that the balance of international payments was persistently unfavorable to the United States (BC 1975, p. 868). How then was it reasonable to expect "our medium would increase in proportion to our produce?" It is a question Jefferson, nowhere that I am aware, even attempted to answer.

Jefferson was well acquainted with the works of David Hume, but he seems not to have appreciated Hume's idea that keeping a nation's money supply "gradually increasing" could stimulate its economy to greater output. "Jugglers only will propose" to increase industry and output "by legerdemain tricks with paper," he opined (Padover 1943, p. 364). Altogether, it seems fair to say that Jefferson's understanding of monetary affairs was distinctly inferior to that of Benjamin Franklin.

There are, however, places where Jefferson had something good to say about paper money.

Previous to the Revolution, most of the states were in the habit, whenever they had occasion for more money than could be raised immediately by taxes, to issue paper notes or bills, in the name of the state. . . . [Some] states named in the bill the day when it should be paid, laid taxes to bring in money enough for that purpose, and paid the bills punctually. . . . In these states paper money was in as high estimation as gold and silver. On the commencement of the late Revolution, Congress had no money. . . . Congress had no resource then but in paper money . . . which they were obliged to emit for the purpose of the war. (Padover 1943, pp. 49–50)

The object of . . . [the paper emissions of the old Congress] was a holy one; for if ever there was a holy war, it was that which saved our liberties and gave us independence. (Padover 1943, p. 367)

Nor did Jefferson believe that all forms of paper money should be a thing of the past. As late as 1813 he wrote that, "treasury bills bottomed on taxes . . . thrown into circulation, will take the place of so much gold and silver." But he seems to have believed that any issue of paper money should be retired from circulation after the collection of the taxes upon which they were "bottomed." The idea of permanent issues of treasury bills, or some other form of government-issued paper money, gradually adding to the nation's money supply as the economy grew seems either not to have occurred to him or not to have enjoyed his approval (Jefferson to J. Eppes, 11 September 1813, see Lipscomb 1905, 13: 353).

Jefferson's well-known opposition to the Bank of the United States stemmed from two sources: (1) opposition to the use of "implied constitutional powers" by the federal government, and (2) opposition to the very principle of any bank (whether with a federal or state charter) issuing banknotes on the basis of fractional reserves. In view of the fact that Jefferson was willing to countenance implied federal powers or powers not specifically granted by the Constitution, as he did in making the Louisiana Purchase, we may assume that it was his opposition to banks of issue per se rather than the constitutional matter, that played the major role in his thinking.

I have ever been the enemy of banks, not of those discounting for cash [coin], but of those foisting their own paper into circulation. . . . My zeal against those institutions was so warm and open at the establishment of the Bank of the United States, that I was derided as a maniac by the tribe of bank-mongers, who were seeking to filch from the public their swindling . . . gains. (Letter to Adams, 24 January 1814, see Lipscomb 1903, 14: 17)

I believe that banking establishments are more dangerous to our liberties than standing armies. (Letter to Taylor, 28 May 1816, see Lipscomb 1903, 15: 229)

The distress of our country [has been] produced . . . by . . . bank paper. . . . We must not suffer the moral of the present lesson to pass away without improvement by the eternal suppression of bank paper. . . . Interdict forever, to both the state and national governments, the power of establishing any paper bank. . . . Certainly no nation ever before abandoned to the avarice and jugglings of private individuals to regulate, according to their own interests, the quantum of circulating medium for the nation. . . . Evil has been produced by . . . this ruinous machinery of banks; and justice, wisdom, and duty all require that [the legislature] should interpose and arrest it before the schemes of plunder and spoilation desolate the country. (Letter to Rives, 28 November 1819, see Lipscomb 1903, 16: 76)

It is said that [bank] paper is as good as silver, because we may have silver for it at the bank where it issues. This is not true. One, two, or three persons might have it; but a general application would soon exhaust bank's vaults and leave a ruinous proportion of their paper in its intrinsically worthless form. (Letter to Eppes, 6 November 1813, see Padover 1943, p. 354)

As unsatisfactory as was the way money supply problems were dealt with in the early years of the United States, the way they were dealt with in England during the same period was no more satisfactory.

Chapter 14

Money and Banking in Britain, 1792–1821

With various allies from time to time, England was at war with France and its allies almost continuously for the twenty-three years that ended with the defeat of Napoleon at Waterloo on June 18, 1815. The engagements of the British Navy and the battles of the British Army and its allies occasioned the expenditure of what were for that era enormous sums of money. How the British government came into possession of the money it spent — how the war was financed — is the principal focus of this chapter. We shall find that this war, like that to suppress the United States, was financed in very nearly the worst possible way.

The cost of the war cannot be determined with any high degree of accuracy. One historian gives the cost for 1793 to 1815 inclusive as £831.5 million (Andreades 1968, p. 119), another as £850 million (Bray 1968, p. 73), and yet another as £880 million (Mitchell 1962, pp. 391–396). All these estimates, however, omit items for the 1793–1815 period that should be included. Furthermore, demobilization and other military expenditures during 1816 should also figure as a part of the cost of the war.

My best estimate of British war costs for 1893–1816 inclusive is £1.36 billion, more than 1.5 times the highest of the cited estimates. Let me now try to justify this figure and provide a context that will show its significance.

Total spending by the British government for the wartime period, according to the authority I consider most reliable, was £1.57 billion (Mitchell 1962, pp. 391–396). This is the sum of £154 million spent for all civil government, £480 million spent in payment of interest on the national debt, and £936 million spent directly on the war effort. But this breakdown of expenditures overlooks, or fails to give a proper emphasis to, at least three important indirect war expenditures.

First, much of the payment of interest on the national debt resulted from rapid increases in the debt during the war years. For 1792 interest on the debt amounted to only £9.3 million; and had the war not increased the debt year after year, the total interest for the twenty-four years from 1793 through 1816 would have been only about £220 million rather than £480 million. It seems proper, therefore, to add to the £936 million spent directly for the war effort £260 million in indirect cost in the form of interest on the increase in debt occasioned by the war. This would raise expenditures attributable to the war to £1.196 billion.

Second, although the national debt increased by roughly £540 million, many of the government bonds were marketed at a discount so that only about £436 million in actual spending resulted from their sale (Cannan 1969, p. xliii). It seems only proper to add the £104 million difference to the war cost and thus increase the total to £1.3 billion.

Third, the war brought about a large increase in the administrative costs of civil government (more tax collectors, more bookkeepers, and so on). Had the cost of civil government continued at the 1792 level for twenty-four years, it would have totaled £100 million less. As a very conservative estimate, we may attribute £60 million of this increase to the war. This brings the total direct and indirect costs of the war for 1793–1816 to £1.36 billion.

Note that the first and second of these items increased the cost of the war by £364 million, almost 40 percent. That is to say, the way in which the war was so largely financed by borrowed money significantly increased its cost during the twenty-three year wartime period.

The second item of added cost is especially noteworthy. It shows that although soldiers, sailors, and marines were required by government, if necessary, to give their lives for the war effort, people with money were not willing and not required to make loans for the war effort at the rate of interest the government offered. Moneylenders, who insisted on discounting the bonds and handing over only £436 million in return for government promises to return £540 million plus accrued interest, were permitted by the government to behave in this greedy and unpatriotic manner. When it came to making sacrifices "for God and country," the moneylenders demanded to be excused; and an overly tolerant government acquiesced.

Remember that in all the discussion above we have been concerned only with war costs incurred during the years from 1793 through 1816. Interest costs and other costs attributable to the war (disability pensions, for example) went on and on after 1816. In the century following the war, interest on the public debt of Britain amounted to more than twice the £1.36 billion cost of the war although a part of the interest cost is attributable to other wars. On average about 40 percent of all the money spent by the British government from 1815 to 1915 was spent paying interest on money borrowed to finance wars. That is to say, the productive classes were heavily taxed to provide income for an unproductive class of moneylenders and heirs to moneylenders.

For all practical purposes, it may be said that Britain's war with France was financed entirely by taxes and borrowing. Paper money created by government, contrary to what should have been the case, played no really significant role in paying for the war. The creation of money was left almost entirely to the private banking system, and the government borrowed and paid interest on the money thus created instead of creating interest-free money for itself.

Property taxes, sales taxes, and excise taxes were raised to levels previously not experienced in England; and for the first time, income taxes were imposed. Few stones were left unturned in the effort to bring in tax revenues. Borrowing, as well as taxation, soared to new levels. Some of the money the government borrowed had been in existence when the war began, some was created by banks and loaned to the government directly, some was created by banks and loaned to private borrowers who in turn loaned it to the government, some was created by banks and loaned to private borrowers, spent into circulation, saved out of the income resulting from spending, then loaned to the government.

In an astonishing display of lack of patriotism, the Bank of England often refused loans to the government at the 5 percent maximum rate it was permitted to charge. Instead, it loaned money at 5 percent to favored clients who then bought discounted government bonds and thereby gained a return of 8 percent or more.

The merchants . . . were certainly under a strong temptation to borrow from the Bank of England at five per cent interest for the sake of investing the sum so borrowed in Exchequer Bills, yielding . . . for a time, even seven or eight per cent or more. . . . The Bank, instead of lending to the government would only lend to those who lent to the government, the government paying an additional interest and the merchants receiving it. (Thornton 1978, p. 129)

This incredibly shameful procedure provides another example of the disinclination—the outright refusal—of moneyed people to make sacrifices for the war effort.

Although restricted to charging a maximum rate of 5 percent on the money it created, the Bank of England would rank high in any list of war profiteers. This came about because the bank used its system of fractional reserves to lend the same money to several different borrowers and collect 5 percent from each of them.

The Bank, serving the financial needs of government during the Restriction, had prospered. In addition to . . . dividends [ranging from 7 to 12 per cent per annum] it distributed substantial bonuses in 1799, 1801, 1802, 1804, 1805, and 1806; and in 1816 it paid a stock dividend of 25 per cent and maintained the same cash dividend [10 per cent] on the increased stock.

The Bank . . . made unprecedented profits during the Restriction [and] seemed to regard its legal and moral rights to these profits as beyond challenge. (Fetter 1978, pp. 70–71)

The Bank of England (the stock of which was held by, among others, many members of Parliament) was treated by Parliament with great deference, and its profiteering was consistently condoned. A committee of Parliament in 1810, for example, opposed "any compulsory limitation . . . of the rate of Bank profits and dividends. . . . In the judgment of your Committee, such schemes . . . would be objectionable as a most hurtful and improper interference with the rights of commercial property" (Sumner 1968, p. 389). Britain's chancellor of the Exchequer was much of the same opinion, and on April 10, 1818, he told Parliament that "it would not be consistent with the honour or welfare of the country [for the government] to make itself a partner in any profits which the Bank of England happened to derive" (Fetter 1978, p. 84).

The fulsome oratory of the period was replete with phrases not only about "honour of the country," and "the rights of commercial property," but also about "venerable customs," "practices from time immemorial," and so on. The oratory notwithstanding, the patent fact is that the British government during the war paid the Bank of England, a private corporation, to create money that the government could easily have created for itself and paid outrageous rates of interest on money it borrowed from other lenders. It is equally clear that officials of the government connived in making the ripoff possible.

So far as I have been able to determine, the statistics necessary for a comprehensive accounting of the amount of money created by banks, an accounting that is even approximately accurate, do not exist. By 1810, in addition to several private banks in London, there were said to be 721 banks outside London (Andreades 1966, p. 219), but we have no figures to show how much in banknotes and deposits they created on the basis of what fractional reserves in specie or reserves in Bank of England banknotes during the years 1793–1816. About the Bank of England itself, we know somewhat more.

The total of loans to private citizens and to the government by the Bank of England increased from £13 million in February 1792 to £44.5 million in February 1815 (Cannan 1969, p. xlv) or by just under 6 percent per annum on average. This may be taken as the approximate rate of money creation by the Bank of England. Since the bank was very conservatively managed, the rate of money creation by other banks may be assumed to have been greater. One historian gives a rate of increase of the banknotes of country banks from 1795 to 1810 as between 9 and 13 percent (Sumner 1968, pp. 231, 241). But the statistics do not exist that would permit a calculation of the overall rate of growth of the money supply of Britain or the amount by which it increased. Nevertheless, to make it possible for £436 million to be invested in government bonds by banks and private citizens, it is obvious that very large increases in the money supply were a necessity—that a very large amount of money creation by banks occurred.

Henry Thornton, a prominent London banker of whom more will be said later, clearly understood the role of money creation by banks in the financing of the war.

In consequence of the additions to the public debt made during the war, the occasional enlargements of the quantity of bank paper [money] arising from this cause, have become much more considerable. (1978, p. 223)

Country banks, also, as well as the Bank of England, have been highly beneficial, through the issue of their paper [money], to the productive capital [money supply] of the country. (1978, p. 176)

Elsewhere Thornton speaks of "the more than usual largeness of the bank loans to government" and of "the additional capital [money] given to the kingdom through the use of country bank notes" (1978, pp. 132, 181).

While the Bank of England and all other banks were printing irredeemable paper money virtually as they pleased, individuals who tried to do the same thing were called counterfeiters and promptly punished. Between 1797 and 1815, 257 of them were executed (Fetter 1978, p. 71).

Banks created money and loaned it to government to help finance the war under circumstances that require elucidation to make a proper understanding of the history of banking in England possible. Let us begin this part of the chapter by recalling some words of Adam Smith. "There are several different sorts of paper money; but the circulating notes of banks and bankers are the species which . . . seems best adapted to this purpose" (1909, p. 241). And the reason Smith favored the paper money issues of private banks was that "A paper money consisting in bank notes . . . payable upon demand without any condition, and in fact always readily paid as soon as presented, is, in every respect equal in value to gold and silver money; since gold and silver money can at any time be had for it" (1909, p. 263).

The gold reserves of the Bank of England amounted to £7 million as late as February 1794, and would have been enough to redeem about half the banknotes and bank deposits created by the bank. As the war progressed, however, large amounts of gold were spent on the continent and elsewhere, and the gold reserves of the Bank of England declined both for this reason and because citizens of Britain hoarded gold as fear of an invasion increased. Gold reserves had fallen to only £5.1 million by August 1795, to £2.5 million by February 1796, and to £1.1 million by February 1797 (Cannan 1969, pp. xliv, xlv). During the same period, the amount of paper money issued by the bank increased. The result of the disappearance of gold and the simultaneous issue of more paper money was obviously a decline in the ability of the bank to redeem its paper in gold. Thus on February 26, 1797, the bank, with the approval of Parliament, stopped redeeming its notes or deposits in gold. Both the other London banks and the country banks were similarly relieved of the necessity of redeeming their paper. In other words, England forsook the gold standard.

The period during which banks were permitted to default totally on their promises to redeem their paper "on demand in gold" was euphemistically called a period of "restriction," and it lasted until "resumption" of the gold standard on May 8, 1821. In other words, during the forty-eight years after Adam Smith praised the paper money of private banks because it is "always redeemable on demand," it was not, in fact, so redeemable in Britain during half that period.

Remember now another contention of Adam Smith: "No law could be more equitable than the act of Parliament, so unjustly complained of in the colonies, which declared that no paper currency be emitted there in time coming, should be a legal tender of payments" (1909, p. 266). But the effect of "restriction" was that the irredeemable banknotes of the Bank of England became de facto legal tender. The British did exactly what they had forbidden the colonists, although Parliament repeatedly refused to make the banknotes legal tender de jure as well. This refusal was denounced by, among others, Sir Francis Baring. The government, he said, was guilty of miserable subterfuge, but Parliament remained adamant (Fetter 1978, p. 29).

The rate at which the needs of war resulted in increases of the money supply was in excess of the rate occasioned by "the needs of trade." The result was a fall in the purchasing power of the banknotes of the Bank of England. A £1 banknote that up until February 1797 would purchase .258 ounces of gold on foreign exchanges by February 1814 would purchase only .185 ounces. That is to say, the price of gold increased nearly 40 percent. A rather crude "consumer price index" calculated for the years 1808 to 1814 increased by 54 percent (Sumner 1968, p. 351).

Inflation of prices obviously caused the people with the most money to experience the greatest loss of purchasing power, and upon the end of the war they became the primary agitators for a deflation of prices to restore the purchasing power they had lost. The way to drive prices down is to reduce aggregate demand in the economy, and the way to reduce aggregate demand is to reduce the size of the supply of circulating money. Thus between the end of the war and 1821 the supply of banknotes and deposits ("money in the bank") of the Bank of England was reduced from £43.2 million to £26.1 million—by roughly 40 percent. The price of gold and other commodities fell more or less in proportion. The purchasing power of a £1 banknote was restored to its prewar level of .258 ounces of gold (Sumner 1968, p. 351).

Thereupon Parliament brought an end to the period of "restriction," and England returned to the gold standard.

Deflating the money supply, drastically curtailing aggregate demand, brought on a postwar depression, threw countless members of the labor force out of work, and caused widespread misery. As Sir Francis Baring wrote, "The effect [of postwar deflation and resumption of the gold standard] was that the industrious were obliged to labour under difficulties, that the drones might live in greater affluence" (Fetter 1978, p. 102). The postwar deflation offset the wartime inflation of prices. Thus, people with money were relieved of paying what Franklin had called "a tax on money"—a tax according to which "those people paid most who being richest had the most money passing through their hands" (1907, 9: 135).

The way the war was financed and prices fluctuated provided alluring opportunities for speculators and diverted some of the best minds in England from concentrating on producing for the war effort or otherwise supporting it. For example, a shrewd operator could have begun with 116 ounces of gold in 1814 and used it to purchase a discounted £1000 government 5 percent bond for £625. By 1821 the bond could be sold for banknotes near its face value and the banknotes exchanged for 258 ounces of gold. The speculator would have realized a capital gain of 122 percent and additionally received £50 interest each year.

England "muddled through" and Napoleon went to St. Helena, but the so-called "sound financial policies" that the country embraced resulted in a bonanza for the banking fraternity and a war debt not yet paid in full and still providing "unearned increment" for the great-great-great-great-grand-children of the moneylenders of the era.

Chapter 15

Money and Banking in Britain in the Later Nineteenth Century

Theoretically or nominally, Britain was on a gold standard from 1821 until World War I. "Monetary orthodoxy" during this period meant a belief that acceptance of the gold standard would assure a smoothly functioning, steadily growing economy. This orthodoxy was assailed during the period from several points of view that we consider in turn: (1) that in practice intolerably wide swings in gold reserves tended inevitably to occur and to produce corresponding but much larger swings in total money supply, thus creating a very unsatisfactory boom–bust economy; (2) that since "the free market" or "free trade" would not satisfactorily control the supply of gold reserves, the overall money supply must be controlled by Bank of England or by government policies directed toward keeping it increasing as required to assure steady economic growth and full employment; (3) that the practice of permitting money creation by private banks on the basis of fractional reserves in gold was inconsistent with the general welfare and that money creation should be solely the prerogative of the government, without heed to fluctuations in gold reserves.

The orthodox view assumed that "money will manage itself" and that there was neither need nor place for monetary policy. Money would manage itself because too high a ratio of banknotes to gold reserves would devalue the notes, raise prices, cause gold to flow to other countries, reduce gold reserves, and thus make necessary a reduction in the number of banknotes. Similarly, too low a ratio of banknotes to gold would raise their value, lower prices, cause gold to flow into the country, increase reserves, and thus make possible an increase in the number of notes.

How the gold standard—monetary orthodoxy—worked (or failed to work) has often been misunderstood and is a subject deserving of close attention. First, it must be made explicit that when it is said that a country adopted a gold standard this in no way implies that all transactions were made in gold coin or bullion or that the banknotes or bank credit used in transactions could exist only in a 1-to-1 ratio to gold. Many of the remarks of Henry Thornton with respect to this matter are of interest.

> The amount of gold . . . is not now considered by the commercial world as having all that importance which was [earlier] given it. . . . It is perfectly well understood among all commercial men, that gold coin is not an article in which all payments (though it is so promised) are at any time really to be made; that no fund ever was or can be provided . . . which shall be sufficient for such a purpose. (1978, p. 111)

> If [gold] had been our only medium of payment, we might sometimes have been almost totally deprived of the means of carrying on our pecuniary transactions; and much confusion in the affairs of our merchants, great interruption of manufacturing labour, and very serious evils to the state, might have been the consequences. Our paper credit [bank-created money] has on this account been highly important to us. (1978, p. 276)

That banks perform a money-creating function was perfectly evident to Thornton, and in his customary low-key way he takes Adam Smith to task for not clearly recognizing the importance of this function of banks:

> Dr. Smith remarks that it is not by augmenting the capital of a country, but by rendering a greater part of that capital active and productive than would otherwise be so, that the most judicious operations of banking can increase the industry of a country [but] if a less stock of gold will, through the aid of paper, equally well perform the work of the larger stock, it may be fairly said that the use of paper furnishes even additional stock to the country. (1978, p. 176)

Closely related to this last quotation from Thornton is the second point that must be made concerning the way in which the gold standard functioned. This is that in practice it proved not only impossible to maintain a 1-to-1 ratio of paper money to gold but impossible to maintain any constant ratio whatever. That some constant ratio should be maintained came to be called the "currency principle," and most textbook explanations of the gold standard incorrectly assume the constant operation of the currency principle. But here is Thornton:

> The idea which some persons have entertained of its being at all times the paramount duty of the Bank of England to diminish its notes, in some sort of regular proportion to the diminution which it experiences in its gold, is, then, an idea which is merely theoretic. (1978, p. 116)

Table 15.1
Bank of England Gold Reserves

Date	Reserves
May 1821	£12,000,000
December 1825	1,000,000
April 1833	11,000,000
September 1839	2,400,000

Source: Fetter, Frank W. 1978. *Development of British Monetary Orthodoxy, 1797–1875.* Fairfield, N.J.: Augustus M. Kelley, pp. 96, 114, 166, and 174.

Some political persons have assumed it to be a principle, that in proportion as the gold of the Bank lessens, its paper . . . ought to be reduced. . . . A maxim of this sort, if strictly followed up, would lead to a universal failure. (1978, p. 227)

There is too strong and evident an interest in every quarter to maintain, in some way or other, the regular course of London payments. . . . Whether there might chance to be much or little gold in the country, steps should be taken to induce the Bank to issue its usual quantity of paper. (1978, p. 115)

After 1821 (as well as before) the fluctuations in the gold reserves of the Bank of England were startlingly large, as Table 15.1 shows. We may also note that reserves dropped so low as to require suspension of the practice of redeeming banknotes in gold in 1847, 1857, 1866, and other years.

Obviously if the Bank of England had adopted a policy of fluctuating its note issue as violently as its gold reserves fluctuated—a policy of strictly honoring the currency principle—then the total English money supply, and in turn the English economy would have been subjected to severe bouts of prosperity and depression. Far more than it is customary to acknowledge, the gold standard in nineteenth-century England simply did not work. The standard was "maintained," first by paying virtually no attention whatever to the currency principle—by fluctuating the ratio of paper money in circulation to gold reserves through an extremely wide range from about 1.5:1 to about 15.0:1—and second by going off the gold standard—by "restriction" or "suspension"—as deep crises occurred. In short, the money supply was never self-regulating, and as a consequence the economy as a whole was never self-regulating either. The belief that only with the coming of the twentieth century did "monetary authorities" need or attempt to control the economy is completely false.

The Bank of England was the preeminent institution in that country insofar as decisions relating to monetary policies and their execution were concerned. But contrary to the ideology of Adam Smith, there was a clear conflict of interest between the bank as a private corporation beholden to its stock-holders and the bank as a semipublic institution with an obligation to control the size of the money supply in the public interest. Sumner expressed the bank's dilemma very well. Whenever gold began to flow out of the country, when the bank's reserves began to ebb, "the question was whether the Bank should extend its issues, and run the risk of ruining itself, or contract its issues and ruin the public" (Sumner 1968, p. 303).

From the time of its charter, the role of the Bank of England as the source of money or credit for the government in war time was perfectly clear; as long as a war continued the Bank had little choice but somehow to make the advances in notes or credit that the government's war effort required. But during the relatively peaceful years after 1815, there occurred more or less constant debate respecting the extent to which the bank likewise had an obligation to be the source of the money or credit that could keep the peace-time private economy steadily growing.

Controversy arose on account of an increasing awareness both that the economy showed little tendency to grow except as the money supply grew and that "money will not control itself" in any acceptable way (Bagehot 1962, p. 27). Because of its prestige and its great power to influence the money supply, the bank increasingly came to be regarded less as "just like any other private bank" (as the bank liked to say of itself) and more as an institution with responsibilities far transcending any obligation to its stock-holders. In other words, the conflict of interest between the bank's duty to its share owners, on one hand, and its duty to the national economy, on the other, became a highly controversial issue.

Thornton's view of the role of the bank is expressed in the following quotations.

Since the Bank of England have obtained a monopoly of supplying the metropolis with its whole means of circulation, and have, by their superior credit, excluded entirely all other paper . . . and also become so considerable, that their individual conduct operates upon the credit of the whole nation; it is no longer prudent in them to pursue their own individual interest, by any means which are contrary to the general interest. (1978, p. 306)

The true policy of the directors of an institution circumstanced like the Bank of England [must be]: [1] to limit the total amount of paper issued, and to resort for this purpose, whenever the temptation [of entrepreneurs] to borrow is strong, to some effectual principle of restriction; [2] in no sense, however, materially to diminish the sum in circulation, but to let it vibrate only within certain limits; [3] to afford a slow and cautious extension of it, as the general trade of the kingdom enlarges itself; [4] to allow some special, though temporary, increase in the event of an extraordinary alarm or difficulty, as a best means of preventing a great demand at home for guineas [gold]; and, [5] to lean to the side of diminution, in the case of gold coins going abroad, and the general exchanges continuing long unfavourable. (1978, p. 259)

Items two and three in Thornton's list, I believe, constitute the essentials of a policy of any central bank or any "monetary authority" of any market economy at any time, although it may be argued that the way in which easy money may stimulate real growth should have been given prominence in the list. It is important to realize that Thornton was not unaware of this stimulative function of increases in the money supply. In the best tradition of David Hume, Thornton wrote:

Paper [money] possesses the faculty of enlarging the quantity of commodities by giving life to some new industry. (1978, p. 239)

There seems to be only two modes in which we can conceive the additional paper to be disposed of. It may be imagined either, first, to be used in transferring an increased quantity of articles, which it must, in that case, be assumed that the new paper itself tended to create; or secondly, in transferring the same articles at a higher price. (1978, p. 235)

The antecedently idle persons to whom we may suppose the new capital [paper money] to give employ, are limited in number; and we may suppose that, therefore . . . a liberal, or, at most, a large increase of it, will have all the advantageous effects of the most extravagant emission. (1978, p. 236)

That an increase of the circulating medium tends to afford temporary encouragement to industry, seems to be proved by the effects of the Mississippi scheme in France; for it is affirmed by French writers, that the notes of Mr. Law's bank appeared for a time to have a very powerful influence in extending the demand for labour, and in augmenting the visible and *bona fide* property of the kingdom. (1978, footnote to p. 239)

Before there could be any reasonable prospect that the Bank of England could perform the function of satisfactorily meeting the monetary requirements of a fully employed or steadily growing economy, it was necessary that any constraint due even to nominal adherence to the gold standard should be removed and that the bank should be nationalized. Thus from the beginning of the nineteenth century there was a tendency for the bank to be increasingly constrained to pay less attention to the gold standard or the currency principle and to behave more and more as a public rather than a private agency.

Beginning with the last quarter of the nineteenth century, reasonably accurate statistics on Britain's "money stock" are available (Friedman and Schwartz 1982, Table 4.9). For the fifty years following 1870, the money stock was manipulated by the Bank of England in such a way that it increased over the level of the previous year during forty-five of those years, more or less regardless of whether gold reserves increased or decreased. In the thirty-five years after 1885, the money stock was made to increase to a new alltime high every year save one (1904) in disregard of sometimes precipitous decreases in gold reserves. Thus, the gold standard was abandoned in practice long before it was formally discarded. It was abandoned because the type of go-stop economy that it inevitably produced was intolerable and because the overwhelming necessity of a more sane and humane policy became increasingly apparent in the course of decades of everyday experience.

The term "Birmingham School" has been given to those responsible for the second line of attack against the orthodoxy of the nineteenth century. This school contained the most vocal critics of the fact that establishment policy tended to prefer mildly deflationary over inflationary policies and tended too much to result in periods of no growth and high unemployment. Thomas Atwood, a member of Parliament from 1832 to 1839, was a principal spokesman for the Birmingham School. The following exchange, for example, took place before a committee of Parliament considering renewal of the charter of the Bank of England in 1832.

Question: Do you consider that as long as there exists a labourer in the country not fully employed, an increased issue of currency may be made with advantage?

Atwood: As a general principle, I think, unquestionably, that so long as any number of industrious honest workmen in the Kingdom are out of employment, supposing such a deficiency of employment not to be local but general, I should think it the duty, and certainly the interest, of Government, to continue [the issue of paper currency] until full employment and general prosperity is obtained. (Humphrey 1977, pp. 13–14)

On a different occasion Atwood testified:

Prosperity has occurred whenever the Government has filled the Country with what is called Money; and this plenty of Money has necessarily produced a general elevation of prices; and this . . . has necessarily produced a general increase of profit in all occupations; and this . . . has given activity to every trade in the Kingdom; and whilst the workmen in one branch of trade are producing one set of articles, they are inevitably consuming an equal amount of all other articles. This is the prosperity of the Country, and there is no other prosperity which has ever been enjoyed, or ever can be enjoyed. (Humphrey 1977, pp. 13–14)

Another self-described "Birmingham economist," Samuel A. Goddard, denounced as "absurd . . . a system whereby the energies of the whole people may be neutralized, and even prostrated, without any fault on their part or without any real necessity, as a result of monetary contraction" (Fetter 1978, p. 238).

Two Birmingham men, Thomas Wright and John Harlow, in 1844 published *The Gemini Papers*. Their thesis:

The proper plan, it appears to us, is to raise the capacity of the consumer, by securing high wages and ample profits, and by these means making light the fixed national obligations of the people. It is idle to talk of overproduction when we have a population clothed in rags, and most sparingly supplied with the mere necessaries of life. . . . The only limit [we] would affix to the issue of paper money would be the degree of prosperity which the different amount of issues would produce; and this amount can only be ascertained by careful experiment. (Fetter 1978, p. 179)

Clearly, the central objective of the Birmingham School was economic growth and full employment. But implicit in all the quotations given here and explicit in other writings of the economists of the Birmingham School was, first, "an openly inconvertible currency"—that is, the abandonment of the gold standard—and, second, a money supply so managed as to produce full employment.

The orthodox reply to the Birmingham economists was, of course, that if money is created in sufficient quantity to guarantee full employment the result would be intolerable price inflation. The Birmingham economists were rather too ready to concede that full employment would necessarily and inevitably mean a higher price level and to look upon inflation more or less as a necessary evil. Indeed, the fact that inflation would "make light the fixed national obligations of the people" (that the national debt could be retired with cheap money) was considered somewhat of a plus.

The third line of attack against the status quo of the nineteenth century held that the government rather than private bankers should be the creator of the nation's money supply. This viewpoint was first voiced in England, so far as I know, by David Ricardo. In his *Plan for the Establishment of a National Bank,* published posthumously in 1824, he wrote:

It appears that the commerce of the country would not be in the least impeded by depriving the Bank of England of the power of issuing paper money, provided an amount of such money, equal to the Bank circulation, was issued by the Government: and that the sole effect of depriving the Bank of this privilege, would be to transfer the profit which accrues from the interest on the money so issued from the Bank to the Government. (Ricardo 1951, p. 281)

It was part of Ricardo's plan that the government should be subject to redeeming its issues of paper money in specie on demand. His proposal, therefore, although a progressive one representing a considerable departure from orthodoxy, fell short of the more proper proposal of others that the paper money issued by the government should be made legal tender without any promise of redemption in specie.

By 1856 the thinking even of an editorial writer for the *Times* of London was not unlike that of Ricardo three decades earlier:

[We] . . . would like to know how . . . the continuance of the privileges of the Bank of England can be defended, and why the Government, after paying the Bank amply for all that it does for it in its capacity of banker, should delegate to it the privilege of creating 14,000,000 pounds sterling [in banknotes] for no consideration at all. (Fetter 1978, pp. 253-254)

And the *Westminister Review* carried an article by an anonymous author who went even further by saying:

In breaking this monopoly of the Bank, we should be taking a great stride towards the attainment of that ideal system of currency . . . under which the State shall be the sole fountain of issue, under which no money shall circulate on credit [or as interest-bearing money], or, if it does, shall circulate on the credit of the State . . . and under which all profits upon the issue of money shall form a part of the Imperial revenue. (Fetter 1978, p. 253)

This line of attack on the status quo, of course, figured prominently in the nationalization of the Bank of England after World War II. But money creation by the private banks of England, Scotland, and Northern Ireland continued even after the Bank of England was nationalized. Unfortunately for the British, in neither the nineteenth century nor the twentieth, did there ever occur even a close approach to the ideal of a money supply created solely by government.

Chapter 16

The Bank of the United States and Other Matters, 1800–1836

Prefatory to an analysis of the evolution of money and banking during the first third of the nineteenth century, some discussion of the rapidly changing setting within which this process occurred will be advantageous.

In the course of the period of concern, the United States almost exactly doubled in area—from roughly 890,000 square miles to about 1,780,000 through the acquisition of 830,000 square miles by the Louisiana Purchase from France and another 60,000 by purchase of Florida and adjacent areas from Spain.

By 1836 the number of states admitted to the Union had increased to 25. The population had roughly tripled—from 5.3 million to 15.4. The number of persons who immigrated to the United States was about 600,000; and immigration accounted for about 6 percent of the total increase in population (BC 1975, pp. 8, 105).

Private and public expenditures for improvements to the nation's infrastructure increased progressively. Canal investments, for example, although quite small before 1820, totaled $29.7 million for 1821–1828 and $40.4 million for 1829–1836. Construction of railroad trackage began toward the end of the second decade of the period, and about 1000 miles of track had been laid by 1836 (BC 1975, pp. 732, 766).

The number of banks increased from 30 in 1800 to 307 in 1820 and 713 by 1836 for an average annual growth rate of 9.2 percent for the 36 years. The circulating supply of the banknotes of state-chartered banks soared from $10.5 million in 1800 to $140 million in 1836—nearly 7.5 percent per year on average. Deposits in banks (bank credits) increased even more dramatically—

from an estimated $8 million in 1800 to $166 million in 1836 — an average annual rate of 8.8 percent (BC 1975, pp. 1018, 1020).

While the obligations of banks were increasing about 8 percent per annum, the specie reserves of banks probably increased less than 3 percent. By 1836 banks had created $306 million in banknotes plus deposits but had only about $40 million in specie in their vaults. The ratio of banknotes and deposits to specie reserves was thus about 7.5:1 (Sumner 1968, p. 123).

Many banks, all of which were either completely unregulated or, at best, poorly regulated, followed conservative banking policies; far more, however, did not. A horrible example is provided by the Farmers Exchange Bank, founded in 1804 in Rhode Island. An investigating committee of the state legislature found that on the basis of only $3 million capital stock in specie, by 1809 the bank had loaned into circulation banknotes it had itself created to the amount of $580 million. That is to say, the bank held enough specie to liquidate its obligations at only about one-half cent per dollar (Gouge, 1968, p. 45).

Fierce controversies over banking raged througout the 1800–1836 period. Indiana, which entered the Union in 1816, made banking a state monopoly, as did Missouri, admitted in 1821. Illinois entered the Union in 1818 and sharply restricted banking. Arkansas, admitted in 1836, refused to permit the chartering of any bank whatsoever.

Federal chartering of banks provoked as much dissension as state chartering. The first Bank of the United States was a storm center from its founding in 1791 until its charter expired unrenewed in 1811. So also was the second Bank of the United States during the entire time of its charter — 1816–1836.

Specie in the hands of the public was never plentiful and always coveted throughout the period. Because of the inexpediently determined mint ratio of gold to silver, the stock of the former metal diminished and the latter metal tended increasingly to predominate in circulation until a revaluation in the 1830s.

The first Bank of the United States was "wisely and skillfully managed" according to Secretary of the Treasury Albert Gallatin. In 1809, for example, the bank had obligations in the form of deposits and banknotes equal to only 2.6 times its specie. In other words, holding enough gold and silver to liquidate its obligations at nearly 40 cents on the dollar, it was probably the most liquid bank in the United States.

The headquarters of the bank were in Philadelphia; but branches were maintained in Boston, New York, Baltimore, Washington, Norfolk, Charleston, Savannah, and New Orleans. The bank had 25,000 stockholders, 18,000 of whom resided abroad and were prohibited by the bank's charter from having any voice in the management of the bank. The average dividend up to 1809 was an attractive 8.4 percent per annum on its nominal per-share value of $400, and the stock often sold at a premium (Krooss 1983, pp. 195–201).

The case favoring a renewal by Congress of the charter of the bank in 1811 rested primarily on the fact that its banknotes constituted virtually the only "national currency" in circulation. The notes of the bank, when specie was demanded for them, were not normally discounted anywhere in the country, although discounting was common in the case of the vast majority of the banknotes of state-chartered banks. In addition to furnishing a national currency, the bank acted as fiscal agent for the Treasury of the United States, held as deposits all tax collections, and saw to the paying of government obligations with its notes or deposit credits.

During the interval between the deposit of taxes and the payment of government obligations, the bank had the use of the government's money at no cost. Thus Gallatin proposed that if the charter were to be renewed the bank should pay interest on government deposits whenever they exceeded, he suggested, $3 million. He made no suggestion as to the rate of interest the bank should pay the government (Krooss 1983, pp. 195–201).

"The greatest objection against the renewal of the charter seems to arise from the great portion of the bank stock held by foreigners," wrote Gallatin (Krooss 1983, pp. 195–201). Although foreigners had no voice in management, annual interest at 8.4 percent on the stock amounted to about $34 per share, about $600,000 on the 18,000 shares owned abroad. Thus, it was argued, a twenty-year renewal of the charter would result in the export of some $12 million in specie, perhaps nearly half the specie in the country in 1809.

There were other objections to the bank as well, each stemming from a different constituency. Here it will suffice to mention only three of the most important claims of the various opponents: (1) that the federal government had no constitutional authority to charter a bank, (2) that by its policy of returning to the issuing bank for specie all banknotes of state banks it received, often after discounting them, the bank was imposing undue hardships on state-chartered banks, and (3) that all fractional reserve banks should be prohibited and the country confined to coin for its circulation (Krooss 1983, pp. 195–201). For a variety of reasons Congress never even considered the wisest alternative—nationalizing the Bank of the United States.

Congress declined to renew the charter of the bank, allowing it to expire on March 4, 1811. Fourteen months later, the United States declared war on Britain; and the government's task of financing the war was rendered considerably more difficult by the absence of any sort of "central bank."

The War of 1812 brought about an above-average export of specie, as well as domestic hoarding of specie. Except a few in New England, most banks were forced to suspend redemption of their banknotes or demand deposits in specie. Resumption of the practice of redeeming bank obligations in specie did not take place until February 1817.

In February 1816, John C. Calhoun reported to the House of Representatives that there were in circulation about $170 million in the banknotes of state-chartered banks although the vaults of the banks contained not more than $15 million in specie. That is to say, banks had created about $155 million in paper money on which they could draw interest but could not, as they had promised, redeem in gold or silver (Gouge 1968, p. 77).

For what amounted roughly to the era of the War of 1812, from December 1811 to December 1815, the federal government spent $119.4 million and took in as taxes only $51 million, thus incurring a deficit of $68.4 million. The debt of the government, however, increased by $82.1 million, from $45.2 million to $127.3 million (BC 1975, p. 1104). The debt increased by $13.7 million more than the deficit because government bonds and notes could be sold to not overly patriotic banks and moneyed people only at an average discount of about 17 percent and sometimes at a discount as high as 25 percent.

For 1812 through 1815, expenditures for army and navy totaled $93.1 million. Roughly $24.6 million of this, about 26 percent, was paid out of taxes (Gouge 1968, p. 77). As is discussed directly, about $4 million, less than 5 percent, was paid by the government creating money for itself. The remaining $64.5 million, about 69 percent, was raised by one or another from of borrowing. A part of the borrowing came from banks, money they created in the process of making the loans, and a part was borrowing from the nonbank public; but the amount or percentage in each case is not readily determinable.

The government issued a number of treasury notes good for all payments of federal fees and taxes and exchangeable for federal bonds. Nearly $18 million in treasury notes was in circulation January 1, 1816. About $14 million in notes bore interest, and these notes were widely used by banks as interest-bearing reserves in place of non-interest-bearing specie. About $4 million in notes were of small denomination, widely used by banks for making payments in lieu of specie. The notes, in fact, became another sort of "national currency" since the notes of the expired Bank of the United States could no longer serve this function. These treasury notes represented the first federal government issues of paper money since the War for Independence. All treasury notes were withdrawn from circulation by the early 1820s (Kagin 1984, p. 87).

As a result of the many problems encountered in financing the war and of increasing dissatisfaction with state-chartered banks, the federal government issued a twenty-year charter to a second Bank of the United States in 1816. The authority of the federal government to charter the second Bank of the United States was then challenged, and the matter was carried to the Supreme Court. In deciding the famous case of *McCulloch* v. *Maryland,* Chief Justice Marshall wrote that although there is nothing in the Constitution specifically empowering Congress to charter a bank, issuing such a charter is within the *implied powers* of Congress. "After the most deliberate consideration, it is the unanimous and decided opinion of this court that the act to incorporate the Bank of the United States is a law made in pursuance of the Constitution, and is a part of the supreme law of the land" (Krooss 1983, p. 252).

The second Bank of the United States, the majority of the stock of which was privately owned, quickly alienated the state-chartered banks by following the same practice as the first bank and returning to state banks in exchange for specie all their banknotes that came into its posession. The state-bank opposition to this policy is understandable; for if a state bank followed a policy of having in circulation $1000 in banknotes for each $100 of specie in its vaults, for example, then a demand by the Bank of the United States for $100 in specie forced the bank to call in $1000 in loans and reduced its earnings from interest accordingly.

Demands upon state banks for specie, with the consequent reduction in their banknote circulation, were (in part at least) responsible for the so-called Panic of 1819 which added large numbers of workers and farmers to the list of opponents of the Bank of the United States (Harris 1961, p. 110). Partly symptom and partly cause of the panic or crisis of 1819 was the fact that the banknote circulation of the nation increased from about $45 million in 1812 to over $100 million in 1817 and then was reduced to $45 million by 1819. In Pennsylvania, the average selling price of land was $38 per acre in 1809, $150 in 1815, and $35 in 1819 (Sumner 1968, p. 80). The Bank of the United States, which had loans and discounts amounting to $41.2 million outstanding in 1818, had only $28 million outstanding by 1822 (BC 1975, p. 1018).

Throughout the twenty-year period of its charter, the Bank of the United States did not adhere to the currency principle—did not pursue a policy of maintaining any strict ratio of banknotes and deposits to specie reserves. The ratio bounced around from 1.6:1 to 8.2:1 between 1817 and 1836. The bank sometimes increased its banknote circulation when it was losing specie and at other times contracted circulation when it was gaining specie. Likewise, the bank sometimes increased its loans and discounts when losing specie and reduced loans and discounts when gaining specie. It varied at its pleasure the ratio of its loans and discounts to specie from a low of 3.3:1 to a high of 16.4:1 during the twenty years of its charter. All this amounts to saying that the Bank of the United States, like the Bank of England, largely ignored the currency principle.

As of 1836, the banknote circulation of all banks in the United States was $140 million and that of the Bank of the United States $23 million, 16 percent of the total. "The Bank of the United States was the largest corporation in America, and one of the largest in the whole world." "The government owned $7,000,000 Bank of United States stock, foreigners owned $8,000,000 and private persons in the United States owned $20,000,000" (Hammond 1957, pp. 292, 408).

The banknotes of the Bank of the United States were everywhere acceptable at face value, whereas the banknotes of the 712 other private banks were subject to discounts varying anywhere from 0 to 100 percent. The banknotes

of a few large banks in Boston, New York, or Philadelphia might pass without discount throughout the country, but at any considerable distance from
their bank of origin almost all other banknotes were either unacceptable in
everyday transactions or acceptable only at discount. A person needing to
travel from state to state carried the banknotes of the Bank of the United
States as a "national currency" and avoided the issues of other banks. The
effect of the failure to recharter the bank in 1836 was the virtual disappearance of anything that might be called a national currency aside from gold or
silver coins. From this point of view, the demise of the bank resulted in great
inconvenience to traders and, in at least some small measure, restricted trade
and real economic growth.

From 1823 until its demise, the Bank of the United States was under the
control of Nicholas Biddle, who, whatever his merits, is said to have "boasted
that he had the power of life or death over state banks and that he had more
power than the President of the United States" (Studenski and Krooss 1952,
p. 88). The fact that there was considerable truth in the boast only made
more fierce the opposition to the bank on the part of the state banks and on
the part of Andrew Jackson when he became president in March 1829.

President Jackson's fight against the Bank of the United States is perhaps
the best remembered facet of his administration. But neither Jackson and
other opponents of the bank nor Biddle and other defenders advocated what
would have resulted in the best banking system or the best type of money
supply for the growing nation. What would have been best would have been
a denial to the Bank of the United States and to all state-chartered banks the
power to create banknotes or bank deposits and the concentration of the
power of money creation in the hands of the secretary of the treasury or
some agency responsible to the secretary.

Jackson went on record as opposing the power of both the Bank of the
United States and state-chartered banks to create money: "My position is
now and has ever been since I have been able to form an opinion on this
subject that Congress has no power to charter a Bank and that the states are
prohibited from issuing bills of credit or granting a charter by which such
bills can be issued by any corporation" (Hammond 1957, p. 349). We must
also note that Jackson never proposed vesting any power to create paper
money in the office of the secretary of the treasury. It appears to have been
his view that the money supply of the United States should consist solely of
specie.

It is maintained by some that the Bank [of the United States] is a means of exercising
the Constitutional power "to coin money and regulate the value thereof." Congress has
established a mint to coin money and passed laws to regulate the value thereof. The
money so coined with its value so regulated, and such foreign coins as Congress may
adopt, are the only currency known to the Constitution. (Hammond 1957, p. 349)

Since it was completely unrealistic to believe that a money supply consisting solely of specie would be adequate, Jacksonian policy was so deeply faulted as to be completely unrealistic. On the other hand, Biddle and his supporters were also quite wrong in that they proposed to leave the power to create money in private hands—to leave the power to the largely private Bank of the United States and to privately owned state-chartered banks.

In the end Biddle was a big loser insofar as his defense of the second Bank of the United States was concerned. The bank's charter was allowed to expire. Jackson was a loser as well, however, in that the money supply came to consist not mainly of specie but primarily of the banknotes and deposits of state-chartered banks. The biggest loser of all was the general public, inasmuch as the power to create money remained in private hands.

A prominent historian of the period has written that "to exploit America's resources money was needed, and to provide money there must be banks" (Hammond 1957, p. 164). But this is untrue. The proper provider of money is the federal government. As John Taylor had written, "Banking . . . is a fraud [and the public] suffers the imposition of paying interest on the circulating medium" (Hammond 1957, p. 36).

How complete was the defeat of Jackson (and his idea that "money coined at the mint and such foreign coins as Congress may adopt, are the only currency known to the Constitution") became apparent only in 1837. In that year the "Jacksonian Supreme Court," in *Briscoe* v. *Bank of Kentucky,* ruled that state-chartered banks, or even wholly state-owned banks, and the banknotes or deposits they created, were in full accord with the Constitution. *Briscoe* effectively reversed an essentially opposite (but generallly unenforced) ruling of the Marshall Court in *Craig* v. *Missouri* in 1830. State-chartered banks emerged as the big winners of the Jackson–Biddle contest. As has been remarked, "The law is not what the Constitution says but what the judges say the Constitution says" (Hammond 1957, p. 592).

Even before the decision in *Briscoe* and before the expiration of the charter of the Bank of the United States, Jackson had ordered government deposits withdrawn from that bank and deposited in state-chartered banks that came to be called "pet banks." Thus in another way was exhibited the Jackson ambivalence that opposed all banks but at the same time exhalted states rights above federal rights. The result was a shift of funds and power from Philadelphia's Chestnut Street to New York's Wall Street (Hammond 1957, p. 361).

Before we conclude our review of the 1800–1836 period, two other matters relevant to money and banking must be mentioned. The first is that in 1834 Congress redefined the gold dollar and altered its content from 24.75 grains of pure gold to 23.22 grains while the silver dollar remained defined as 371.25 grains pure silver. In other words, the ratio of the value of gold to the value of silver was changed from 15:1 to 16:1 (Sumner 1968, p. 112). But just as the 15:1 ratio, being less than the world market ratio of 15.5:1, led to the export of gold and tended to leave only silver in circulation, the new 16:1 ratio led to the export of silver and tended to leave only gold in circulation. During the ten years from 1826 through 1835, gold exports exceeded imports by $2 million while silver imports exceeded exports by $37 million. During the ten years from 1836 through 1845, the flow was reversed; gold imports exceeded exports by $23 million, and net import of silver dropped to $11 million (BC 1975, p. 886).

The second matter deserving mention is that by 1834 the federal government had paid off virtually all its creditors to the point where its debt amounted to $38,000. In 1834, 1835, and 1836, for the only time in its history, the federal government of the United States was for all practical purposes debt free. Roughly half the debt of the peak year 1815 was liquidated during the Monroe and J. Q. Adams administrations, and the remaining half during the Jackson administration. Import duties and the sale of public lands provided most of the money required for debt liquidation.

Chapter 17

The Discovery of Gold in California and Other Matters, 1836–1860

During the period that is the subject of this chapter, the United States increased in size from roughly 1,780,000 square miles to its present size (less Alaska and Hawaii) of over 3,000,000 square miles. By treaty with Britain for Oregon Territory in 1846, about 290,000 square miles were acquired; by conquest from Mexico in 1848 roughly 920,000; and by purchase from Mexico another 30,000. By 1860 the thirty-three states then admitted to the Union included all territory east of the Mississippi and eight states to its west, including California and Oregon on the West Coast. The population approximately doubled from 15.4 million to 31.5 million. This amounts to an annual growth rate of about 3 percent. Nearly 4,600,000 immigrants entered the country during the twenty-four years, compared to only 600,000 the preceding thirty-six years (BC 1975, pp. 8, 111, 428).

Improvements in the nation's infrastructure were impressive. Canal investments, for example, increased from $40.4 million for the eight years 1829–1836 to $65.2 million for 1837–1844 but decreased rapidly thereafter as railroading gained in prominence. Miles of railroad track built through 1836 totaled only about 1000; but during the 1837–1848 period 5,200 miles were laid and during the 1849–1860 period another 22,650 (BC 1975, pp. 732, 766).

The nation's supply of banknotes issued by state-chartered banks increased at a much slower rate for the 1837–1860 period than it had during the previous period—the result, in part at least, of the severe and prolonged depression of 1837–1843 and the less severe setback of 1857–1858. Banknote circulation increased from $140 million in 1836 to $207 million in 1860. Deposits in banks (bank credits), all of which were state-chartered, increased from $339 million in 1836 to $517 million in 1860. The number of banks more than doubled, from 713 to 1562 (BC 1975, p. 1020). Total specie in circulation and in bank reserves in 1836 is not accurately known but perhaps amounted to $80 million. By 1860 it had increased to about $225 million (BC 1975, p. 995).

It may also be noted that of the thirty-one states admitted to the Union by 1860, five (Arkansas, California, Iowa, Oregon, and Texas) prohibited banks entirely; three others (Florida, Illinois, and Wisconsin) sharply restricted banking; and two (Indiana and Missouri) made banking a state monopoly (Woolley 1984, p. 31). Note that seven of the ten states listed here were west of the Mississippi. Banking was far more unpopular in the west than the east, or perhaps one should say far more unpopular in the less-developed regions. All ten antibank states were admitted to the union after 1812, seven of them after 1835.

Then (as today) the economy prospered primarily as banks created money by making loans to investors and thereby increased the amount of money in circulation and the amount of aggregate demand for commodities. In the depression years from 1837 to 1843, the loans and discounts of banks in the United States contracted from $525 million to $255 million, more than 50 percent. Banknote circulation fell by nearly 60 percent — from $149 million to $59 million. Deposits in banks likewise shrank — from $190 million to $78 million (BC 1975, p. 1020).

The 1837–1843 depression was probably triggered not by an unwillingness of domestic banks to further extend credit but by credit contraction on the part of foreign lenders. For the seven years 1830 through 1836, the value of imports by U.S. residents exceeded the value of exports by a total of $162 million. For the seven years 1837 through 1843, the cumulative balance of payments deficit was reduced from $162 million to $26 million, and the credit standing abroad of borrowers in the United States greatly improved (BC 1975, p. 886).

Recovery from the depression was not rapid. Loans and discounts of domestic banks rose slowly from the low of $255 million in 1843 — to $265 million in 1844 and $289 million in 1845 (BC 1975, p. 1020).

With the annexation of Texas in December 1845, a war with Mexico was provoked. The United States defeated Mexico in the 1846–1848 war and reduced Mexico to less than half its size by annexing 920,000 square miles of its territory.

Expenditures for the army and navy soared from $12 million in 1845 to $17.3 million in 1846 and $46.2 million in 1847 before dropping to $35.9 million in 1848 and $24.7 million in 1849. By 1850 military expenditures had returned to a level near that of 1845. If we take the cost of the war as the annual federal expenditures in excess of the 1845 level, we get $74.7 million. That is to say, the cost of the annexed territory came to about thirteen cents per acre. The Mexican War cost only about four-fifths as much as the War of 1812, but it was immensely more rewarding. And the Mexican War, coming at a time when the United States economy and consequent collection of taxes were much larger than they had been in 1812, resulted in an increase in federal debt of only $47.1 million from 1845 to 1849 (BC 1975, p. 1114).

During the administrations of Jackson's protégé Martin Van Buren, 1837–1841, and of Jackson's fellow Tennesseean James K. Polk, 1845–1849, the Jacksonian idea of divorcing federal finances entirely from private banks was implemented. Jackson's idea was "to separate the government from all banks, receive and disburse the revenue in nothing but gold and silver coin." The government would hold all its specie in vaults of the Treasury in Washington and in "Sub-Treasuries" in other large cities. It would neither accept nor make payments employing banknotes or bank deposit credits.

Although the ill-conceived idea of conducting federal financing in this way originated with Jackson, it did not become fully implemented until 1846. It remained in effect until its impracticality became evident immediately upon the commencement of the Civil War.

An early opponent of the "Sub-Treasury System" was Abraham Lincoln. In a speech in 1839 he asserted that there was then not more than $80 million in specie in the country and federal revenues amounted to $40 million. Thus to implement the sub-treasury plan would at times withdraw from circulation "half the specie in the nation." With so much specie idle in government vaults rather than serving as reserves in banks, bank credit would be severely restricted. Lincoln also believed that the plan would be more expensive than utilizing banks for deposit of federal funds, and less safe. Although Lincoln and other Whigs were more nearly right than the Democrats, their objections were to no avail.

Another development of importance in the years following the Jackson Administration was increasing regulation of banks by those states that permitted banking. Virginia, in 1837, appears to have been the first state to decree a maximum ratio of banknotes to specie reserves — 4:1. Louisiana was the first state to institute a maximum ratio of banknotes plus demand deposits to specie, and it instituted the most restrictive ratio of any state — 3:1 (Harris 1961, p. 110).

In October 1853, the banks of New York City organized the "Clearing House" for interbank exchanges. Each clearing house member bank was required to maintain specie reserves equal to one fifth of their banknotes plus deposits. About the same time, banks in Massachusetts were put under the requirement of maintaining reserves equal to 15 percent of notes plus deposits (Hammond 1957, p. 715).

The defeat of Mexico in 1848 took place just in the nick of time, for in that year gold was discovered at Sutter's Mill in newly annexed California Territory. The disovery of gold was also timely in that it rendered the sub-treasury plan somewhat more practical than might otherwise have been the case.

About $650 million in gold is recorded as having been produced in the United States in the twelve years from 1849 through 1860. The nation was immediately transformed from a gold-importer to a gold-exporter. For the twelve years from 1837 through 1848, the United States was a net importer of $28 million in gold. For the 1849–1860 period, it was a net exporter of $436 million in gold. This enabled the country vastly to increase its merchandise imports (commodities other than gold or silver). For the 1837–1848 period, U.S. merchandise exports exceeded imports by $16 million. For the 1849–1860 period, merchandise imports exceeded exports by $385 million (BC 1975, pp. 884–885). Some of the merchandise imports, of course, were consumption items, but other imports (e.g., machinery) contributed greatly to the capacity of the country to produce goods and to transport what it produced.

It has been noted that for 1849–1860 gold production amounted to $650 million and net exports to $436 million. No very exact figures are available, but it appears that upwards of two thirds of the $214 million difference went to increase monetary gold in circulation or to increase the supply of gold in government or bank vaults. Only somewhat less than one third went into plate, jewelry, and other consumption items.

The combination of direct and indirect ways in which the discovery of gold led to the growth of the United States economy is incalculable, but that the effect of domestic gold production was profound and lasting cannot be doubted. For a developing country eager to purchase the technology of more advanced foreign countries and needing precious metals for this purpose, the discovery of California gold was a purely fortuitous event of immense importance.

Because, as earlier observed, silver was overvalued in terms of gold, because the amount of silver in silver coins was greater than the face value of the coins, silver coins tended to be withdrawn from circulation. In consequence, in 1853 Congress reduced the silver content of half-dollars and other silver coins. The silver content of two half-dollars was reduced from 371.25 grains to 345.6 grains, thus making two half-dollars worth only 95¢ in silver and making it unprofitable to withdraw coins from circulation and melt them down for sale as bullion. Coinage of silver dollars was stopped simultaneously. Silver thereafter was used only as "small change"; and gold coins took over in transactions where banknotes or bank credit was not used.

The American writer on the subjects of money and banking during the period between the Revolution and Civil War most deserving of our attention is Edward Kellogg. Just as the writings of Adam Smith on money and banking have been overrated, those of Kellogg have been underrated. And for much the same reason — Smith said what bankers and moneyed people wanted to hear and wanted propagated, and Kellogg said the opposite.

Kellogg was a Connecticut Yankee who became a wholesale dry goods dealer in New York City and eventually acquired sufficient means to retire and devote his time to writing. He was fifty-one when his first book appeared in 1841. His principal work, *Labor and Other Capital: The Rights of Each Secured and the Wrongs of Both Eradicated,* appeared in 1849.

Kellogg hated private money-creating banks with the same passion as Jefferson and Adams, as quotations from *Labor and Other Capital* abundantly show.

In the State of New York the banks are authorized to discount to two and one half times their capital. For instance, if the stockholders pay in, say one million dollars as capital stock, the bank is at liberty to discount or loan out to the people two and a half millions of dollars [by printing banknotes]. Without a bank charter, the men who own the million of money, which constitutes the capital of the bank, could only loan one million dollars. In granting the charter, the legislature grants to these few individuals the privilege of charging the people seven per cent interest on one and a half millions of dollars never owned by the stockholders. (1971, pp. 179-180)

Kellogg goes on to say that this is only a part of the story; that banks not only print and loan banknotes but also make loans by creating deposits. And deposit creation, he says, often amounts to 1.5 times the amount of the issue of banknotes. On only $1 million in capital, then, a bank might loan not only $2.5 million by banknote issue but also $3.75 million by deposit creation. Hence the bank could draw 7 percent interest on $6.25 million, although the stockholders had advanced only $1 million: "Nearly three times the whole amount of the specie in the banks of the State of New York from 1835 to 1845 would have been required to pay their deposits, at any one time during that period, without redeeming in specie one circulating bank-note" (1971, p. 182). To have paid off all issued banknotes, as well as deposits, would have taken over five and perhaps six times the amount of specie in the banks.

The procedure of bankers was likened by Kellogg to the case of the owner of only one acre of land making deeds of one acre each to five different individuals or charging five different people rent on the same acre of land. The same "immorality," he said, "attached to charging five different people interest on a dollar while owning only one dollar of specie" (1971, pp. 183-184).

Kellogg called attention to the large number of bank failures recorded over the years immediately preceeding publication of his book and wrote:

It is perfectly obvious that our legislative bodies have founded our banking system on false pretenses — upon promises the banks neither can, nor expect, to fulfill. . . .

The government enacts a law [requiring] payments in specie, when it is perfectly well known that specie does not exist in sufficient quantities. (1971, p. 193)

Equally disturbing to Kellogg was the power that banks possessed to vary the rate of interest. "They can make money very abundant [and hence make interest rates low], or very scarce [and interest rates high]." This makes it possible for banks to "purchase State Bonds, and other securities, at a great discount from their par value" at one time and subsequently to sell them above par. He gives as an example New York State Bonds of $1000 face value and paying $60 per annum. By raising the "discount rate" or normal rate of interest to 8 percent the banks could drive down the selling price of the bonds to $750, at which price the banks were buyers. Later the discount rate would be manipulated down to 5 percent. This pushed up the bond price to $1200, at which time the banks became sellers. Counting capital gains on the bonds, the banks made as much or more money when the rate was 5 percent as they did when it was 8 percent (1971, pp. 185–187).

But Kellogg went far beyond criticism of the banking system and challenged the whole concept that equitable rates of interest are possible when a scarce commodity such as gold or silver is made the basis of a monetary system.

In all ages and nations, the rates of interest maintained have been so high as continually to concentrate the wealth in a few hands. When the wealth becomes thus concentrated, the producers and distributors [are left] destitute of property. (1971, p. 170)

Nothing . . . now prevents the full employment and just compensation of labor but the monopoly of money and unjust interest rates. (1971, p. 153)

The idea that a just and equitable rate of interest would result from a policy of laissez-faire was derided by Kellogg. He quoted Jeremy Bentham's *Defense of Usury* as follows:

No man of ripe years and of sound judgment, acting freely and with his eyes open, ought to be hindered with a view to his advantage, from making such a bargain, in the way of obtaining money, as he thinks fit; nor (what is a necessary consequence) anybody hindered from supplying him, upon terms he thinks proper to acceed to. (Kellogg 1971, p. 60)

In reply Kellogg wrote:

According to Bentham's theory, when money is loaned, the rate of interest to be paid must be a matter of agreement between borrower and lender. This makes the rate of interest belong to the system of free-trade, whereas it no more belongs to this system than the length of the yard-stick or the weight of the pound. By increasing the rate of interest, both the principal of the money, and the interest upon it, have an increased power over property, as much as a pound weight increased has over the quantity of products. (1971, p. 60)

There is simply no way, Kellogg repeats again and again, that an acceptable rate of interest may be expected to result from a confrontation between "the necessity of the borrower and the avarice of the lender" (1971, p. 226). On the contrary, government has an obligation to keep the rate of interest low and see that it fluctuates over only a narrow range (1971, p. 59).

The rate of interest, Kellogg said, should be proportioned to "the productiveness of land and labor" or the productiveness of the total economy. Inequity results because "the present rates of interest greatly exceed the increase of wealth by natural production" (1971, p. 248). In other words, the rate of interest must be kept somewhat below the real growth rate of the economy; otherwise the wealth of moneyed people will increase faster than the wealth of the generality of people, and a redistribution of income and wealth favoring moneyed people will occur. This is a timeless principle of political economy, but even yet today a much overlooked and unappreciated one. So far as I know Kellogg was the first to formulate it and stress its importance. He deserves far more acclaim on this score than has been accorded him.

Kellogg proposed a detailed plan for controlling the rate of interest. His plan embodied several features of any proper approach to the numerous problems of money and interest: (1) the federal government should divorce money from any relationship with gold or silver because such a relationship necessarily means that money will remain excessively dear; (2) it should modify the charters of private banks so as to deprive them of the power to create money; and (3) the federal government should become the sole creator of a paper money for the economy.

But his overall plan cannot be considered satisfactory. For in addition to these proposals, he wanted what came to be called "Kellogg's Interconvertible Bond Scheme." According to this scheme, the government would lend money that it created to any and all individuals willing to mortgage land of twice the value of the loan. Such loans would be made at 1 percent per annum interest; and since money would always be available at this rate, the rate would never rise higher. At the same time, the government would stand ready to sell to all individuals government bonds paying 1.1 percent interest, and thus the rate of interest should never fall lower. Kellogg mistakenly thought that by thus controlling interest within narrow limits the purchasing power of money would tend to be similarly invariant, although this is not at all the case. "The fallacy of Kellogg's reasoning [was that it confused] the value of money as the rate of interest and as purchasing power. . . . Stabilizing the rate of interest . . . renders unstable the value of money as purchasing power" (Commons 1934, p. 594).

Whatever the shortcomings of his plan, Kellogg in his time recognized as did few others many of the monetary practices weighing down on the producing classes and many of the elements of a more satisfactory order. As noted earlier, his most important contributions to monetary theory were (1) that the rate of interest tends to determine the distribution of income and wealth between the producing classes on the one hand and the nonproducing moneylenders on the other and (2) that a rate of interest greater than the growth rate of the economy will not only promote injustice but prove intolerably inhibiting to an optimum rate of economic growth.

Kellogg's aim was a society very significantly different from the one he saw about him. His aim was a society in which poverty could not exist in any family whose members were able and willing to work. This remains the aim of any humane economic theory or monetary policy.

Chapter 18

Union Financing of the Civil War, 1861–1863

At the time of the election of Abraham Lincoln in November 1860, in the states that were to remain loyal to the Union, the money supply consisted of gold coins amounting to just under 28 percent of the total and silver coins amounting to just under 3 percent of the total. The remaining 69 percent of the money supply consisted of bank-created money (BCM) about two fifths of it in the form of banknotes and three fifths in the form of bank deposits or checkbook money. As we see in some detail in this chapter and those to follow, this structure of the money supply was destined to be altered radically during the next few years (BC 1975, p. 995).

Lincoln was inaugurated March 4, 1861. On April 12, Fort Sumter was fired upon and Lincoln's "war to crush the rebellion and preserve the Union" began. That April the strength of the Union Army was less than 17,000. By December the size of the army had multiplied to just under 200,000, by the end of 1862 to over 600,000, and by the end of 1863 to over 900,000 (BC 1975, p. 1142).

This immense increase in the armed forces and the provision of supplies for them entailed an enormous escalation in federal expenditures. The cost of the war to the Union amounted to about $35 million in 1861, $446 million in 1862, and $683 million in 1863 — a total for the three years of $1.164 billion (BC 1975, p. 1114). Among other things, this chapter deals with how this expenditure was financed, and the next chapter with the expenditures and financing during the remaining years of the war.

If the nature as well as the scale of the financial crisis confronting the Union is to be appreciated fully, a number of relevant factors must be noted.

First, at the time of Lincoln's inauguration the government was obliged by legislation inherited from the Jackson Era to deal solely in terms of specie when receiving or disbursing money. Silver having virtually disappeared from circulation except as minor coin, paying for war costs with specie meant in practice paying with gold. Accordingly, the government was constrained to receive only gold for all taxes and for any bonds it might sell or any money it might otherwise obtain by borrowing.

Second, the federal debt at the beginning of Lincoln's administration was approximately $65 million, and the government's credit standing was poor; so poor indeed that federal bonds were ranked inferior to those of Massachusetts, New York, Ohio, and Pennsylvania; so poor that state guarantees of federal issues had in the past sometimes proved necessary in order to avoid large discounts; so poor that a treasury issue during the Buchanan administration sold at a 10 percent discount (BC 1975, p. 1118; Hepburn 1924, p. 180; Sharkey 1967, p. 18). And now the would-be borrower, already financially troubled, was engaged in a war the outcome of which was uncertain. Such conditions notwithstanding, Secretary Chase was determined not to permit treasury issues to sell below par or sell for anything but gold.

Third, the federal government in the past had depended upon customs revenues and the sale of public lands for nearly all its expenditures. There was no internal revenue tax structure whereby the government could increase its revenues by merely raising tax rates, no bureaucracy of internal revenue tax collectors that could be set in motion to collect additional taxes rapidly and efficiently.

Fourth, the hoarding of gold began even before Lincoln's inauguration and before the outbreak of war. The demands by hoarders on banks for the banks' gold reserves mounted relentlessly thereafter.

It is not surprising, in view of the large imbalance between expenses and prospective revenues, that on July 17, 1861, Congress passed an act that authorized the borrowing of $250 million via the sale of treasury notes and bonds. Under the circumstances, however, this act created more problems than it solved. Treasury Secretary Chase entered into an agreement with the banks of New York, Philadelphia, and Boston whereby the banks would immediately buy with gold $50 million in bonds. The hope was that as Chase paid for government purchases with gold, the gold would return to the banking system soon enough to permit purchase by banks of another $50 million in bonds as Chase came to need the additional money. Obviously, $250 million in bonds could not be sold to banks all at once since they would be stripped of their entire gold reserves long before the issue could be subscribed. Nor could the issue be sold to the nonbank public, for it likewise had not enough gold if a sufficiency were to remain for day-to-day transactions in the private sector. And in any case, citizens constituting the nonbank public were not accustomed to buying bonds and not disposed to buy them at par.

The banks agreed to the arrangement just described, and as insisted upon by Chase, only with great reluctance. What they wanted was to subscribe to the treasury issues not by paying in gold but under the condition that they would pay by creating bank deposits in the name of the treasury — deposits upon which the treasury would write checks in payment of its incoming bills. This was a procedure quite common in the private sector but one to which the secretary was constrained, or declared himself constrained, to refuse assent. Chase, a believer that banks should be federally chartered, had no wish to enhance the position of the banks, all of which were state chartered in 1861, 1862, and 1863.

The $50 million in gold borrowed from banks and hauled by horse-drawn drays to the treasury or subtreasuries and disbursed by Chase did not, however, return promptly to the banks. That it did not was due partly to unavoidable friction in the system but especially to hoarding. By December 28, 1861, the gold reserves of the banks had so dwindled that the banks were forced to suspend payment in specie; the "gold standard" had to be abandoned just as it had been abandoned by Britain during its wars on the continent earlier in the century. When banks defaulted, the treasury's principal source of gold disappeared and the treasury was likewise forced to default. Suspension of specie payments by the treasury followed closely upon suspension by banks.

Thus covering the treasury deficit by selling bonds at par for gold had proved impossible. And selling bonds below par or selling them for banknotes or bank deposit credits remained unacceptable to Chase. Congress then turned, as had the Continental Congress nearly a century before, to a government emission of paper money. An issue of $150 million in "United States notes" ("greenbacks" or "legal tenders" as they came to be called) was authorized by Congress and signed by President Lincoln on February 25, 1862. This was the first of three so-called "Legal Tender Acts." On April 5 the first printing was received by the treasury and the first payment of debts made with greenbacks. Subsequent issues of greenbacks in like amounts were authorized in July 1862 and March 1863. The total amount in non-interest-bearing U.S. legal tender notes authorized during all the war years was thus $450 million. In other legislation, Congress authorized the issue of non-interest-bearing "fractional currency" and interest-bearing legal tenders.

Table 18.1 summarizes war costs and war financing for the first three years of the Union war effort. This table shows that Union financing of the early years of the war relied primarily on borrowing, secondarily on money creation, and only in a very minor way on taxation. We see in the next chapter that there were significant differences in the way the war was financed after January 1, 1864.

Attention must next be given to changes in the structure of the nation's money supply during the first three years of the war, as shown by Table

Table 18.1
War Costs in Millions of Dollars and How Paid in Percentages of Total

Year	1861	1862	1863	3 Years
Cost of War	$35	$446	$683	$1164
Percentage Paid By:				
Taxes	29%	5%	11%	9.5%
Borrowing	71	59	52	55.2
GCM	0	36	37	35.3

Source: Bureau of the Census. 1975. *Historical Statistics of the United States—Colonial Times to 1970.* Washington, D.C.: U.S. Government Printing Office, p. 1114.
Note: GCM = government-created money

18.2. The table may be a little misleading for it shows total money issued rather than actual money in circulation. At times, large amounts were held in the treasury for future payment of bills, and an indeterminant amount of gold was hoarded. Nevertheless, the numbers are accurate enough that *trends* can be identified, and the trends rather than the annual amounts are significant. The most noteworthy trends are (1) the absolute increase but declining percentage of coin, (2) the absolute increase but declining percentage of BCM, and (3) the huge increase both in absolute and percentage terms of government-created money (GCM).

Having given the essentials of war costs, war financing arrangements, and changes in the money supply thus necessitated, we may proceed to a more detailed discussion of government financial policies. Although Wesley C. Mitchell and other historians of the period have expressed the belief that money creation by government would have been unnecessary if only Chase had been willing to sell bonds below par, no convincing case for this contention can be made, and no case at all unless discounts on the order of 50 percent or more are contemplated (Mitchell 1903; Sharkey 1967, p. 33). And in any event, selling bonds below par would have been unwise since it would have obligated the government to repay greater principal amounts than it received.

It is essential to understand that the enormously increased civilian and military expenditures of the Union required a large addition to the money supply—merely an increase in velocity of turnover (of the money supply of the size of 1860) would not do the job. There was no quick way to increase the amount of specie in the country, and thus a choice had to be made between "inconvertible government created money" or "inconvertible bank created money"—a choice between "money of the people and money of the bankers" as some commentators said (Sharkey 1967, pp. 55, 106). It was altogether right and proper that money created by government was preferred over bank-created money.

Table 18.2
Constituents of the Money Supply, 1860 and 1863

	Millions of Dollars		Percentage of Total	
Year	1860	1863	1860	1863
COINS	$228	$271	30.6%	20.3%
BCM	517	643	69.4	48.2
Banknotes	207	239	27.8	17.9
Deposits	310	404	41.6	30.3
GCM	0	421	0.0	31.5
Greenbacks	0	312	0.0	23.4
Other	0	109	0.0	8.1
TOTAL	745	1335	100.0	100.0

Source: Bureau of the Census. 1975. *Historical Statistics of the United States—Colonial Times to 1970.* Washington, D.C.: U.S. Government Printing Office, p. 992–995.
Note: BCM = bank-created money; GCM = government-created money

The decision of the government to embark on a policy of creating money — the passage of the Legal Tender Acts authorizing greenbacks — was by far the most significant monetary event since the Jackson Era. The proudest accomplishment of that era, the policy that all federal receipts and payments had to be made in specie, was completely overturned. The acts were, indeed, the most significant monetary legislation since the adoption of the Constitution. For despite the absence of any specific authorization in the Constitution of money creation by the federal government and despite the long-held belief that the federal government had only those powers specifically authorized, the federal government proceeded to create enormous amounts of paper money.

Although the idea of federal creation of a legal tender currency in 1862 occurred independently to numerous public officials and financial experts and occurred to them more or less simultaneously, it is interesting to note that in a letter dated December 6, 1864, to a Col. E. D. Taylor of Ohio, President Lincoln stated that the idea of greenbacks originated with Taylor and was conveyed to Lincoln in January of 1862. Lincoln went on to say that Treasury Secretary "Chase thought it [the issue of legal tender notes] a hazardous thing but we finally accomplished it and gave the people of this Republic the greatest blessing they ever had — their own paper money to pay off their debts" (Hertz 1931, 2: 957).

As Lincoln remarked, Secretary Chase indeed did have misgivings about the government creating legal tender money. In a letter to the *New York Post,* February 4, 1862, however, after reciting a list of his reservations, he wrote, "I consent to the expedient of United States Notes in limited amounts being made a legal tender" Hammond 1970, p. 202).

When Chase raised with the president the question of the constitutionality of federal paper money, Lincoln is quoted as having said: "The rebels are violating the Constitution to destroy the Union. I will violate the Constitution, if necessary, to save the Union, and I suspect, Chase, that our Constitution is going to have a rough time of it before we get done with this row" (Sandburg 1939, 3: 397).

In his December 1862 message to Congress, Lincoln made the following reference to greenbacks:

The suspension of specie payments by banks soon after the commencement of your last session, made large issues of United States Notes [greenbacks] unavoidable. In no other way could the payment of the troops, and the satisfaction of other just demands, be so economically or so well provided for. The judicious legislation of Congress, securing the receivability of these notes for loans and internal duties, and making them a legal tender for other debts, has made them a universal currency; and has satisfied, partially, at least, and for the time, the long-felt want of an uniform circulating medium, saving thereby to the people immense sums in discounts and exchanges. (Nicolay and Hay 1907, 2: 264)

Although the issue of United States notes was primarily owing to the exigencies of war, the notes answered a perennial need throughout the nation for a "national" or "universal" currency. In 1860 there were said by one historian to be "7,000 kinds of banknotes in circulation, not to mention 5,000 kinds of counterfeit notes" (Angell 1924, p. 294). Another historian estimated that the circulation contained "more than 8,300 sorts of paper money of solvent banks . . . while the issues of fraudulent, broken, and worthless banks brought the total up to more than 13,000. Also 6,000 counterfeits were circulating" (Sandburg, 1939, 3: 191).

Extended and spirited debates in Congress over the first of the Legal Tender Acts preceded the enactment of the legislation authorizing the printing of greenbacks. Brief excerpts from various speeches disclose something of the nature of the arguments of both supporters and opponents of the acts.

Senator Fessenden: This thing is wrong in itself, but to leave the government without resources at such a crisis is not to be thought-of. (Hammond 1970, p. 214)

Senator Doolittle: While in theory the only money of our people is gold and silver, the fact is otherwise. It is paper almost exclusively and at this moment it is the irredeemable paper of suspended bank corporations. . . . This country must assert its constitutional authority over the currency . . . in some practicable way, and it seems to me that the mode proposed in this bill is the simplest and most direct in the present exigencies. (Hammond 1970, p. 219)

Senator Sherman: Money is due and payable to your soldiers, to contractors, to the men who have furnished provisions and clothing for your army, to your officers, your judges, and your civil magistrates. Selling bonds on the market would produce something like sixty cents on the dollar . . . because there is no money [gold or silver coin] with which to buy bonds. (Hammond 1970, p. 218)

Senator Howe: Whatever our wishes may be, it is impossible to command the revenues for this war in coin. (Hammond 1970, p. 215)

Representative Thaddeus Stevens: The government and not the banks should have the profit from creating a medium of exchange. (Hammond 1970, p. 192)

It is worth special mention that while most of those favoring the Legal Tender Act supported it on the basis of the urgency of the moment, Thaddeus Stevens emphasized not that the act was expedient (although he undoubtedly believed it was) but that it accorded with a principle or axiom of the highest importance in statecraft. The single sentence of Stevens just cited sums up the whole matter with the utmost accuracy and terseness. It is as fully applicable in times of peace as in times of war, as applicable in the twentieth as in the nineteenth century.

The United States notes were promises to pay only in a limited or special sense. The five-dollar greenback, for example, bore on the obverse side the words, "The United States promise to pay the bearer five dollars" and "Payable at the Treasury of the United States." It was a serious mistake, however, to call the greenbacks "notes" or to print such phrases on them. Any hint of any sort that the greenbacks were promises to pay or needed to be payable in something else was a mistake. To add to the confusion, nothing was said about *when* a note would become payable or in what medium it would be paid. Presumably the notes would be paid in legal tender. But the reverse side of all notes bore the words, "This note is legal tender for all debts public and private except duties on imports and interest on the public debt and is receivable in payment of all loans made to the United States." On the presumption that the notes were to be paid in legal tender, they could be paid with themselves! In any case, the notes were not payable immediately in either gold or silver. Whether they ever would be so payable was an open question for several years.

The legislation introduced and passed by the House made the greenbacks "legal tender for all debts public and private" without exception. Excepting "duties on imports and interest on the public debt" was inserted into the act in the Senate, passed by that body, and insisted upon in the House-Senate conference that produced the final version. This was a second mistake of great importance. The two exceptions to making the greenbacks full and unredeemable legal tenders were extremely detrimental to the purpose of the issue of the notes. The notes should have been made legal tender without any qualification as in the House version. The fact that the greenbacks were declared less good than gold for the payment of custom duties and interest on government debt downgraded the issue and provided ammunition and encouragement to all its critics (Munson 1945, p. 55).

The exceptions that made the greenbacks less good than gold or silver were introduced into the legislation under pressure from diehard specie advocates and the lobbyists of bankers and bondholders. The clear intention of the sponsors of the exceptions was to undermine the "full legal tender" principle.

The requirement that interest should be paid in gold guaranteed that the government would be required periodically to go into the money market and buy gold with greenbacks. The requirement that custom duties should be paid in gold made it necessary for the payers of duties to do likewise. This gave money market manipulators substantial influence on the gold–greenback exchange rate and thus provided them with a way to make the greenbacks exchange for gold at less than par and undermine confidence in them.

The requirement that the government pay its interest obligation, and no other obligation, in gold justifiably aroused great controversy. It obviously was intended to favor moneylenders above every other class of citizen, even above soldiers and sailors on active duty who were paid in greenbacks, not specie. The not inconsiderable power over Congress wielded by bankers and other moneylenders nevertheless carried the day, and the greenback's inning began with two strikes against it.

Greenbacks were not actually redeemable in gold at the treasury from the time of issue until 1879. "The whole country was now on an inconvertible paper basis; it remained there for seventeen years" (Angell 1924, p. 293). Greenbacks became redeemable in gold in 1879 and continued redeemable until 1933. They are no longer thus redeemable, although the few original issues that remain in circulation are available as collector's items at many times face value. By the act of May 31, 1878, the amount of United States notes is maintained to this day at $322,539,000. This amount has been re-printed in the form of $100 notes. These notes are declared to be "outstanding" although they are unjustifiably and illegally withheld from circulation by the treasury (Letter dated May 28, 1986, written by Charles W. Bennett, assistant director of the Division of Federal Reserve Bank Operations of the Board of Governors of the Federal Reserve System).

At all times greenbacks interchanged at face value with the banknotes of reputable banks. Other banknotes traded not only at a discount for gold but at a discount for greenbacks.

Overmuch has been made by historians of the fact that greenbacks came to trade for gold only at a discount, the size of the discount being determined by "money market conditions." At the lowest ebb of their value it took about $28 in greenbacks to secure a $10 goldpiece; but trading at so large a discount was short lived, and by 1866 only $14 in greenbacks would secure a $10 gold-piece, by 1870 only $11, and by 1879 exactly $10 (Barrett 1931, p. 90). And, of course, the banknotes of even the most reputable banks fluctuated in value in terms of gold precisely as did the greenbacks. The decline and recovery in value of the paper money created by sound banks was the same as the decline and recovery in value of the paper money created by government.

As Table 18.2 shows, the Union's money supply was approximately doubled between 1860 and 1863. It was impossible, however, to double the production of goods and services in so short a time. Under such circumstances,
"price inflation" of gold and all other goods and services was inevitable.
Table 18.2 also shows that while government-created money increased by
$421 million, bank-created money increased by $126 million. "Relieved of
the responsibility for redemption [in gold], the banks could profitably issue
additional millions in notes" or deposits (Sharkey 1967, p. 28).

The common practice of blaming all price inflation on acts of money creation (whether by government or by banks) is misguided. The conversion of
an economy from civilian to military production in the 1860s, the distribution
of purchasing power that does not result in the production of goods and
services that consumers wish to buy, the haste and destruction war entails,
these and other factors tend to cause prices to rise just as does money creation at high annual rates. "Some writers have ascribed the price inflation
almost entirely to the influence of greenbacks, but this is a mistaken view"
(Studenski and Krooss 1952, p. 147). Thomas W. Olcott of Albany, New
York, a prominent banker, properly observed that "military expenditures
would produce [price] inflation even if [all expenditures were] made in coin"
(Hammond 1970, p. 230).

It must be emphasized also that the legal tender greenbacks created by the
government became an important source of increased reserves for private
banks which enabled them to increase the amount of money they created. In
other words, the government not only permitted private banks to create
money, the government in effect facilitated the process.

This fact goes some distance toward explaining why there was not more
opposition by banks than actually occurred to the creation of the greenbacks.
As Senator Doolittle told his collegues, "Every $5 United States Note [green-
back] the banks receive they will put in their vaults like so much gold and
with it as reserves will issue three $5 notes of their own" (Hammond 1970,
pp. 220–221). In fact, for every $5 greenback the banks kept in their vaults
as reserves, they issued more than $15 in newly created money, but more of
it in the form of deposit credits than in the form of banknotes. And, of
course, a part of what they created they loaned to the government at interest.

Bankers no doubt viewed the issue of greenbacks with very mixed emo-
tions. In their own very singular way, they were patriotic unionists who
wanted victory for the North and wanted to help attain it. On the whole they
had to agree that an issue of greenbacks was the best solution to the treasury
crisis of 1862–63 and that the war could not be financed while the government
maintained a gold standard. On the other hand, they viewed money creation
by the government as infringing on what they considered their turf, and thus
they tended to view greenbacks with considerable consternation. Finally,
they saw the legal tenders as a way of increasing their reserves to an extent
that it was impossible to increase them with relatively scarce gold and realized

that this would greatly enhance their own money-creating capacity. Thus they tended to view the greenback issue with at least halfhearted favor. In any case, it is a fact of history that bankers did not mount the type of all-out attack of which they were capable on the greenback issue. They were content to settle for amendments that downgraded the greenbacks while still causing them to yield the benefits the bankers desired.

Chapter 19 _____

Union Financing of the Civil War, 1864–1866

Although the war ended in April 1865 and demobilization was rapid, war-connected costs were still greater in 1866 than they were in 1862 and far greater than they had been in 1861. A review of the financing of the war and its overall cost, therefore, requires consideration of 1866 as well as the years of actual warfare. Table 19.1 supplements Table 18.1 and shows the cost of war to the Union for 1864, 1865, and 1866 and how the costs were financed.

Table 19.2 brings forward the data of Table 18.1 for the three years 1861–1863 in the first column, repeats the data of Table 19.1 for the three years 1864–1866 in the center column, and gives data for all six years in the last column.

Later in this chapter we return to the overall cost of the six years of war-related expenditures; but for now let us note that Table 19.2 shows that from

Table 19.1
War Costs in Millions of Dollars and How Paid in Percentages of Total

Year	1864	1865	1866	3 Years
Cost of War	$826	$1227	$457	$2510
Percentage Paid By:				
Taxes	27%	22%	100%	37.9%
Borrowing	67	78	1	61.4
GCM	6	0	-1	0.7

Source: Bureau of the Census. 1975. *Historical Statistics of the United States — Colonial Times to 1970.* Washington, D.C.: U.S. Government Printing Office, p. 1114.
Note: GCM = government-created money

Table 19.2
War Costs in Millions of Dollars and How Paid in Percentages of Total

Period	3 Years 1861-1863	3 Years 1864-1866	6 Years 1861-1866
Cost of War	$1164	$2510	$3674
Taxes	9.5%	37.9%	28.9%
Borrowing	55.2	61.4	59.4
GCM	35.3	0.7	11.7

Source: Compiled from Tables 18.1 and 19.1
Note: GCM = government-created money

Table 19.3
Constituents of the Money Supply, 1863 and 1866

Year	Millions of Dollars 1863		Millions of Dollars 1866		Percentage of Total 1863		Percentage of Total 1866	
COINS	$271		$129		20.3%		7.6%	
BCM	643		1055		48.2		62.0	
Banknotes		239		296		17.9		17.4
Deposits		404		759		30.3		44.6
GCM	421		516		31.5		30.4	
Greenbacks		312		328		23.4		19.3
Other		109		188		8.1		11.1
TOTAL	1335		1700		100.0		100.0	

Source: Bureau of the Census. 1975. *Historical Statistics of the United States—Colonial Times to 1970.* Washington, D.C.: U.S. Government Printing Office, p. 1114.
Note: BCM = bank-created money; GCM = government-created money

Table 19.4
Changes in the Constituents of the Money Supply in Millions of Dollars

Period	1860-1863	1863-1866	1860-1866
COINS	+ 43	- 142	- 99
BCM	+126	+412	+538
GCM	+421	+ 95	+516
TOTAL	+590	+365	+955

Source: Compiled from Tables 18.2 and 19.3
Note: BCM = bank-created money; GCM = government-created money

the first to the second three-year period: (1) the percentage of the cost of the war paid by taxes increased greatly, (2) the percentage paid by borrowing increased moderately, and (3) the percentage paid by government-created money dropped significantly.

The first of these changes is attributable to the fact that the government by 1864 and later had in force several new excise taxes and tariffs; and for the first time in the country's history, an income tax had been put into effect. The third of the changes resulted from the fact that by 1866 the government had ceased creating money; and there was less government-created money in circulation than in 1865. The near equality of the percentage increase in taxes and the percentage decrease in reliance on government-created money accounts for the relatively small change in the percentage of war costs paid by borrowing.

Table 19.3 shows components of the Union money supply in December 1863 and December 1866 and shows thereby the changes in the structure of the money supply during this three-year period.

The reader is reminded that authorities differ on the amounts of money of the various types for any given year. Thus the amounts shown in Table 19.3, like those shown in Table 18.2, are primarily presented for the purpose of showing percentages. What may be observed for the period from 1863 to 1866 is a large decrease in coins as a percentage of total, a very small decrease in the percentage of government-created money, and a large increase in the percentage of bank-created money.

Since the point that I wish to make now is one of great importance, let me emphasize it by the data of Table 19.4. What may be calculated from this table is that although from 1860 to 1863 the government created $295 million more than the banks, from 1863 to 1866 the banks created $317 million more than the government, and thus for the entire period from 1860 to 1866 the banks created more than the government.

The fact that there was more money creation between 1860 and 1866 by banks than there was by government has not been given the emphasis it deserves by most historians. It is of great significance in two ways. First, prices were about 87 percent higher in 1866 than they had been in 1860, and the usual practice is to blame this on the creation of money by the government. To whatever extent there is justification for attributing price inflation to money creation, however, Table 19.4 shows that more of the inflation in 1866 should be attributed to money creation by banks than to money creation by government.

Second, if more than $1 billion in money creation was to occur between 1860 and 1866, and Table 19.4 shows it did occur, then the entire amount should have been money creation by government applied to the cost of the war. Instead of only about 12 percent of the cost of the war being paid by government money creation, as Table 19.2 shows, about 24 percent should have been thus paid. Correspondingly less money should have been borrowed.

Remember Thaddeus Stevens's axiom, "The government and not the banks should have the profit from creating a medium of exchange."

Table 19.2 shows the cost to the Union of the Civil War by yearend 1966 amounted to $3.674 billion. This, however, is far from being the ultimate monetary cost of the war. Benefits paid to Union veterans and dependents from the end of the war to 1970 amounted to about $8.57 billion. Interest on war loans has been estimated by government statisticians at $1.17 billion (BC 1975, p. 1140). According to these figures, the ultimate dollar cost of the Union's war was about $13.41 billion, although I believe the amount attributed to interest has been greatly underestimated.

The fact that the triennium 1864–1866 may be distinguished from the triennium 1861–1863 by far larger tax levies has already been mentioned. The second triennium also differs from the first in that it witnessed the enactment of a great deal of legislation concerning banks. The passage in February 1863 of the National Banking Act, for example, was an event of far-reaching significance beginning with 1864.

The publicly declared purpose of the sponsors of this act was "to provide a National Currency, secured by a pledge of United States Stocks, and to provide for the circulation and redemption thereof." The real purpose, however, was not so simple. The issue and circulation of legal tender United States notes (greenbacks) had already provided a national currency, and there was neither need nor justification for any other. Flawed though they were by the Senate action that declared them less good than gold in the payment of custom duties or interest on government debt, the greenbacks constituted a national currency that could be improved upon only by making them legal tender for all purposes without exception and removing any indication that their validity depended upon redeemability in specie.

The alternative to the non-interest-bearing national currency issued by the government (greenbacks) would, according to the National Banking Act, take the form of an interest-bearing national currency issued by private banks and introduced into the circulation by lending them to borrowers from the bank. An interest-bearing currency, of course, is a currency that remains in circulation only so long as someone is willing and able to pay interest on it. Nevertheless, it was a principal intention of the sponsors of the Banking Act to get rid of greenbacks altogether as soon as possible and leave the interest-bearing national currency as the only national currency.

The National Banking Act was a pet project of Treasury Secretary Chase. In the Senate, the act was backed by Finance Committee Chairman John Sherman who became secretary of the treasury a decade later. Most bankers, however, were content with the banking system under state charters and displayed no enthusiasm for the federal charters called for by the act. Nevertheless, it passed the Senate and House by narrow margins and was signed into law by Lincoln on February 25, 1863. It was extensively amended by the act of June 3, 1864 (Krooss 1983, 2: 297–328).

An important reason why the National Banking Act was passed by Congress and approved by the president is to be found in "the climate of the times." The Civil War period was one of an enthusiastic pro-Union nationalism that exalted the importance of the federal government and correspondingly denigrated the role of the states. In the North, during the war years, the doctrine of states' rights tended to be associated overwhelmingly with slavery, rebellion, and secession. The pendulum that had swung far in favor of states' rights and against a strong central government during the first half of the nineteenth century now moved equally far in the opposite direction.

The Banking Act created a system of federally chartered and federally regulated banks called "National Banks." According to the act, the banknotes issued by National Banks, to be called "National Currency," would be engraved and printed by the federal government. No matter what bank issued them, they would be uniform in appearance (except for showing the specific bank of issue) and would uniformly have the prestige of the federal government, rather than merely that of a state charter, behind them. The national currency of the banks would not be legal tender, but their acceptance and circulation would be guaranteed by the fact that they would be redeemable on demand by the bank of issue in "lawful money of the United States." Minimum reserve requirements in "lawful money" as a percentage of deposits plus banknotes were specified, and the total national currency issue was limited to $300 million.

A provision in the National Banking Act that particularly appealed to Secretary Chase and other government officials required the newly chartered national banks to use government bonds as security for the creation of the national currency banknotes. This provision was made a part of the act in order to make it easier to sell government securities by requiring banks to buy them. The act would thus provide assistance to the government in the continued financing and refinancing of its debt.

Here is an example of how the system would work according to the National Banking Act. Five or more persons could associate to obtain a federal charter by raising as little as $50,000 capital in legal tender, but let us say for an example that they raised $300,000. They were then permitted to purchase treasury bonds to the amount of one third their capital, $100,000-worth in our example. The remaining $200,000 they would use for making loans. With $100,000 in government bonds as security, they were permitted to issue national currency in the amount of nine tenths of their holdings, $90,000-worth in our example.

Of course, our bank could then lend $90,000 in national currency banknotes and collect interest on both $100,000 in government bonds and $90,000 in banknotes—it could thus collect what amounted to nearly double interest on nearly one third of its capital. In a year when the average return on loans was 6 percent, the return on money invested described here would be in excess of 11 percent. Despite the contentment of bankers with the system of state-chartered banks that the act replaced, it is easy to see why they were not vehement in their opposition to the National Banking Act.

The sea-change in sentiment from exalting states' rights to exalting the Union was manifest not only in the legislation creating national banks but also by a law enacted July 13, 1866. This new law decreed a tax of 10 percent of face value on the banknotes of all state-chartered banks (Krooss 1983, p. 343). Such legislation effectively drove all banknotes of state-chartered banks out of circulation. Paper currency in the United States for many years thereafter would consist exclusively of (1) non-legal-tender, interest-bearing national currency issued by private banks and (2) legal tender, non-interest-bearing United States notes (greenbacks).

It was the clear intention of the unionists who sponsored the 10 percent tax on the banknotes of state banks to put an end to state-chartered banks entirely and leave the banks chartered under the National Banking Act in exclusive control of the field. Just as the National Banking Act asserted the right of the federal government to charter banks and control money creation by them, the act of July 1866 was intended to assert that the states had no right to charter banks or control money creation by them. This intention was far from completely fulfilled because it was not understood by the framers of the legislation that state banks could create money by creating deposits as well as by printing banknotes. Had the new law taxed deposits as well as banknotes of state-chartered banks it would have succeeded in forcing all banks to switch from a state charter to a national charter.

It may seem altogether incredible that the members of the House and Senate at that time could have been so ignorant about so fundamental a monetary matter as not to understand that banks created money by creating deposits as well as by creating banknotes. Such ignorance, nevertheless, seems an undeniable historical fact. There is nothing to indicate that the state banks were intentionally left a loophole by virtue of which they survived.

After 1865 state-chartered banks, although deprived of the privilege of creating banknotes, thrived on deposit creation. By the eve of the Great Depression of the 1930s, there were about 17,500 of them compared to 7,500 National Banks, although the country's largest and most influential banks were federally chartered (BC 1975, pp. 1019, 1023).

Although in early 1863 there were in circulation banknotes of "sound" state-chartered banks in the amount of $239 million, by December 1866 virtually no such banknotes remained in circulation. Although in early 1863 there were in circulation no national currency banknotes of national banks, by December 1867 the amount was $291 million, near the limit specified in the National Banking Act. At the same time, deposits in all banks, whatever the source of charter, amounted to about $744 million (BC 1975, p. 993).

The often-stated goal of a "uniform national currency" thus did not characterize the immediate postwar years. The paper circulation contained not only nearly $300 million in the banknotes or national currency of the national banks but also more than $400 million in United States notes and other GCM (fractional currency and interest-bearing legal tenders). The two forms of paper money were different enough in appearance not to be confused easily, but both had "The United States of America" printed in large letters front and center. They could be interchanged at face value, but greenbacks were preferred since they were legal tender and national currency notes were not. During the time when specie payments were suspended, the national currency was redeemable only in United States notes; and United States notes were redeemable only in other United States notes. As is discussed in the following chapter, both forms of paper money were made redeemable in gold late in 1879 and remained so redeemable for several decades thereafter.

The banknotes of the national banks also carried the words "Secured by United States Bonds deposited with the Treasurer of the United States." Perhaps this will prompt readers to recall that the Bank of England began by being granted the authority to issue banknotes in the amount of its loans to the government. Similarly, the size of the permitted issue of banknotes by a national bank was determined by the size of its loans to the government, by its holdings of treasury bonds. The argument that because a government already owes money it is able to "secure" the issues of banknotes by private banks is not an overly impressive one. And surely it is evident that to the extent it makes any sense for the government to create a treasury bond out of a little paper and ink and then permit a bank to hold the bond and use it as basis for bank-created money, then it should make even more sense for the treasury to hold the bond itself and use it as a basis for government-issued money. It would make even greater sense for the government merely to issue money without bothering to issue a bond. If the government can create a bond of real value out of paper and ink, it can create money of real value in the same way.

An overwhelming disadvantage of bank-created money (whether through deposit creation as loans are made or through banknote circulation owing to the making of loans) is that such money remains in existence only so long as someone is willing to pay interest on it. Thus bank-created money is "impermanent money" or "ephemeral money." An overwhelming advantage of government-created money is that its continued existence does not depend on anyone's willingness to pay interest. With customary provisions for its replacement as it becomes excessively worn, government-created money is "permanent money."

When a country depends on bank-created money, any event that results in the reduction of borrowing from banks results in a shrinkage of the country's money supply. As the money supply shrinks, the volume of trade and production shrinks. As the volume of trade and production shrinks, borrowing from banks further declines, and a further shrinkage in the size of the country's money supply occurs. Thus the economy spirals into depression. When a country depends on government-created money, there is no similar tendency toward a downward spiraling in the size of the money supply. Greenbacks in every way constituted a superior form of money to the national currency of the national banks.

During the triennium 1864–1866, the national banks issued only a little less than $300 million in national currency. For the "security" of this issue, the banks were required by the National Banking Act to purchase roughly $330 million in treasury bonds. Now recall that in Table 19.4 it was shown that from 1863 to 1866 the amount of BCM increased by $412 million. This shows that for the period under consideration over three quarters of all the money that banks created they created for lending to the government. And the government, instead of creating interest-free money for itself, permitted the banks to create interest-bearing money, borrowed it from the banks, and obligated itself to pay interest to the banks. And remember, the money the banks created was just as irredeemable as the money government could have created for itself.

That during the Civil War the Union created for itself an irredeemable paper currency has been called "a formal act of national bankruptcy" (Hammond 1970, p. 186). But I have found no similar denunciation of the fact that during the same period the government permitted banks to create an irredeemable paper currency, borrowed it from them, and paid them interest for it. Nowhere have I found this labeled, as it should be, "a formal act of national stupidity."

At an assumed average rate of interest of 5 percent per annum paid annually for the 125 years from 1866 to 1991, the sum of roughly $300 million the government permitted the banks to create and then borrowed from them would have cost the government about $2 billion in interest. If interest had not been paid annually but compounded, the 5 percent rate on $30 million would have resulted in a debt of $134 billion by 1991.

Because of his almost unparalleled stature in United States history, a considerable interest attaches to the monetary ideas or convictions of Abraham Lincoln, and it seems appropriate to comment further on this matter.

People who believe that the creation of money should be solely the prerogative of government and that private banks should be denied any power to create money would be very pleased indeed if they could point to the revered Lincoln as an early champion of this position. It has been asserted, for example, that Lincoln's views included the following: "The monetary needs of increasing numbers of people advancing toward higher standards of living can and should be met by the government. . . . The issue of money should be maintained as an exclusive monopoly of the National Government" (Munson 1945, p. 124).

Those who attribute such views to Lincoln cite in their support the fact that he urged congressional approval of the Legal Tender Acts of 1862 and 1863 and signed them into law and that it is said that in 1864 he called the greenbacks created by the acts "the greatest blessing the people of this Republic ever had" (Hertz 1931, 2: 957). This is about all they can cite, however, and it is hardly a sufficient basis for saying that Lincoln believed "the issue of money should be an exclusive monopoly of the government." Whatever he may have thought, Lincoln was never so categorical about the matter as to say, as did Thaddeus Stevens, "The government and not the banks should have the profit from creating a medium of exchange."

It must not be overlooked that Lincoln signed the National Banking Act into law in 1863 and thus gave national banks the power to create banknotes and deposits. This alone seems a sufficient action to make it altogether unwarranted to attribute to him the idea that "the issue of money should be an exclusive monopoly of the National Government."

It can be argued, of course, that the National Banking Act conferred no new powers on banks; they could already create deposits and banknotes. And it can be contended that the primary purpose of the act was to make banking require a national rather than a state charter—that the purpose was not to change the fundamental character of banking. But the point remains that the act with Lincoln's signature on it gave renewed authority, some would say "higher" authority, to money creation by banks.

It can also be argued that Lincoln signed the National Banking Act and gave national banks power to create money despite the fact that he believed they should not be granted such a power, that he signed the act only because of pressures to which a president must sometimes, even if unwillingly, accede. But the evidence for such a contention is somewhere between scanty and nonexistent. Lincoln did not have to sign the act to placate bankers—they were at most lukewarm in its support. He did not have to sign it to placate Congress—the act barely passed in both the House (78–64) and the Senate (23–21). There is no evidence that he had to sign it to placate any other influential pressure group. He might have signed it in order to placate Secretary Chase, whose pet project it was, but this amounts to no sufficient reason.

Although the one person most responsible for the National Banking Act was Chase, Lincoln appointed him to the Supreme Court in 1864. Never an enthusiastic supporter of greenbacks, Chase, while on the court, was to vote twice to declare greenbacks unconstitutional. Lincoln could not have been unaware of Chase's views when the appointment to the court was made.

In March 1865 Lincoln made Hugh McCulloch secretary of the treasury. McCulloch was a banker who in 1868 in a speech at Ft. Wayne, Indiana said: "I look upon an irredeemable paper currency as an evil. . . . Gold and silver are the only true money. I have no doubt that these metals were prepared by the Almighty for this very purpose" (McCulloch 1888, p. 201). McCulloch was an arch conservative who served Andrew Johnson as secretary of the treasury throughout his term. Like Johnson, he opposed universal manhood suffrage for the freed slaves (Foner 1988, p. 182). McCulloch supported John Alley's House resolution of December 18, 1865, that proposed a beginning to the withdrawal of greenbacks from circulation (Schell

1930, p. 405). McCulloch evinced no similar wish to withdraw the banknotes of private banks from circulation and later wrote that "what the country needed for a circulating medium was not United States Notes . . . but a currency supplied by the National Banks" (McCulloch 1888, p. 210).

McCulloch's views were public knowledge before Lincoln appointed him to the treasury post. That Lincoln would make such appointments, as in the case of Chase and McCulloch, provides additional evidence that it is unwarranted to attribute to Lincoln the idea that "the issue of money should be an exclusive monopoly of the National Government."

All this having been said, a non-interest-bearing, irredeemable legal tender paper money created by government first became a part of the United States money supply during Lincoln's administration; and a non-interest-bearing, irredeemable legal tender paper money created by an agency of government remains a part of our money supply. Lincoln undoubtedly had the most advanced ideas about money of any president since Jefferson, and the creation of greenbacks during his administration marked a significant event in the monetary history of the United States.

To conclude this chapter, perhaps a few remarks should now be made with regard to the cost of its war to the Confederacy and how it was financed. Like the North, the South was early on confronted by a shortage of specie and by the hoarding of specie. Banks in the South were forced to suspend redemption of their banknotes in gold even earlier than those in the North (Hammond 1970, p. 255). The South, like the North, was also handicapped by the lack of a structure for raising internal revenue.

It has been estimated that the cost of the war to the central government of the Confederacy was about $2.25 billion. Of this, about $250 million was raised by taxes, about $500 million by borrowing, and about $1.5 billion by printing-press money (Studenski and Krooss 1951, p. 157). An indeterminate part of the war cost was provided by individual states, and the Rebel armies frequently found it necessary to resort to sequestration of supplies.

As early as 1863, the paper money of the Confederacy had depreciated to the extent that $100 in paper was required to buy a $5 goldpiece (Myers 1970, p. 169). It seems likely that a part of the depreciation resulted from counterfeit Confederate money dumped on the South by the North as a counterinsurgency measure (Hammond 1970, p. 257). With the defeat of the last rebels in April 1865, the debt certificates and paper money of the Confederacy became worthless.

Chapter 20

From War's End to Resumption of Gold Payments, 1865–1879

Whatever else may be said of it, the period from 1865 through 1879 cannot be called serene from the viewpoint of a historian of economics or money. Like so many other periods in our past, it was one of on-again–off-again prosperity and of ongoing and embittered discussions of "the money question" and the role of banks. But the controversies of this era were far from a mere repetition of those of the Jackson Era. The alternative to "bank paper" favored by the critics of private banks in the 1830s and 1840s was coins of gold or silver. The alternative favored by the critics in the 1870s was United States notes — greenbacks.

The years between 1862 and 1879 are sometimes referred to as the "Greenback Era" although "era of the inconvertible greenback" might be more appropriate. For, although greenbacks first came into circulation in 1862, they remained in circulation far later than 1879 when they first became convertible into gold at face value. But the term Greenback Era is not altogether inappropriate in that greenbacks provided the focus of countless debates and resulted in formation of the Greenbacker Movement and the organization of a Greenback party.

The views of the most influential Greenbackers are presented shortly, but first something must be said of their adversaries. It will be remembered that the $5 greenback, for example, carried the words, "The United States of America will pay to the bearer five dollars . . . payable at the United States Treasury." When the first greenbacks were issued, everyone understood that this promised that a $5 greenback would sometime in the future be exchangeable for a $5 goldpiece. It was the view of Hugh McCulloch, the former banker and gold monometalist who became secretary of the treasury in 1865, that steps should be taken to make greenbacks trade at face value for gold coins as soon as possible. This view was shared by others — by most bankers, by those who advocated a gold standard as a matter of high principle, and by bondholders and holders of debt paper generally who wanted to receive gold rather than greenbacks when their loans matured.

Since the greenbacks in circulation had a face value of hundreds of millions of dollars and there was little gold in the treasury with which to redeem them, and since it was easier to reduce the number of greenbacks than to increase the gold in the treasury, McCulloch's policy first and foremost became one of reducing the greenback circulation. Greenbackers objected to McCulloch's "tight money" policy not only "on principle" but also because of his manner of effecting it. For McCulloch sold bonds for greenbacks and then destroyed the greenbacks. That is to say, he exchanged non-interest-bearing debt (as greenbacks were confusingly called) for interest-bearing debt.

The aim of Greenbackers was, of course, the exact opposite of McCulloch's. It was to increase the amount of government-created non-interest-bearing money as required to keep interest rates low, maintain full employment prosperity, and pay off the "profiteering and usurious" bondholders with money of no greater value than the money with which the bonds were purchased.

The most logically consistent and theoretically sound of the Greenbackers was Henry C. Carey, a Philadelphia entrepreneur, economist, and author. He has been called "the founder of The American School of Economics"; and when he died in 1879, *The Nation* spoke of him as "the writer who probably had more influence on the economic thinking of his countrymen than all other authors put together." In 1857 Karl Marx, with considerable exaggeration, called Carey "the only original economist among the North Americans" (1973, p. 884).

In *The Past Present and Future,* published in 1848, long before the issue of the first greenback, Carey wrote:

The larger the quantity of [money] the lower will be the rate of interest [and] the greater will be the facilities for constructing new roads and mills and the more rapid those exchanges from hand to hand which constitute commerce and for the making of which money is absolutely indispensable. (Unger 1964, p. 51)

In 1858, in *Principles of Social Science,* Carey said:

The high cost of borrowing money [due to an insufficiency in the money supply] causes a deduction from the profits of the trader, from the rents of houses, from the freight of ships. The owner of money, then, profits at the expense of all other capitalists. (Unger 1964, p. 51)

After the first issues of greenbacks, Carey wrote pamphlets aggregating over 1000 pages championing, as he saw it, the cause of entrepreneurs by the advocacy of monetary expansion and protectionism. More specifically, in 1866 he wrote that (1) expansion of the greenback issue should be government policy since inconvertible currency had been in good part responsible for victory in the Civil War and concurrent prosperity; (2) on the eve of the War, the country had been in the depths of a severe depression because the specie and banknotes in circulation had been insufficient to conduct the country's domestic business; (3) the scarcity of circulating media had enabled owners of money to charge such burdensome interest rates that entrepreneurs instead of increasing the number of factories had been compelled to restrict production; and (4) the depression had ended and production accelerated largely because of the government issue of greenbacks. Carey was an unrelenting opponent of greenback contraction and of resumption of the gold standard (Dorfman 1946, 3: 6; Unger 1964, p. 51).

Perhaps the next most noteworthy writer of the period was Alexander Campbell, a mining engineer and entrepreneur who credited most of his ideas, and properly so, to Edward Kellogg. While not a man of great originality, Campbell was an indefatigable pamphleteer and agitator. He was elected to Congress from Illinois for a single term on a Democrat-Independent ticket in 1874. In *The True Greenback* he wrote:

The war has resulted in the complete overthrow and utter extinction of chattel slavery on this continent, but it has not destroyed the principle of oppression and wrong. The old pro-slaver serpent, beaten in the South, crawled up North and put on anti-slavery clothes and established his headquarters in Wall Street where . . . he now, through bank monopolies and non-taxed bonds, rules the nation more despotically than under the old regime. . . . I assert . . . that an investment of a million dollars under the National Banking Law, or in non-taxed government securities, will yield a larger net income to its owner than a like amount invested in land and slaves employed in raising cotton and sugar did in the South in the palmiest days of the oligarchy. (1866, p. 31)

Campbell proposed an "interconvertible bond" scheme not dissimilar to that of Kellogg although he was willing to accept a higher range of interest rates than his mentor. More than others of his time, Campbell appreciated and tirelessly repeated Kellogg's contention that an interest rate in excess of the growth rate of the economy would redistribute income in favor of money lenders.

The present rates of interest are greatly in excess of the [rate of] increase in national wealth, and consequently oppressive and unjust to the producing classes. (Campbell 1866, p. 7)

I am persuaded that the present accumulative power of money greatly exceeds the increase in national wealth and is tending to the impoverishment and degradation of the industrial classes. (1866, p. 22)

Some of the other noteworthy opponents of the deflationary policies of the era are deserving of brief citation.

1. Congressman Frederick Pike of Maine who declared:

There is not a man in this country . . . that prefers a banknote [nonlegal tender] to a greenback [legal tender]. All of them are content with the money to which they have become accustomed and which costs the government nothing except the expense of making. (Sharkey 1967, p. 70)

2. Congressman Thaddeus Stevens, the staunch Republican advocate of "radical reconstruction" in the South, who in almost his final public act directed his withering scorn and sarcasm at repayment in gold of bonds purchased with depreciated greenbacks (Sharkey 1967, p. 86).

3. President Andrew Johnson: "An aristocracy based on nearly two and one-half billion dollars in national securities has risen in the northern states to assume that political control which was formerly given to the slave oligarchy" (Studenski and Krooss 1952, p. 161).

4. Congressman George H. Pendelton of Ohio:

There are now $300,000,000 in bonds in the Treasury as security for the National Currency of banks. The bonds are represented by a nearly equal number of banknotes. The bonds call for $18,000,000 in gold annually as interest. I maintain these bonds should be redeemed in greenbacks. The result would be that the greenbacks would take the place of the banknotes which would be called in and $18,000,000 of annual interest would be saved. . . .

To expand the currency when people are incurring debt and to contract the currency when they come to pay it, is public robbery, whether such be the motive or not. (Sharkey 1967, p. 100)

5. Simon Newcomb, astronomer and economist, who complained that the National Banking Act made the sovereign right over the currency a free gift to the national banks and deprived the government of the profit on the issue of currency (Dorfman 1946, 2: 977).

6. Francis Bowen, businessman, who decried the fact that "The government has borrowed huge sums in heavily depreciated paper dollars but agreed to repay them with an equal number of gold dollars" (Unger 1964, p. 63).

7. Simeon B. Chittenden who told the National Board of Trade in 1870,

Perhaps we should have resumed [the gold standard] at war's end but, had we resumed then, we should not have had the great development of railroads which has come as an incident to our paper money, and which may yet prove . . . that a great war and paper money may possibly be a great blessing. (Unger 1964, p. 166)

8. James C. Sylvis, president of the Iron Molders International Union and ardent "Campbellite" who said:

For twenty years I have been trying to . . . find the reason why a small portion of the population enjoyed ninety percent of the wealth of the nation, while the many whose labor produced everything, lived in poverty and want. The answer is interest. Interest . . . produces nothing; all it does is to transfer the products of labor to the pockets of the money lenders, bankers, and bondholders. (Unger 1964, pp. 106–107)

9. The Chicago newspaper *Workingman's Advocate,* 3 August 1867:

Every man who has a United States bond has just the same right as the bankers, or ought to have, to deposit it in Washington and receive notes for it, all the while drawing interest on it, as well as speculating with the money thus received. (Sharkey 1967, p. 196)

10. Monetary Commission created by Congress:

The true and only cause of the stagnation of industry and commerce now everywhere felt is . . . a shrinkage in the volume of money. . . . A rise in the value of money and a fall in general prices are the greatest evils which can befall the world. No fall in the value of metallic money nor a resulting rise in prices have ever proved other than a blessing to the world. (Myers 1970, p. 201; Nugent 1968, p 168)

11. The authors of the National Greenback-Labor party platform of 1878 who demanded that the government provide a supply of money "adequate to the full employment of labor, the equitable distribution of its products, and the requirements of business" (Unger 1964, p. 17).

12. The authors of the same party's platform of 1880 who wrote, "All money . . . should be issued by the government, and not by or through banking corporations, and when so issued should be full legal tender for all debts, public and private" (Unger 1864, p. 18).

13. Susan B. Anthony, Elizabeth Cady Stanton, Abby Hopper Gibbons, and Victoria Woodhull — women who one and all opposed Resumption and backed Campbell's Interconvertible Bond (Unger 1964, p. 108).

Another way of expressing the most fundamental point of view of Carey and many Greenbackers is to say that *the lack of money need never be an impediment to full employment and must never be allowed to be an impediment to full employment.* If at any time there should come to exist a will to end unemployment, as there once existed a will to win the Civil War, the necessary money could be similarly arranged. Greenbackers believed that most government policies after 1865 were such as to destroy prosperity, increase unemployment, depress wages, reduce the quantity of non-interest-bearing money in circulation, increase the quantity of interest-bearing money in circulation to the enrichment of bankers, and create a bonanza for a small but powerful class of speculators in government bonds.

The high tide in the greenback movement was reached in the congressional elections of 1878 when twenty-four representatives were elected on either the third party ticket or a fusion ticket with the Democrats. This, however, amounted to only about 8 percent of all representatives. In the presidential election of 1876, the third-party candidate, Peter Cooper, polled about 1 percent of the total. In the 1880 election, James B. Weaver polled about 3.4 percent.

These election statistics, however, are a poor measure of the overall accomplishments of the Greenbackers. Their influence on candidates of the

Democratic party was pervasive, and the support accorded them by many Democrats and a few Republicans gave them an influence far beyond that indicated by their poor showing as a third party. Nevertheless, from 1865 onward the secular trend moved in the direction of less government-created money and more bank-created money. The best the Greenbackers and their allies could accomplish was in the nature of delaying actions.

So much for the viewpoints of McCulloch and those like-minded on the one hand and Greenbackers and their allies on the other hand. But perhaps it should be mentioned here that there was something of a middle ground between the extremist deflationists and the extremist antideflationists, a middle ground that received little attention between 1865 and 1879. One could believe in the gold standard without necessarily believing that the pre-war gold content of the dollar (23.22 grains) was sacred. A compromise might have been possible—one that maintained the gold standard but redefined the dollar in terms of gold and reduced its gold content. Thus, for example, monetary historians Milton Friedman and Anna Schwartz have written: "Our own judgment in retrospect is that, given a gold standard was to be reestablished, it would have been preferable to have resumed at a parity . . . somewhere between the pre-war and end-of-war rate" (Friedman and Schwartz 1963, p. 80).

Another view not represented by either McCulloch or the Greenbackers was that of the Marxist Social Democratic Workingman's party. The party's newspaper, the *Labor Standard,* although having nothing favorable to say about McCulloch, denounced Greenbackers as "middle-class men" who had little sympathy for the problems of labor. "The disease from which we suffer is not the want of currency but a planless system of production," opined the editor (Unger 1964, p. 325).

The views of Greenbackers and Marxists differed substantially in other ways as well. Marxists saw class conflict as involving industrial workers versus "the capitalist class." To Greenbackers, however, the conflicting parties were "the producers" on the one hand and "bankers, bondholders, and the money barons" on the other. And "producers" included not only industrial workers but farmers and "capitalist entrepreneurs." Put another way, to Greenbackers the all-important distinction was one between creditors and debtors. It made no sense to Greenbackers for debtor entrepreneurs (whether engaged in farming or industry) to be placed in the same class as creditor bankers or other "parasitic money-lenders."

Perhaps only Henry Carey and a few other Greenbackers were fully aware of the theoretical implications of their position. Essentially they were arguing that the size of a nation's domestic money supply should be planned and controlled by government. Contrary to the view of advocates of the gold standard, free trade, and laissez faire, the size of the money supply should not be left to the chance discovery of domestic gold mines or to a favorable gold balance in international payments over which foreigners had substantial influence.

Monetary matters were a concern not only of the executive department of government, represented primarily by McCulloch, but also of Congress and the judicial branch. I consider these in reverse order.

As already discussed in Chapter 6, the value of money as a medium of exchange of goods and services is largely a function of the market forces of supply and demand. The value of money as a medium of payment of debts, however, is a legal matter only remotely related to market forces. The purchasing power of greenbacks in the marketplace fluctuated widely, as might have been expected, during the 1860s and 1870s; and the worth of greenbacks in the settlement of debts eventually came before the courts.

Here is a hypothetical case. On January 1, 1862, John Doe loaned Richard Roe $1000 in gold – in what was unquestionably "lawful money of the United States" at the time. This sum was to be repaid with interest at 5 percent compounded at the end of five years. Thus on January 1, 1867, Roe would owe Doe $1276. Suppose now that on the due date Roe offers Doe $1276 in greenbacks – "lawful money of the United States" by act of Congress. Doe refuses to accept payment on the grounds that it then takes $13 in greenbacks to purchase $10 in gold and that $1276 in greenbacks is worth only $982 in gold. Thus, Doe argues, payment in greenbacks would defraud him of $294. But how can he refuse payment in greenbacks if they are "lawful money of the United States?"

In a number of decisions, which historians call the "legal tender cases," the Supreme Court dealt with such matters as are suggested by the imaginary Doe–Roe controversy. Leaving aside numerous preliminary decisions and a host of legal technicalities, the first court ruling of historical interest came on February 7, 1870 in *Hepburn* v. *Griswold.* The overall effect was that the Legal Tender Acts were declared unconstitutional. In other words, the court ruled that the government cannot print money and make it legal tender for the payment of debts (Warren 1922, p. 233).

Because of the importance of this decision and of subsequent events, it is not without interest that *Hepburn* v. *Griswold* was decided by the narrow margin of four to three. Only seven justices voted because the size of the court had a short time earlier been reduced by Congress from nine to eight justices while a vacancy had occurred still later and not yet been filled.

After General Grant took office as president in March 1869, a full court was again declared to require nine justices. After two new justices had been appointed by Grant and approved by the Senate, the matter of the constitutionality of the Legal Tender Acts was reopened. On April 19, 1871, in *Knox* v. *Lee* the court reversed *Hepburn* v. *Griswold* by a five to four vote. The Legal Tender Acts were thus declared to be constitutional, and greenbacks were certified as "legal tender for the payment of debts" (Warren 1922, p. 247).

The reversal of a four to three court opinion by a five to four opinion, and reversal under rather bizarre circumstances, has long been a subject of controversy among historians. Controversy notwithstanding, the right of Congress to make paper money legal tender in payment of debts has remained "the law of the land" ever since *Knox* v. *Lee*. According to the opinion in this case, Richard Roe could discharge his debt to John Doe with what amounted to only $982 in gold, although both parties understood at the time the loan was made that $1276 in gold was intended. Members of the court were not unmindful that individual injustices of this nature would ensue from the *Knox* v. *Lee* decision; but "matters of state," the majority believed, transcended individual rights. As Justice Strong remarked:

If it be held by this Court that Congress has no constitutional power under any circumstances or in any contingency, to make treasury notes a legal tender for payment of all debts (a power confessedly possessed by every independent sovereignty other than the United States), then the government is without those means of self-preservation which, all must admit, may, in certain contingencies, become indispensable. (Warren 1922, p. 242)

Congress was as deeply involved in money matters as McCulloch and the Supreme Court. The Public Credit Act of 1869 promised that greenbacks and nearly all treasury issues would eventually be redeemed in coin. The Funding Act of 1870 authorized banks to increase banknotes from $300 million to $354 million. A Coinage Act passed in 1873 is discussed in the next chapter. The Resumption Act of 1875 brought nearer the day when greenbacks and bonds would actually be redeemed in coin.

Resumption was the stated policy of Congress and the president from 1875 on, and resumption was finally scheduled for January 1879. With the highly controversial election of 1876 that resulted in Rutherford Hayes assuming the presidency and with his appointment of John Sherman as secretary of the treasury, planning toward resumption proceeded apace. From 1875 to 1879, the interest-bearing debt of the federal government was increased $179 million despite budgetary surpluses of nearly $100 million. The money thus acquired was used to purchase gold for the purpose of redeeming greenbacks and paying off bonds as might be required once resumption became an accomplished fact. By December 1878, the treasury had on hand $170 million in gold.

In January 1879, gold payments were resumed as planned. Only a few holders of paper money demanded gold in its place. The nation was back on the gold standard at prewar parity after seventeen years with surprisingly little commotion on resumption day.

And now let us turn to what actually happened to the nation's money supply during the tumultuous years between 1865 and 1879. The period almost divides itself into two quite different subperiods — 1865 to 1869 and 1869 to 1879.

Money supply statistics for the first of these subperiods is given in Table 20.1. As can immediately be observed, deflation of the money supply was a principal characteristic of the four years. Total money underwent a contraction of $261 million — from $1.774 billion to $1.513 billion. And as may be

Table 20.1
Constituents of the Money Supply, 1865 and 1869

Year	Millions of Dollars				Percentage of Total			
	1865		1869		1865		1869	
COINS	$158		$ 98		8.9%		6.5%	
BCM	978		1067		55.1		70.5	
Banknotes		289		295		16.3		19.5
Deposits		689		772		38.8		51.0
GCM	638		348		36.0		23.0	
Greenbacks		379		315		21.4		20.8
Other		258		33		14.6		2.2
TOTAL	1774		1513		100.0		100.0	

Source: Bureau of the Census. 1975. *Historical Statistics of the United States—Colonial Times to 1970.* Washington, D.C.: U.S. Government Printing Office, p. 1114.
Note: BCM = bank-created money; GCM = government-created money

calculated, total money was thus reduced by about 3.9 percent per annum.

A closer study of the table reveals that the decrease in total money comprised a decrease of $60 million in coin circulation and of $290 million in GCM, offset by an increase of $89 million in BCM. McCulloch's policies actually reduced greenbacks and other government paper at a shocking annual rate of 14 percent while permitting bank paper to increase at 2.2 percent. Little wonder at the fury of the Greenbackers.

Partly because of the outcry of Greenbackers and partly because of other factors, the statistics for the 1869 to 1879 period are quite different, as Table 20.2 shows. Government paper in this period was made to contract at an annual rate of only 1.4 percent, compared to the earlier rate of 14 percent. And activity in the private sector caused bank paper to increase at 2.8 percent yearly. As a result of these changes, as well as an increase in coin circulation, the total money supply increased at an annual rate of 2.3 percent from 1869 to 1879 whereas it had declined at 3.9 percent from 1865 to 1869.

One might get the impression from the data of Table 20.2 that the 1870s could be called boom years. Such is not the case. According to monetary historians Friedman and Schwartz, real output of the economy reached new all-time highs in only five of the ten years. The other five years were marked by recession or depression, 1873 being a particularly bad year (Friedman and Schwartz 1982, p. 122).

In part the unrest of the period and the failure to achieve uninterrupted growth was due to unevenness in distribution of money throughout the country, as well as slow growth of the overall money supply. Per capita circulation of national currency in 1866 was $33.30 for the area from Philadel-

Table 20.2
Constituents of the Money Supply, 1869 and 1879

	Millions of Dollars		Percentage of Total	
Year	1869	1879	1869	1879
COINS	$ 98	$ 196	6.5%	10.3%
BCM	1067	1401	70.5	73.8
Banknotes	295	321	19.5	16.9
Deposits	772	1080	51.0	56.9
GCM	348	302	23.0	15.9
Greenbacks	315	302	20.8	15.9
Other	33	0	2.2	0.0
TOTAL	**1513**	**1899**	**100.0**	**100.0**

Source: Bureau of the Census. 1975. *Historical Statistics of the United States — Colonial Times to 1970.* Washington, D.C.: U.S. Government Printing Office, p. 1114.

Note: BCM = bank-created money; GCM = government-created money

phia to Boston, $6.36 for seven midwestern states, and $1.70 for ten southern states. The per capita figure for Rhode Island was $77.16 but that for Arkansas only $0.13. In 1869 there were 829 national banks in Pennsylvania, New York, Massachusetts, and Ohio but only 26 in eight of the states of the former Confederacy. Southerners believed the National Banking Act and the taxation of the banknotes of state-chartered banks were particularly designed to cripple them financially, but states of the midwest and far west were hurt as well. States of the interior and far west were less accustomed to checks and credit instruments than eastern states. They depended more on paper currency and thus were doubly injured by its uneven distribution (Sharkey 1959, pp. 235–237; Nugent 1968, p. 138; Goodwyn 1976, p. 27).

I have not been able to find any statistics on real gross domestic product (GDP) for the period prior to 1869. From 1869 to 1879, however, real GDP is said to have increased at the high average annual rate of 5.1 percent, despite recession years and an average annual decline in the price level of 3.3 percent (Friedman and Schwartz 1982, p. 122). Because the amount given for the rate of growth of real GDP is based on estimates, it may be inaccurate; but there can be little doubt that the price level declined substantially and that despite this fact the real GDP grew significantly.

During the fourteen years 1865–1879, the real GDP of the United States came to equal, if not exceed, that of any other country in the world; but people remained very poor by later standards. Per capita income in 1990 was $21,900. In terms of 1990 dollars, per capita income in 1879 was $3,090. And the great majority of people, since income was as unevenly distributed then as it is now, had annual incomes of much less than $3,000.

Between 1865 and 1869, exports of merchandise increased at a spectacular average annual rate of 12 percent. Steel production was 70 times greater in 1879 than it had been in 1865. The number of farms increased by more than 50 percent. The period was replete with events of great significance – the completion of the first transatlantic telegraph cable in 1866 and the first transcontinental railroad in 1869; the purchase of Alaska in 1867, increasing the territory of the United States by almost a fifth; the invention of the typewriter in 1873, the telephone in 1876, and the phonograph in 1877.

The achievements of the 1865 to 1879 period, often in the face of very adverse circumstances, were little short of amazing. To the extent the quantity of money had anything to do with these achievements, they were due almost entirely to irredeemable paper money – to an "unsound currency" – not to gold. To a very significant extent, they were due to irredeemable paper money created by government – greenbacks.

Chapter 21

Bimetallism and Populism, 1879–1896

An outstanding characteristic of the 1865–1879 period, as we have seen, was that many people in the debtor class tried and failed to arrange matters so as to pay off their own debts and the Union's Civil War debt with interest-free money in the form of greenbacks. This effort continued thoughout the 1879–1896 period, although its champions were often called Populists rather than Greenbackers. A more outstanding characteristic of the later period, however, was the attempt of many people in the debtor class to so arrange matters as to pay off their own debts and the government's with cheap money in the form of silver. They were called bimetallists or silverites, and the defeat of William Jennings Bryan in the presidential election of 1896 signaled both their failure and a defeat of Populism.

The nomenclature of the period fits the facts only very loosely. The terminology that is most telling, I believe, distinguishes three broad categories — monometallists, bimetallists, and, let us say, nonmetallists.

The monometallists one and all were gold standard advocates. Bankers, bondholders, and creditors generally were monometallists. Most members of the academic community, particularly those concerned with "political economy," were also "gold bugs." So were most members of the clergy. Gold was widely regarded among them as "God's money" although, curiously, silver was not.

The bimetallists all advocated a legal tender status of one sort or another for silver as well as gold. Among them were nondebtor owners of silver mines and a considerable portion of the debtor class, including some Populists.

The nonmetallists were opposed to both other categories and in fact opposed to any commodity money, metallic or otherwise. Among them were

Greenbackers, some Populists, and others of the debtor class.

The monometallists—the creditors, the moneyed class—eventually prevailed, in part at least because their opposition was split into two principal groups, and each of these into a confusion of subgroups. The bimetallists are considered first, the nonmetallists later.

It must again be emphasized that the fundamental difficulty with a monetary system based on a precious metal is that ordinarily and in the long run the supply of gold or silver cannot be made to increase at a steady and optimum rate—the rate at which modern economies are capable of growing in real terms. Thus a system of either gold or silver monometallism is incapable of providing a money supply that grows sufficiently to accommodate even moderately steady economic growth at constant prices.

If in the long run the gold supply increases only 1.15 percent per annum and silver only 1.2 percent, as is shown in Chapter 2, the supply of gold plus silver increases by only about 1.17 percent. Thus a bimetallic system is subject to the same basic objection as a monometallic system. It is subject to an additional objection, as is pointed out in Chapter 13—the historical evidence shows that the ratio of the value of gold to that of silver for any number of reasons, always changes with the passage of time. Thus, in the case of a bimetallic system, either the official ratio of gold to silver must be altered or the cheaper metal will drive the dearer metal out of circulation. If the government-determined mint ratios are tampered with from time to time, the system is not automatic or consistent with laissez-faire principles; and if the ratios are not tampered with, a de jure bimetallic system tends to evolve into a de facto monometallic system.

As noted in Chapter 16, in 1834 Congress established the official value of gold at $20.67 per troy ounce and that of silver at one-sixteenth that amount, about $1.29 per troy ounce. The bimetallists of our period wanted free coinage of all gold or silver brought to the mint at these values. Since there was no controversy about free coinage of gold at $20.67 per ounce, the bimetallist program boiled down to a demand for free coinage of silver at $1.29 per ounce.

This was hardly a subject worth discussing before 1874, inasmuch as before that year the price of silver bullion fluctuated above $1.29. With the price of silver at $1.36 in 1859, for example, no one would care to take $1.36 in silver to the mint and receive a coin worth only $1.29 in gold. Between 1834 and 1860 overvalued silver was driven out of circulation, and a de facto gold monometallism came to prevail.

With discovery of the Comstock Lode and other silver sources, annual output of silver in the United States soared. Almost simultaneously, Germany adopted a gold standard, demonetized silver, stopped buying silver, and began selling its monetary stock of silver. The increasing supplies of silver, together with softer demand, affected prices adversely as Table 21.1 shows.

Had the 1834 mint prices and ratios prevailed in 1896, anyone could have

Table 21.1
Silver Production and Prices in the United States

Period	Production Millions of Ounces	Average Price $ per Troy Oz.
1856-1860	.310	1.348
1861-1865	28.810	1.341
1866-1870	49.112	1.324
1871-1875	95.453	1.292
1876-1880	157.681	1.156
1881-1885	182.841	1.112
1886-1890	231.819	.979
1891-1895	287.057	.786
1896-1900	279.544	.612

Source: Bureau of the Census. 1975. *Historical Statistics of the United States—Colonial Times to 1970.* Washington, D.C.: U.S. Government Printing Office, p. 606.

bought an ounce of silver for 64.5 cents, taken it to the mint, and doubled his money by having it coined into a silver dollar worth $1.29 in gold. In other words, debtors could have discharged their obligations with a money that was very cheap indeed.

Creditors, who bought treasury bonds with cheap money in the form of greenbacks during the Civil War, managed afterward to so arrange things that they would be paid with dear money in the form of gold, often doubling their purchasing power. "Turn about is fair play," thought the debtors who borrowed dear money and envisioned repaying in cheap silver. Owners of silver mines were also as eager as debtors to have 64.5 cents worth of their silver converted into a coin worth twice as much in gold or other legal tender.

Not only were debtors as eager to rip off their creditors as the government's creditors had earlier been to rip off the government; they had, or thought they had, a strong legal basis for paying bondholders in silver. For many of the government's debts, still amounting to over $2 billion in 1880, specified only that they should be paid in "specie" or in "coin"; and silver seemed to meet this criterion as well as gold.

When the bimetallists began to warm to possibilities of cheap silver, they discovered to their chagrin that in 1873, in an act of Congress little noticed or debated at the time, silver had been demonetized in the United States and the country placed on a de facto, although not officially proclaimed, gold standard. When they discovered it, bimetallists denounced the act that demonetized silver as the "Crime of '73." The demonetization of silver was described as the result of a secret plot hatched by monometallist bondholding scoundrels.

Table 21.2
Silver Coins and Silver Certificates in Money Supply (Average Amounts in Millions of Dollars)

Period	Coins	Certificates	Total
1870-1875	$ 15.0	$ 0.0	$ 15.0
1976-1880	48.7	1.2	49.9
1881-1885	81.3	72.8	154.1
1886-1890	105.0	197.2	302.2
1891-1895	116.6	321.5	438.1

Source: Bureau of the Census. 1975. *Historical Statistics of the United States—Colonial Times to 1970.* Washington, D.C.: U.S. Government Printing Office, p. 994.

There exists a large literature on the "Crime of '73," and the controversy over it cannot be said to be entirely dead yet. What the record seems to show, however, is that some very alert creditors foresaw the probability of cheaper silver in the not-distant future and the possibility they might be required to accept repayment of their loans in cheap money. They therefore proposed demonetizing silver in 1873 in order to forestall this possibility. But there was nothing secret about the act of Congress that accomplished this end. The bimetallists, to the extent there were any bimetallists in 1873, were simply caught napping. Of course, although the monometallists in Congress were quite open about printing and distributing copies of the proposal to demonetize silver and doing so for a considerable time before Congress voted on it, they made no great effort to explain clearly and in detail all the reasons for and implications of their proposal.

The bimetallists failed completely in their efforts to establish free coinage of silver into legal tender coins at the ratio of sixteen to one, or any other ratio. Their agitation and political activities, however, were not entirely without effect. The silverite-sponsored Bland-Allison Act of 1878, for example, instructed the secretary of the treasury to buy between 2 and 4 million ounces of silver per month at the prevailing market price, and actual purchases thereafter averaged about 2.5 million ounces per month. The Silver Purchase Act of July 1890 specified that the secretary should purchase 4 million ounces each month. The result of these acts was a large increase in the number of silver coins and silver certificates in circulation, as Table 21.2 shows.

Over a twenty-year period, the circulation of silver coins and certificates was increased at the astonishing average rate of 18.4 percent per year. From 1879 to 1896, the ratio of the dollar value of all silver coins and certificates in circulation to the value of all gold coins and certificates increased from 1.12:1 to 1.82:1.

The silver that the treasury purchased pursuant to the act of 1878 was all bought for less than $1.29 per ounce as the act directed, but it was then used to pay government obligations with coins or certificates that could be exchanged for gold worth $1.29. Silver certificates bore the words: "Receivable for Customs, Taxes, and All Public Dues" and thus the silver certificates were not full legal tender. Nevertheless a $5 silver certificate could be exchanged at the treasury for 5 silver dollars or a $5 legal tender greenback or a $5 legal tender goldpiece. Many banks, however, segregated silver deposits and refused to pay them in gold.

The silver that the treasury purchased pursuant to the act of 1890, because of the continuing fall in the price of silver, was all bought for even less than the earlier price. It was put into storage, and for each ounce stored, $1.29 in treasury notes was issued and then used to pay government obligations. These notes bore the words: "Receivable at face value in payment of all debts public and private except when otherwise expressly stipulated in the contract." By 1893 almost $141 million in these treasury notes had been issued. Silver purchased pursuant to the act of 1890, unlike that purchased pursuant to the act of 1878, resulted in an increase in the amount of legal tender in circulation.

Pursuant to the acts of 1878 and 1890, therefore, the treasury paid for most of the silver it bought by printing money—money that had a face value and an exchange value much greater than the actual cost of the silver the treasury purchased. That is to say, some government obligations were paid with money the treasury had obtained cheaply but directly or indirectly provided full legal tender value to the recipient. It has been estimated that the treasury realized a profit of $70 million on its silver purchases under the Bland-Allison Act (Walton and Robertson 1983, p. 330).

The acts of 1878 and 1890 benefited not only the treasury but also the owners of silver mines. It made the sale of their output easier, and purchases by the treasury boosted the demand side of the market and kept silver prices from sinking even lower. Furthermore, there was even some benefit to debtors generally in that the total amount of money in circulation became more plentiful.

The Silver Purchase Act of 1890 was repealed in October 1893. Between then and Bryan's defeat in November 1896, only a few silver dollars were coined, and only a few new silver certificates and no new treasury notes were issued. Silver dollars, incidentally, were never very popular except in some few areas where there were silver mines. "The preference for paper money is so strong that neither silver or gold is demanded in place of it," wrote Treasury Secretary Sherman (Myers 1970, p. 213).

Although the bimetallists were decisively and lastingly defeated in 1896, they had profoundly affected treasury monetary policy over a period of nearly two decades. Although they lost their war, they meanwhile won a few battles and had much to show for their efforts. The same can hardly be said of the nonmetallists.

The period when the Greenback party was an organization of even minor importance extended from 1875 to 1884. Even then, the party's influence was slight west of the Mississippi and south of the Mason-Dixon Line, and it numbered relatively few farmers in its ranks. Beginning about 1887, Greenbacker ideas came to be increasingly embraced in precisely those areas where earlier there had been few adherents and increasingly advocated by farmers.

Most of the twenty-five or so years after 1870 were very difficult for farmers. An index of wholesale prices of farm products fell from 128 in 1869 to 72 in 1879 and then to a low of 39.6 in 1896. Wheat sold for $1.79 per bushel in 1873 and for $0.60 in 1894 (BC 1975, pp. 200, 208). But these prices are annual averages; at harvest time in the 1890s, a Dakota farmer often could get no more than $0.35 for a bushel of wheat. Not only was money far from plentiful on the farm, it could be borrowed by farmers only at interest rates that ranged as high as 36 percent (Goodwyn 1976, p. 114). Any scheme involving a more plentiful supply of money and thus, it was hoped, involving higher prices for farm produce and lower interest rates, any scheme hostile to "usurious bankers and money-lenders," found an attentive ear among agrarians.

Hostility to bankers was paralleled by an infuriated opposition to railroads. "The government had given four western railroads as much land as Ohio, Indiana, Michigan, and Wisconsin together, in addition to millions of dollars in loans or outright subsidies" (Myers 1970, p. 198). Farmers felt the giveaways to railroads excessive, but what rankled most were the high freight rates they were charged. "Large elevator companies transported grain from Chicago to England for less money than it cost a Dakota farmer to send his wheat to Minneapolis" (Myers 1970, p. 115).

Thus it came about that ideas implying the nationalization of money creation, such as greenbackism, were often embraced along with an accompanying demand for nationalization of the railroads. The platform of the People's Party of America in 1892, for example, called for "a national currency, safe, sound, and flexible, issued by the General Government only, a full legal tender for all debts, public and private, and this without the use of banking corporations. . . . the government to own and operate the railraods in the interest of the people (McPherson 1892, p. 271). The Knights of Labor, presided over by Terence Powderly, advocated similar measures although with less energy (Wiebe 1967, p. 68).

Along with some fairly clear programmatic ideas, there was a great deal of confusion and inconsistency in the Populist party's platform. Another plank, for example, called for "free and unlimited coinage of silver and gold at the present legal ratio of sixteen to one." The party tried at one and the same time to embrace nonmetallist greenbackism and bimetallist free silver. One historian of the period noted that the Republican party leaned toward gold monometallism, the Democratic party toward silver bimetallism, and the Populist party toward greenback nonmetallism. There were, however, many and significant exceptions in each party (Goodwyn 1976, p. 452).

The confusion and turbulence of the times are perhaps best shown by the fact that in 1890 Populists in Kansas won 324 races to only 71 for Republicans. In the next election, Republicans won 277 races and the Populists only 127 (Goodwyn 1976, p. 317). In the deep South, however, the opponent of the Populist party or the People's party was the Democratic party, and wide swings in preference occurred there as in Kansas.

Although the Greenback Era was characterized by notable theoreticians such as Carey and Campbell, the subsequent period produced no outstanding advocates of monometallism. Although Ignatius Donnelly is sometimes mentioned, the most notable commentator on money of the 1880s and 1890s was probably C. W. Macune of Texas, although one historian dismisses Macune as an "opportunistic nomad" (Wiebe 1967, p. 74).

Just as Carey, for example, aimed to speak for "the producing classes" of the Northeast (entrepreneurs and workers) without much attention to agrarians, Macune spoke mainly for farmers and showed only a peripheral interest in the problems of industrial workers or factory owners. The Farmer's Alliance, for which Macune became spokesman, expanded rapidly for a few years after 1887. The purpose of the alliance was to cope with the principal problem of farmers—inadequate and too costly credit. The system that victimized farmers was at its most vicious in the cotton-producing South, but it worked with only a difference in degree where farmers of corn or wheat in the Midwest were concerned. At the depressed prices of the time, farmers often received so little for their crops that they were forced not only to borrow money to sustain themselves until the next crop could be sold but also to borrow for the machinery and seed needed to plant the next crop. Many farmers were perpetually in debt to banks or "factors" or "furnishing merchants" who made loans and bought crops. Many farmers were constrained to sell when crops matured, only to see prices rise by 20 or 25 percent by the following spring or summer.

Macune proposed what amounted to a crop withholding scheme, a plan whereby farmers would mortgage their crops to the government rather than to banks or others at low rather than exorbitant rates of interest. His plan called for the erection of federal government warehouses in every county in the country that produced $500,000 worth of agricultural commodities. In these warehouses, farmers would store their produce and await higher prices before selling. Farmers would be charged small fees for grading, storage, and insurance and pay interest at the rate of only 2 percent per annum. The government would advance farmers legal tender "certificates of deposit" for an amount up to 80 percent of the local market price. Thus the plan, it has been said, "represented the political equivalent of full-scale greenbackism for farmers" (Goodwyn 1976, p. 152; see also Wiebe 1967, p. 72).

Harry Tracy, an associate of Macune and also a Texan, pointed out that officials of the treasury under Grover Cleveland had made $47 million available to the New York Clearing House Association at 1 percent interest in order to bail out eastern commercial banks.

If the government can loan these bankers at 1 per cent interest on their collateral [wrote Tracy], why can't the government loan it to the people on their collateral. . . . What a burlesque on democratic government for 4000 men, because they are rich, to enjoy privileges that are denied to 65,000,000 people. (Goodwyn 1976, p. 369)

The Farmer's Alliance was a cultural as well as political movement. It emphasized cooperation, self-education, shared hope, and aspirations for human dignity. It was, however, essentially an organization of whites, and it was often extremely racist. It everywhere championed grassroots influence over the monetary system. "The national banks [said S. M. Adams of the Alabama State Farmer's Alliance] were conceived in sin and born in diabolical iniquity." Feelings ran high on all sides of the controversies of the 1890s. Theodore Roosevelt even went so far as to advocate "taking ten or a dozen of [the Populist] leaders out, standing them against a wall, and shooting them dead" (Wiebe 1967, p. 96).

In 1892 the Populist candidate for president, General James Weaver, polled over a million votes; and five states cast one or more electoral votes for him. It is significant that no state not organized by the Farmer's Alliance developed a strong Populist movement (Goodwyn 1976, p. 254). By 1896, however, the third party "money parties" were supporters of the Democratic party's champion of bimetallism, William Jennings Bryan—a rather confused opponent of national banks and supporter of state-chartered banks. The popular vote that year was about 48 percent for Bryan and 52 percent for Republican William McKinley.

Farmers, of course, were not the only ones with problems during the years between 1879 and 1896. Unemployment was an often severe problem. Thus another important event of the era was the introduction into both the House and Senate of what I believe was the first "full-employment" legislation in the nation's history. H.R. 7438 (53rd Congress, 2nd Session, June 12, 1894) was perhaps the most significant result of the march on Washington by "Coxey's Army" of the unemployed. The writing and introduction of this legislation was primarily due to Coxey's efforts. It provided for the printing by the U.S. Treasury of $500 million in legal tender notes good for payment of all debts public or private. This money was to be spent on the public roads of the nation. "All citizens of the United States making application to labor shall be employed," the bill stated. Further, "All labor . . . shall be paid . . . not less than one dollar and fifty cents per day for common labor and three dollars and fifty cents for team and labor [and] eight hours per day shall constitute a day's labor."

Here was "Keynesianism" long before Keynes, but with the financing of the government as "employer of the last resort" far better conceived than by Keynes—the full employment was to be financed by government money cre-

Table 21.3
Constituents of the Money Supply, 1879 and 1896

Year	Millions of Dollars		Percentage of Total	
	1879	1896	1879	1896
COINS & CERT.	$ 196	$ 940	10.3%	18.9%
Gold	126	497	6.6	10.0
Silver	70	443	3.7	8.9
BCM	1401	3675	73.8	74.0
Banknotes	321	215	16.9	4.3
Deposits	1080	3460	56.9	69.7
GCM	302	351	15.9	7.1
Greenbacks	302	256	15.9	5.2
Other	0	95	0.0	1.9
TOTAL	1899	4966	100.0	100.0

Source: Bureau of the Census. 1975. *Historical Statistics of the United States—Colonial Times to 1970.* Washington, D.C.: U.S. Government Printing Office, p. 1114.
Note: BCM = bank-created money; GCM = government-created money

ation rather than, as Keynes would have it, by government borrowing. But, of course, H.R. 7438 had no real chance of being passed; it never even got out of committee.

Neither the nonmetallist efforts of agrarians like Macune nor those of working-class advocates like Coxey had much significant or lasting effect on monetary affairs between 1879 and 1896. To the extent the monometallists encountered even minor setbacks during the era, they came at the hands of the bimetallists. Overall in this period, as in those before and after it, gold standard advocates prevailed.

Table 21.3 shows that the fastest-growing component of the money supply between 1879 and 1896 was silver. The rate of increase in silver was 11.5 percent per year on average, and no other component increased at anywhere near this rate. On the other hand, the component comprising greenbacks and other government-created money amounted to less than half the percentage of the total in 1896 than it amounted to in 1879. These figures show the partial success of bimetallist agitation and the almost total failure of nonmetallists' efforts toward more money creation by government.

Perhaps the most portentous showing of Table 21.3, however, is the increasing importance of bank deposits as a component of the total money supply. This component increased by 7.1 percent per annum on average. Paying by checks drawn on banks continued slowly to supersede paying by coins or paper money. In 1888 even the treasury ceased demanding payment of taxes or other dues in legal tender and began accepting payment by check.

By 1890, over 90 percent of the dollar value of all transactions in the country was being paid by check (Myers 1970, p. 200).

In 1895, Brooks Adams, great-great-grandson of President John Adams, published *The Law of Civilization and Decay* in which he wrote:

With the advent of the bankers, a profound change came over civilization, for contraction began. Self-interest had from the outset taught the producer that, to prosper, he should deal in wares that tended rather to rise than fall in value, relative to coin. The opposite instinct possessed the usurer; he found that he grew rich when money appreciated, or when the borrower had to part with more property to pay his debt when it fell due, than the cash lent him would have bought on the day the obligation was contracted. (pp. 261–262)

All during the 1865–1896 era, it usually happened that the borrowers had to part with more property to pay their debts than the cash lent them would have bought at the time it was borrowed. In part, at least, this very happy era for creditors was due to the success of usurers and their dupes in thwarting every effort by "the producing classes" to bring about the more rapid increases in the money supply that would have stopped the persistent fall in the price level.

Gold Discoveries and
Other Matters, 1896–1914

By pure coincidence, at about the same time that the nonmetallists and bi-metallists were defeated and the gold monometallists triumphant, gold was discovered in Alaska, the Yukon, and South Africa. Simultaneously, improved methods of separating gold from ores were developed. The amount of gold in the United States began to increase rapidly, and the total money supply of the country, now officially linked to gold, likewise increased rapidly. During the same period, but without similar significance, the rate of increase in the production of silver declined. Relevant statistics are supplied by Table 22.1.

From the first fifteen-year period shown by Table 22.1 to the second, gold production slowed while silver production more than doubled; whereas from the second period to the third, gold production more than doubled and silver production slowed. It was, of course, the faster growth of gold rather than the slower growth of silver that was more significant.

World production of gold increased as well as United States production. The gold stock of the world is estimated to have more than doubled from

Table 22.1
Multiples of Growth in Production of Silver and Gold in the United States

From	To	Gold	Silver
1865-1880	1881-1896	0.81x	2.26X
1881-1896	1897-1912	2.32x	1.18x

Source: Bureau of the Census. 1975. *Historical Statistics of the United States – Colonial Times to 1970.* Washington, D.C.: U.S. Government Printing Office, p. 606.

1890 to 1914, growing at an average rate of about 3.5 percent a year (Friedman and Schwartz 1963, p. 137).

A gold standard, observed de facto since 1879, was embraced de jure in the United States by the Gold Standard Act of March 14, 1900. According to this legislation, the standard of value was declared to be "the dollar consisting of twenty-five and eight-tenths grains of gold nine-tenths fine" (Krooss 1983, 3: 119).

> In point of direct material serviceability, no doubt, a fresh supply of gold is one of the least useful forms of wealth to the production of which industrial effort can be directed, but for the purposes of business prosperity at large it is probably the most serviceable addition that can be made to the aggregate wealth. (Veblen 1978, p. 235)

These words of Thorstein Veblen in 1904 are undoubtedly true under the presumption of a gold standard monetary system. For a faster growth in the supply of gold, the "reserve money" of the banking system makes possible faster growth in overall money supply. To see the effect of this, it is particularly instructive to compare the fourteen years 1882–1896 to the period of similar length 1896–1910. In the first period the gold supply increased at an annual rate of 2.3 percent and the overall money supply at 3.8 percent. In the second period, the gold supply increased at an annual rate of 7.6 percent and the overall money supply at 8.1 percent.

As Veblen also wrote, the more rapid growth of the money supply meant more rapid growth in spending or aggregate demand. Increased aggregate demand always results either in an increase in production to satisfy that demand or in higher prices of commodities to soak up the demand, or both. Thus, although real output increased at an average annual rate of only 1.8 percent in the fourteen years from 1882 to 1896, in the ensuing fourteen years the rate jumped to 4.6 percent. The fourteen-year period preceding 1896 was one of the least prosperous periods of such length in U.S. history, and the period of the same length following 1896 was one of the most prosperous.

In the fourteen years ending in 1896, real output grew more slowly than population, and per capita real output was less in 1896 than 1882, decreasing by 0.3 percent per annum. By contrast, in the fourteen years beginning with 1896, real output increased more rapidly than population, and real per capita output ended the period 41 percent above the 1896 level; its average annual rate of increase being 2.6 percent (Friedman and Schwartz 1982, pp. 122–123). This and more are best revealed by Graph 22.1, which shows curves for index numbers of total money supply and per capita real output for the periods 1882–1896 and 1896–1910.

Whether populist agitation would have resumed after Bryan's defeat in 1896 if money growth and real output growth had remained sluggish we will never know, although it seems most probable. What really sealed the immediate fate of the bimetallist and nonmetallist movements, however, was the rapid growth of the gold supply, the total money supply, and real per capita

Graph 22.1
Growth of Money Supply and Per Capita Output, 1882–1896 and 1896–1910

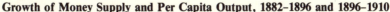

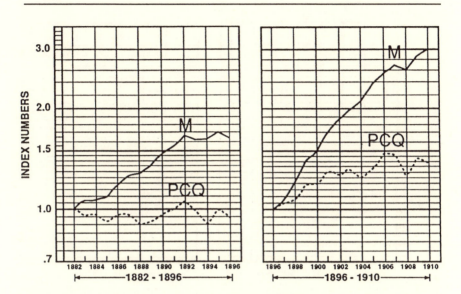

Source: Friedman, Milton, and Anna J. Schwartz. 1982. *Monetary Trends in the United States and the United Kingdom.* Princeton, N.J.: Princeton University Press, pp. 122–123.
Note: M = total money supply; PCQ = per capita real output

output after 1896. The "soft money" movements had been responses to "tight money" and slow economic growth; with "easy money" and faster real economic growth, their raison d'etre vanished. Although they were decisively defeated in 1896, what happened immediately thereafter proved that the "soft money" advocates were essentially right all along. Their argument during the years preceding 1896 that the nation's money supply was growing too slowly (that more greenbacks should be printed or more silver monetized) appears to have been entirely correct. For just as soon as the money supply began to increase more rapidly, per capita output (and hence per capita income) began to increase. There can be little doubt that if the soft money advocates had been more successful and the money supply had increased much faster than it did between 1882 and 1896 then incomes would have been greater and the years altogether more prosperous.

To keep in perspective the changes in per capita output or income during the periods at issue, it may be noted that per capita income in 1990 in 1990 dollars was $21,920. By contrast, PCQ in 1882 was $3506; in 1896, $3380; and in 1910, $4834. With PCQ $126 less in 1896 than in 1882, the unrest among agrarians and urban workers is readily understandable.

It must also be remembered in this context that per capita income in terms of real purchasing power is very much less than a perfect measure of the ac-

Graph 22.2
Growth of Money Supply, Total Output, and the Price Level, 1882–1896 and 1896–1910

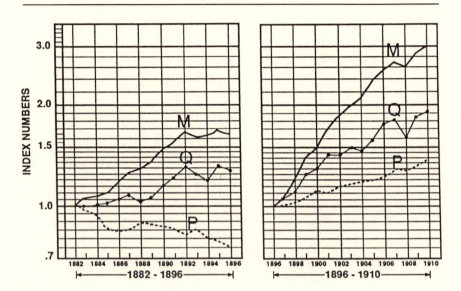

Source: Friedman, Milton, and Anna J. Schwartz. 1982. *Monetary Trends in the United States and the United Kingdom.* Princeton, N.J.: Princeton University Press, pp. 122–123.
Note: M = total money supply; Q = real output; P = price level

tual welfare of most individuals. It takes no account of the fact that the "robber barons"—the "captains of industry and finance"—the Carnegies, Vanderbilts, Morgans, Goulds, Harrimans, and Rockefellers—increased their real incomes very much faster than the average person, and the great majority of urban and rural working people increased their real incomes much more slowly than the average. At a time when the distribution of income between rich and poor changes rapidly, as it did in our subject periods, per capita income amounts tend to be misleading.

The contrast between the years preceding 1896 and subsequent years is also manifest in many other ways. The further significance of 1896 as a watershed year is perhaps best shown by Graph 22.2. Here we see curves in terms of index numbers for total money supply, real output, and the general level of prices for the fourteen years before and after 1896.

* * *

We have already noted the very much more rapid growth of M in the second period than the first. This difference accounts for the great differences in the growth trends of Q and P in the two periods.

Before we discuss the overall trends in Q and P, however, two details should be noted. The first is the sharp contraction in M from 1892 to 1893 that made 1893 an unusually distressful year. Observe from Graph 22.2 that the result of the contraction in M was an even sharper contraction in Q. Similarly it may be observed that in 1908 there occurred another contraction of the money supply and another even sharper contraction in Q. Such year-long contractions in the money supply are rare, and they are always accompanied by contractions in Q. It may not always be possible to increase Q_r by simply increasing M_r; but it seems always possible to decrease Q_r simply by decreasing M_r.

Two other matters of very special interest to students of economic trends are shown by the curves for M, Q, and P for the 1882–1896 period in Graph 22.2. First, substantial real economic growth (Q growth) occurred despite an almost steadily falling price level. Second, this was a period of negative correlation between money and prices. Let us consider these two features of this period in greater detail.

On average from 1882 to 1896 the general price level declined nearly 2 percent per year. As often mentioned, falling prices tend to affect adversely borrowers in general and entrepreneurs in particular — tend to make it more difficult for them to realize a satisfactory profit. When prices decline 2 percent per year, persons who borrowed money at the nominal rate of, say, 7 percent are forced to pay a "real" rate of 9 percent. The increasing burdensomeness of debt during a time of falling prices is perhaps best illustrated by the fact that it took a farmer twice as many bushels of wheat to pay a debt of a given number of dollars in 1894 as in 1882. The fact that Q was able to increase 1.8 percent per year from 1882 to 1896 while prices declined over 1.9 percent per year seems to show that many entrepreneurs were able to reduce costs and maintain profitability despite falling prices — something ordinarily very difficult to accomplish. This they were able to do by constant introduction of improved machinery and improved methods of production and by crushing most labor opposition to their frequent wage cuts.

It may be mentioned in passing that very much the same thing that is shown by Graph 22.2 for the fourteen year 1882–1896 period was also true for the twenty-seven year 1869–1896 period. That is to say, for this longer period it was also true that in the average year Q increased even though prices fell. There is no other period in U.S. economic history of anywhere near comparable length when this occurred.

Now let us turn from the unusual negative correlation between real growth and the price level to the equally (or even more) unusual negative correlation between changes in money supply and changes in the price level that characterized the 1882–1896 period. As remarked in earlier chapters, no idea in economic theory is more widely or stubbornly or perversely held than that "the dominant influence and ultimately the whole influence of monetary change is on prices rather than output" (Friedman and Schwartz 1982, p. 8).

As also earlier remarked, this idea encompasses a belief that growth of output Q depends entirely on "real" factors (such as natural resources, labor supply, progress in science and technology, and so on) and not at all on monetary factors; the price level P, on the other hand, is asserted to depend entirely on monetary factors and not at all on real factors. In everyday usage, this way of viewing the matter means that any increase in the money supply is "monetary inflation" and any increase in the price level is "price inflation" and that "price inflation" is "ultimately and solely" due to "monetary inflation."

Yet we see from Graph 22.2 that for the 1882–1896 period the money supply increased about 65 percent; but instead of likewise increasing about 65 percent as the misconceived theory requires, the price level declined by about 25 percent. It may be added that for the twenty-seven years from 1869 to 1896 the money supply more than tripled (increased 3.4-fold). If "the whole influence of monetary change is on prices rather than output," then the price level should have more than tripled. Instead, the price level did not even double. It declined, and it declined rather steadily and uniformly. Of the period 1869–1896, as well as the 1882–1896 period, it would have been far more nearly true to say "the whole influence of monetary change is on output rather than prices" rather than the opposite.

Let us now compare the curves for 1896–1910 to those of 1882–1896. Here we see that a little more than doubling of the annual rate of money growth (from 3.8 to 8.1 percent) resulted in a little more than doubling in the annual Q growth rate (from 1.9 to 4.5 percent). Again the responsiveness of Q to increases in M is illustrated. But we must also note a significant increase in the P growth rate (from -1.9 to $+2.2$ percent). Entrepreneurs responded to increased aggregate demand not only by producing more but also by raising prices.

It is important to remember, however, that there are real constraints on how fast Q can grow. Once full employment of the labor force is reached, further increases in output become very difficult. Thus it seems only reasonable to presume that if the rate of money growth were again doubled (from 8 to 16 percent) most of the effect of the increased rate would be on prices rather than output.

The point, again, is that Q always declines when M declines, and Q never grows unless M grows; but this does not mean that Q can always be increased by simply increasing M. Beyond the point where the real constraints on Q growth become significant, increases in M tend to increase P more than Q. An excessive rate of money growth can undoubtedly cause demand-pull price rises, just as a negative rate of money growth can undoubtedly cause Q to decline, or just as a switch from a fast to a slow rate of money growth can cause the rate of Q growth to slow. To repeat the lesson of Chapter 1, the relationship of M to Q and P is given by $MV = PQ$ and there is no simple linear relationship or proportionality between either M and P or M and Q.

Chapter 23 _____

The Period 1864–1914
Considered as a Whole

In December 1913 Congress created the Federal Reserve System, and in August 1914 World War I began in Europe. Because of these events, I have taken 1914 to mark the end of one era and the beginning of another; and I now consider some of the changes in the nation's banking procedures and monetary system over the half-century ending in that year.

Table 23.1 provides us with the essential statistics for the first matter that requires discussion—changes in the nation's banking procedures, which amounts to a fifty-year rundown of the liquidity of banks. We see from Table 23.1 that in 1864 banks were turning out about $2.97 in bank-created money (and collecting interest on it) for every $1.00 of reserves (legal tender, whether government-created money or specie) in their vaults. Not satisfied with this, the banks slowly increased the ratio of bank-created money to reserves so that by 1914 they were creating about $9.53 in BCM and drawing interest on $9.53 for every $1.00 of reserves in their vaults. Assuming an average rate of interest of 5 percent a year in 1864, banks were getting

Table 23.1
Banknotes Plus Bank Deposits and Bank Reserves

Year	Notes Plus Deposits	Reserves	R/N+D	N+D/R
1864	$ 590	$ 198	.336	2.97
1914	15195	1595	.105	9.53

Source: Friedman, Milton, and Anna J. Schwartz. 1982. *Monetary Trends in the United States and the United Kingdom.* Princeton, N.J.: Princeton University Press. Tables A-1 and A-2.

about 15 percent on their reserve cash. At the same rate of interest in 1914, they were getting 50 percent, more or less.

Looking at the same BCM and reserve figures a different way, we see that in 1864 banks held as reserves about $33.60 for every $100 in deposits. For the average bank, this meant that about a third of all depositors would need to demand cash before the bank would be forced to close its doors. By 1914, banks held as reserves only about $10.50 for every $100 of deposits; and if only about a tenth of all depositors demanded cash, a bank would be forced into default. In other words, banks had only about a third the liquidity in 1914 they had in 1864. The fifty-year history of banking is one of ever-increasing illiquidity and ever-greater vulnerability to runs.

Naturally, the banks were disposed to push to the limit this game of sacrificing liquidity on the altar of increased interest income. But what was the limit? An answer of sorts to this question came during a watershed event in U.S. monetary history—the "Panic of 1907," more properly called the "Banking Panic of 1907." Several money-center banks experienced so large a demand for cash from depositors that their reserves were exhausted and they were forced to close their doors.

Many of these banks, perhaps most of them, were solvent. Given time to collect repayment on their loans, they would have been able to pay cash to all depositors demanding it. But there is no time to collect repayment when a run on a bank occurs. Thus, the problem of the banks in most cases was illiquidity, not insolvency. Their "fractional reserves," being only a small fraction of their deposits, were inadequate to meet the demands for cash from all the depositors who mistakenly thought they had "money in the bank," and default ensued.

When a run on one bank occurs, it tends to panic those depositors whose money is in other banks as well, and to result in runs on them. Thus, although in a way any banker would like to see a competitor ruined by a run, bankers have a common interest in providing a competitor with additional reserves, stopping the run on one bank, and thus preventing runs spreading to other banks. It therefore became not uncommon for bankers informally to "pool" their reserves and make them available to a troubled bank. But the more a bank contributed to the pool, the more vulnerable to a run it became if the runs spread. Getting people, even bankers, to put the common interest above self-interest has always been difficult.

What bankers came to want, and want urgently, was some sort of entity that could act as "lender of last resort" to a troubled bank and thus render it unnecessary for other banks to draw down their reserves in order to attempt a rescue. What they wanted was a "banker's bank," so to speak. An thus was conceived the Federal Reserve System.

The function of lender of last resort might have been given to the United States Treasury. It possessed a stock of both gold and legal tender GCM. But politicians who controlled the treasury were reluctant to appear too blatantly as lackeys who rushed to the rescue of troubled private banks, and bankers were reluctant for it to become obvious to everyone that they needed government aid. For then what would become of their cherished laissez-faire ideology?

A way out of the dilemma appeared to be the Federal Reserve System — the "Fed" — a so-called "independent" bureaucracy that was not in fact independent of either government or bankers. It was created by an act of Congress and could be abolished in the same way; and thus de jure it was far from being independent of government. But de facto its management and operation were handed over to bankers; and thus to speak of it as being independent of them is absurd. The only group that the Fed was indeed independent of in every way was debtors. No bona fide representative of the debtor class ever came anywhere near obtaining membership on the Fed's board of governors or its highly important open market committee.

And, seemingly, the idea was to make the Fed's structure and procedures so complex, so baffling, so inscrutable, so widely incomprehensible, that both government and bankers could save face, while at the same time bankers could get exactly what they wanted. It was an idea implemented with overwhelming success.

Although it is beyond the scope of this book to go into details, it may be mentioned that in due time gold and silver were phased out of the monetary system and the Fed became not merely the lender to banks of last resort but the creator of the money (actually GCM) it loaned to bail out troubled banks. In order to be able to perform this service, the Fed, in a sense, became the money-creator of last resort. Banks, of course, remained the money-creator of first resort.

In due time, banks also persuaded the government to discourage runs on banks by providing "deposit insurance" or guarantees to depositors they could get their money in the event a bank was flagrantly mismanaged and failed. Thanks again to government assistance, it came about that by the last decade of the twentieth century banks were able to attain unprecedented levels of illiquidity, and hence unprecedented levels of return on the actual cash in their vaults or on deposit at the Fed. So much for bank illiquidity. Let us now consider changes in money supply between 1864 and 1914 shown in Table 23.2. We will first note three trends of comparatively minor significance and then the trend of great significance.

First, the proportion of gold plus silver in the total money supply declined from 13.9 percent to 13.1 percent during the half-century. This may be taken to mean that the proportion of the total money supply that consisted of money created either by government or by banks increased from 86.1 percent to 86.9 percent. This small change is worth noting only because it shows the beginning of a trend that was to accelerate and to result today in the almost complete disappearance of gold and silver as a part of the money supply, with the result, therefore, that virtually all money is now either GCM or BCM.

Table 23.2
Constituents of the Money Supply, 1864 and 1914

Year	Millions of Dollars		Percentage of Total	
	1864	1914	1864	1914
COINS & CERT. $ 193		$2347	13.9%	13.1%
Gold	184	1638	13.3	9.2
Silver	9	709	0.6	3.9
BCM	590	15195	42.6	85.0
Banknotes	210	715	15.2	4.0
Deposits	380	14480	27.4	81.0
GCM	603	340	43.5	1.9
Greenbacks	415	338	29.9	1.9
Other	188	2	13.6	0.0
TOTAL	**1386**	**17882**	**100.0**	**100.0**

Source: Bureau of the Census. 1975. *Historical Statistics of the United States—Colonial Times to 1970.* Washington, D.C.: U.S. Government Printing Office, p. 1114.
Note: BCM = bank-created money; GCM = government-created money

Second, the ratio of gold to silver in the money supply in 1864 was 21 to 1; but in 1914 it was only 2.3 to 1. That is to say, during the very period when silver was demonetized and a gold-only standard embraced, the amount of silver in the money supply increased far more rapidly than the amount of gold. The bimetallist agitation of the period, although by no means decisive, was not without its importance, as already noted in a different context.

Third, the ratio of bank deposits to banknotes in the money supply in 1864 was 1.8 to 1; but by 1914 it had soared to 20.3 to 1. In other words, in their function as creators of money, banks increasingly relied on deposit-creation rather than the printing of banknotes. The result of this was that the function of banks as creators of money became less obvious, more arcane, and far less widely understood by the general public than it had been when banks issued and loaned their "printing press money."

Table 23.3 is presented to emphasize the trend of the period that was by far most significant. I have taken the amounts for BCM and GCM from Table 23.2 and placed them in the first two columns of Table 23.3. A third column has been added to show the BCM:GCM ratio. What we see is that in 1864 the money supply contained very nearly exactly the same amount of government-created and bank-created money but that by 1914 the amount of bank-created money was roughly 45 times the amount of government-created money.

Table 23.2 also shows, seen from a slightly different point of view, that

Table 23.3
Constituents of the Money Supply, Percent of Total

Year	BCM	GCM	BCM : GCM
1864	42.6%	43.5%	1 : 1
1914	85.0	1.9	45 : 1

Source: Compiled from Table 23.2.
Note: BCM = bank-created money; GCM = government-created money

during the half-century banks created $14.605 billion as they increased BCM from $590 million to $15.195 billion. Meanwhile, the government cancelled out of existence or de-created $263 million as it reduced GCM from $603 to $340 million. It was the refusal of the government to take advantage of its prerogative of creating money and its total surrender of this prerogative to the private commercial banking system that produced the overwhelmingly most significant trend of the era.

Now a caveat: In saying that between 1864 and 1914 the banks created $14.605 billion I may have exaggerated. Let me explain. In setting up Table 23.2 and similar tables in earlier chapters, I have used for the amount of bank deposits the only figures available—the figures for the total deposits of banks. There is, however, a plusible argument to the effect that in calculating the amount of bank-created money, only the demand deposits or checkable deposits of banks, not the total deposits (demand deposits plus time or savings deposits) should be used. But I know of the existence of no figures for bank demand deposits before 1915.

In 1915, when separate amounts for demand deposits and time deposits began to be published, the ratio of demand to total deposits was about 2:3. So perhaps the correct figure for the amount of money created by banks between 1864 and 1914 is only two thirds of $14.605 billion, or about $9.74 billion. If this is stipulated as the correct amount, then the BCM:GCM ratio of Table 23.2 would drop from 45:1 to 30:1 for 1914. But whether the correct ratio is one or the other of these figures makes little difference. Either is far too large. The argument is overwhelming that all created money should be government-created money and none should be bank-created.

Now we may take note of another fact—that for 1864 the debt of the federal government was $1.816 billion. For 1914 it was still $1.183 billion; and meanwhile $2.852 billion in interest had to be paid, much of it to banks on money they had created. If the 1:1 ratio of BCM to GCM of 1864 had been maintained and the government had created half of the at least $9.740 billion that banks created, the government could have been debt free long before 1914, could have saved billions of dollars in interest, and could have had billions remaining for public improvements or for reductions in taxes. But the banking lobby prevailed over common sense and over the public interest; banks created money apace, and the government created none. A more inane and shameful abnegation of government power is hardly imaginable.

It must be said that either the bankers completely out-maneuvered the un-witting politicians who controlled the government or the politicians connived with the bankers to give them what they wanted—virtually complete control of the money-creation process—although such control rightfully belongs solely to government.

What Professor Henry Simons came to call a "preposterous financial sys-tem" was largely in place by 1914. It endured until 1929 and was largely responsible for the cataclysm of that year and ensuing years. The system was tinkered with a bit and patched here and there in the 1930s, but essen-tially it is beset today by the same illiquidity problems that confronted it in 1914. And it is still largely a system wherein not the federal government but private banks control the money-creation process. It remains today a pre-posterous system, and the trouble it can cause is far from at an end.

Bibliography

Adams, Brooks. 1895. *The Law of Civilization and Decay*. London: Macmillan.

Adams, Brooks. 1913. *The Theory of Social Revolution*. New York: Macmillan.

Adams, Charles Francis, ed. 1856. *Works of John Adams*. Boston: Little, Brown.

Andreades, A. 1966. *History of the Bank of England*. New York: Augustus M. Kelley.

Angell, Norman. 1924. *The Story of Money*. New York: Frederick A. Stokes Co.

Ashworth, William. 1960. *An Economic History of England*. London: Methuen & Co.

Bagehot, Walter. 1962. *Lombard Street*. Homewood, Ill.: Richard D. Irwin.

Barrett, Don C. 1931. *The Greenback and the Resumption of Specie Payments*. Cambridge: Harvard University Press.

Beloff, Max, ed. 1987. *The Federalist*. New York: Basil Blackwell.

Bray, J. F. 1968. *Labour's Wrongs and Labour's Remedy*. New York: Augustus M. Kelley.

Bullock, Charles J. 1979. *The Finances of the United States from 1775 to 1789*. Philadelphia: Porcupine Press.

Bureau of the Census. 1975. *Historical Statistics of the United States Colonial Times to 1970*. Washington, D.C.: U.S. Government Printing Office.

Campbell, Alexander. 1869. *The True Greenback*. Chicago: Republican Books.

Cannan, Edwin. 1969. *The Paper Pound of 1797–1821*. New York: Augustus M. Kelley.

Carson, Deane, ed. 1972. *Money and Finance: Readings in Theory, Policy and Institutions*. New York: John Wiley & Sons.

Commons, John R. 1934. *Institutional Economics*. New York: Macmillan.

Council of Economic Advisors (yearly). *Economic Report of the President*. Washington, D.C.: U.S. Government Printing Office.

Del Mar, Alexander. 1975. *Money and Civilization*. Hawthorne, Calif.: Omni Publications.

Del Mar, Alexander. 1979. *The History of Money in America*. Hawthorne, Calif.: Omni Publications.

Dorfman, Joseph. 1946. *The Economic Mind in American Civilization*. New York: Viking.

Dunn, Gerald T. 1960. *Monetary Decisions of the Supreme Court*. New Brunswick, N.J.: Rutgers University Press.

Ferguson, E. James. 1961. *The Power of the Purse*. Chapel Hill: University of North Carolina Press.

Fetter, Frank W. 1978. *Development of British Monetary Orthodoxy, 1797–1875*. Fairfield, N.J.: Augustus M. Kelley.

Fisher, Irving. 1935. *100% Money*. New York: The Adelphi Company.

Foner, Eric. 1988. *Reconstruction: America's Unfinished Revolution*. New York: Harper & Row.

Franklin, Benjamin. 1907. *The Writings of Benjamin Franklin*, edited by Albert Henry Smyth. New York: Macmillan.

Friedman, Milton, and Anna J. Schwartz. 1963. *A Monetary History of the United States*. Princeton, N.J.: Princeton University Press.

Friedman, Milton, and Anna J. Schwartz. 1982. *Monetary Trends in the United States and the United Kingdom*. Chicago: University of Chicago Press.

Galbraith, John Kenneth. 1976. *Money, Whence It Came, Where It Went*. New York: Bantam Books.

Gouge, William M. 1968. *A Short History of Paper Money and Banking in the United States*. New York: Augustus M. Kelley.

Greider, William. 1987. *Secrets of the Temple*. New York: Simon and Schuster.

Hammond, Bray. 1957. *Banks and Politics in America*. Princeton, N.J.: Princeton University Press.

Hammond, Bray. 1970. *Sovereignty and an Empty Purse*. Princeton, N.J.: Princeton University Press.

Harlow, Ralph Volney. 1929. "Aspects of Revolutionary Finance—1775–1783." *American Historical Review*, 35 (1929–1930): 46–68.

Harris, Seymour E. 1961. *American Economic History*. New York: McGraw-Hill.

Hegeland, Hugo. 1969. *The Quantity Theory of Money*. New York: Augustus M. Kelley.

Hepburn, A. Barton. 1924. *A History of Currency in the United States*. New York: Macmillan.

Hertz, Emanuel. 1931. *Abraham Lincoln—A New Portrait*. New York: Liveright.

Hirst, Francis W. 1926. *Life and Letters of Thomas Jefferson*. New York: Macmillan.

Hixson, William F. 1991. *A Matter of Interest: Reexamining Money, Debt, and Real Economic Growth*. New York: Praeger.

Hume, David. 1970. *Writings on Economics*, edited by Eugene Rotwein. Madison: University of Wisconsin Press.

Humphrey, Thomas M. 1977. "Two Views of Monetary Policy." *Economic Review* of the Federal Reserve Bank of Richmond (Sept./Oct. 1977): 3–13.

Humphrey, Thomas M. 1984. "Algebraic Quantity Equations Before Fisher and Pigou." *Economic Review* of the Federal Reserve Bank of Richmond (Sept./Oct. 1984): 13–19.

Jacob, William. 1968. *A Historical Inquiry into the Production and Consumption of the Precious Metals*. New York: Augustus M. Kelley.

Kagin, Donald H. 1984. "Monetary Aspects of the Treasury Notes of the War of 1812." *Journal of Economic History* 44 (March 1984): 69–88.

Keynes, John Maynard. 1964. *The General Theory of Employment, Interest, and Money*. New York: Harcourt Brace Jovanovich.

Keynes, John Maynard. 1972. *The Collected Writings of John Maynard Keynes*, Vol. 6. London: Macmillan (for the Royal Society).

Kellogg, Edward. 1971. *Labor and Other Capital: The Rights of Each Secured and the Wrongs of Each Eradicated*. New York: Augustus M. Kelley.

Krooss, Herman E., ed. 1983. *Documentary History of Banking and Currency in the United States*. New York: Chelsea House.

Law, John. 1966. *Money and Trade Considered*. New York: Augustus M. Kelley.

Lekachman, Robert. 1977. *The Varieties of Economics*. Gloucester, Mass.: Peter Smith.

Lester, Richard A. 1938. "Currency Issues to Overcome Depressions in Pennsylvania, 1723 and 1729." *Journal of Political Economy* 46 (June 1938): 324–375.

Lester, Richard A. 1939. "Currency Issues to Overcome Depressions in Delaware, New Jesey, New York, and Maryland, 1715–37." *Journal of Political Economy* 47 (September 1939): 182–217.

Lipscomb, Andrew A., ed. 1903. *The Writings of Thomas Jefferson*. Washington, D.C.: Thomas Jefferson Memorial Association.

McCulloch, Hugh. 1888. *Men and Measures of Half a Century*. New York: Charles Scribner's Sons.

McPherson, Edward, ed. 1892. *A Handbook of Politics*. Washington, D.C.

McPherson, James. 1988. *Battle Cry of Freedom*. New York: Oxford University Press.

Marx, Karl. 1970. *Critique of Political Economy*. New York: International Publishers.

Marx, Karl. 1973. *Grundrisse*. New York: Vintage Books.

Marx, Karl. 1977. *Capital*, Vol. 1. New York: Vintage Books.

Marx, Karl, and Frederick Engels. 1955. *Marx Engels Selected Works*. Moscow: Foreign Languages Publishing House.

Mitchell, B. R. 1978. *European Historical Statistics – 1750–1970*. London: Macmillan (for Columbia University Press).

Mitchell, Broadus. 1974. *The Price of Independence*. New York: Oxford University Press.

Mitchell, Wesley C. 1903. *A History of the Greenbacks*. Chicago: University of Chicago Press.

Monroe, Arthur. 1965. *Monetary Theory before Adam Smith*. Gloucester, Mass.: Peter Smith.

Morris, Richard B. 1987. *Forging the Union 1781–1789*. New York: Harper & Row.

Munson, Gorham. 1945. *Aladdin's Lamp*. New York: Creative Age Press.

Myers, Margaret G. 1970. *A Financial History of the United States*. New York: Columbia University Press.

Nettles, Curtis P. 1964. *The Money Supply of the American Colonies before 1720*. New York: Augustus M. Kelley.

Nicolay, John G., and John Hay, eds. 1907. *Abraham Lincoln: Complete Works*. New York: The Century Co.

Nugent, Walter T. K. 1968. *Money and American Society 1865–1880*. New York: The Free Press.

Padover, Saul K. 1943. *The Complete Jefferson*. New York: Duell, Sloan & Pearce.

Palayi, Melichor. 1972. *The Twilight of Gold*. Chicago: Henry Regenry.

Patterson, C. C. 1972. "Silver Stocks and Losses in Ancient and Medieval Times."
    Economic History Review 25 (May 1972): 205–233.
Perkins, Edwin J. 1980. *The Economy of Colonial America.* New York: Columbia
    University Press.
Petty, William. 1963. *The Economic Writings of Sir William Petty,* edited by Charles
    Henry Hull. New York: Augustus M. Kelley.
Phalle, Thibaud D. 1985. *The Federal Reserve System — An Intentional Mystery.*
    New York: Praeger.
Polanyi, Karl. 1957. *The Great Transformation.* Boston: Beacon Press.
Pollack, Norman. 1990. *The Humane Economy.* New Brunswick, N.J.: Rutgers
    University Press.
Powell, Ellis T. 1966. *The Evolution of the Money Market — 1385-1915.* New York:
    Augustus M. Kelley.
Ricardo, David. 1951. The Works and Correspondence of David Ricardo, edited by
    Piero Sraffa. Cambridge, U.K.: Cambridge University Press.
Rist, Charles. 1966. *History of Monetary and Credit Theory.* New York: Augustus
    M. Kelley.
Samuelson, Paul. 1976. *Economics,* 10th ed. New York: McGraw-Hill.
Sandburg, Carl. 1939. *Abraham Lincoln — The War Years.* New York: Harcourt,
    Brace & Company.
Schell, Herbert S. 1930. "Hugh McCulloch and the Treasury Department, 1865-1869."
    Mississippi Valley Historical Review 17 (December 1930): 404-421.
Schumpeter, Joseph A. 1950. *Capitalism, Socialism and Democracy.* New York:
    Harper & Row.
Schumpeter, Joseph A. 1954. *History of Economic Analysis.* New York: Oxford
    University Press.
Sharkey, Robert P. 1967. *Money, Class, and Party: An Economic Study of the Civil
    War and Reconstruction.* Baltimore: The Johns Hopkins Press.
Simons, Henry C. 1948. *Economic Policy for a Free Society.* Chicago: University of
    Chicago Press.
Smith, Adam. 1909. *Wealth of Nations.* New York: P. F. Collier and Son.
Smith, Adam. 1937. *Wealth of Nations.* New York: The Modern Library.
Studenski, Paul, and Herman E. Krooss. 1952. *Financial History of the United States.*
    New York: McGraw-Hill.
Sumner, William Graham. 1968. *A History of American Currency.* New York:
    Augustus M. Kelley.
Thornton, Henry. 1978. *An Enquiry into the Nature and Effects of the Paper Credit
    of Great Britain.* Fairfield, N.J.: Augustus M. Kelley. (Originally published
    1802).
Unger, Irwin. 1964. *The Greenback Era.* Princeton, N.J.: Princeton University Press.
Veblen, Thorstein. 1978. *The Theory of Business Enterprise.* New Brunswick, N.J.:
    Transaction Books.
Vilar, Pierre. 1976. *A History of Gold and Money.* London: NLB Publishers.
Walton, Gary M., and Ross M. Robertson. 1983. *History of the American Economy,*
    5th ed. New York: Harcourt Brace Jovanovich.
Warren, Charles. 1922. *The Supreme Court in United States History.* Boston: Little,
    Brown.

Wiebe, Robert H. 1967. *The Search for Order*. New York: Hill and Wang.
Wilbur, Charles K., and Kenneth P. Jameson. 1983. *An Inquiry into the Poverty of Economics*. South Bend, Ind.: University of Notre Dame Press.
Woolley, John T. 1984. *Money and Politics*. Cambridge: Cambridge University Press.

Index

ABOUT THE AUTHOR

WILLIAM F. HIXSON is a retired businessman and engineer who for many years operated a successful small-business partnership. He has published articles in the *Eastern Economic Journal, The History of Economics Society Bulletin,* and *Economies et Sociétés* (France), as well as book reviews in the *Review of Radical Political Economics.*